DEADLY FORCE

2nd Edition

UNDERSTANDING YOUR RIGHT TO SELF-DEFENSE

MASSAD AYOOB

Published by

Gun Digest® Books, an imprint of Caribou Media Group, LLC

Gun Digest Media
5600 W. Grande Market Drive, Suite 100
Appleton, WI 54913
gundigest.com

To order books or other products call 920.471.4522
or visit us online at gundigeststore.com

ISBN-13: 978-1-951115-85-2

Edited by Corey Graff
Cover Design by Gene Coo
Interior Design by Jong Cadelina

Printed in the United States of America

10 9 8 7 6 5 4 3 2 1

DEDICATION

To **Gail Pepin**, producer of the ProArms
Podcast ... my wife, shooting partner, and
Adult Supervisor, without whom this book
would have taken a lot longer to put together.

ACKNOWLEDGMENTS

I cannot list all the attorneys, judges, law professors and master police investigators with whom I've worked and from whom I've learned over the decades without forgetting a name and hurting some feelings. But a piece of each of them is in the book you hold in your hands, and I profoundly thank them all for the experience and hard-earned wisdom they have shared, to make this book a reality.

— **Massad Ayoob**

TABLE OF CONTENTS

FOREWORD

By **Attorney Jeffrey Weiner**, former president,
National Association of Criminal Defense Lawyers

n all professions requiring high levels of specialization, there are
those who "talk the talk" and those who "walk the walk." Massad
Ayoob is among the rare few who fall in the latter category.

Massad Ayoob is the real McCoy. I know. I trained with him for
years and survived a gunfight because of his teaching and training.
(More about that later...)

Having attended college, law school, and dozens of legal courses and
seminars as a student and teacher, I have seen many people instruct. Simply
put, Mas Ayoob is the best teacher and instructor I have ever learned from.
He is highly knowledgeable — ask anyone in the firearms profession. And he
is a top shooter and a true expert in all the mental and physical aspects of
weapons.

Mas is a superb lecturer and writer. Having read gun publications for almost four decades, I often shake my head in disbelief when I see how other
"gun writers" essentially take Massad's comments and even his phrases, as
well as his teachings, and re-phrase them in an attempt to use them as their
own.

I smile whenever I think of my training with Mas in weapons retention
and disarm techniques. I vividly recall how, in each class, he would select

the biggest, toughest student and say to him, "I am little and weak, and you are big and strong." Mas would hand him a replica of the student's gun and tell him to grip the gun any way he wished and to hold it as tightly as if he had just drawn it in a threatening situation. Then, he'd tell the student that he would take the weapon away, so there would be no surprise. Usually, the student would laugh, firmly gripping the gun with both hands. Mas would ask, "Are you ready?" And when the student acknowledged that he was, Mas proceeded to disarm him within about two seconds. I witnessed this over and over, even when the students were highly trained police officers or Federal agents (who were smart enough to attend Mas's courses at their own expense).

I learned handgun retention techniques that work in the real world. I had the pleasure of listening to Mas's lectures and answers to questions on virtually every aspect of self-defense using handguns, Kubotans, knives, long guns and other weapons.

Several years ago, Mas, I, and two other folks were panelists in a video produced by the American Bar Association's American Law Institute. The video was for lawyers and judges, and the topic was the judicious use of deadly force. The video has been played around the country and is widely used as an educational source. Mas is not a lawyer, but he is highly knowledgeable about the law in this area.

Jeff Weiner, Former President, National Association of Criminal Defense Lawyers jeffweiner.com

With Mas's experience and qualifications as a champion shooter, police captain and expert witness, I can't think of anyone better to write the book you are about to read.

I speak from first-hand knowledge of his credentials as an expert witness. I am a Board-certified criminal trial lawyer, a former president of the National Association of Criminal Defense Lawyers, and a practicing criminal defense attorney for over forty years. My clients and I have benefited from Mas's expertise in several high-profile murder, shooting, and self-defense cases through the years. When I need an expert witness whom I know has rock-solid credentials and credibility and who is untouchable under cross-examination by prosecutors, I call Massad. He is "The Man."

So, when Mas asked me to write this foreword, I immediately accepted. I am genuinely honored by his request.

When the self-defense laws aren't right, work to change them! Ayoob leaves the Wisconsin State Capitol in Madison after testifying for shall-issue concealed carry. The bill passed the legislature, but the state's anti-gun governor vetoed it. Unfortunately, gun owners' civil rights forces fell one vote short of a veto override. However, Wisconsin later passed shall-issue carry, proving that civil rights reforms can require multiple failed attempts before successful.

Okay, I promised details of why I fervently believe in Massad's training. In 1991, my former wife (who also trained with Mas) and I drove home with another couple returning from a wedding party at a fancy hotel in Miami. Everyone was dressed up for the occasion. I wore a tuxedo and a SIG P220 (.45 caliber) in a Milt Sparks's Summer Special holster (under my cummerbund!).

When we arrived at my home, my former wife and I exited the car. As we said "goodnight," my ex-wife yelled, "Home invaders!" and dove for cover under the car. I was in front of the car and saw a tall man with a ski mask running toward the car's rear that my law partner and his wife were still in. The gunman held a handgun, which he pointed directly at me.

Thanks to my training, I immediately drew my handgun and fired first, giving him the surprise of his life. He returned fire with what we later learned was a 9mm.

Whether I hit him is unknown, but he spun around, crouched, and stumbled into the getaway car, which sped away. And that was it. It was over.

There was no time to think — only time to react. No time to retrieve a gun from an ankle holster, a "man purse," or a briefcase. All the training and hours of practice kicked in, and it was over in an instant.

None of us were hurt. The police recovered the 9mm bullet from the dashboard of my law partner's vehicle (who, along with his wife, wisely ducked down as they saw me draw my weapon). The brand new Lexus (which he had picked up that afternoon) had a cracked rear windshield where the 9mm bullet had entered. The 9mm had then traveled forward, hit the front windshield and ricocheted into its final resting place, the dashboard.

When it was all over, and the police finally left my home in the early morning hours, I made three calls: one to Mas, one to John Farnam and one to Quique Fernandez. I thanked them for saving four lives that night. Had it not been for their excellent training, for which I was and am so grateful, the outcome would undoubtedly have been different.

If it sounds like I'm a huge fan of Massad Ayoob, it's because I am. After all, I am here to write this because of my training with him. And, after forty years as a practicing criminal defense attorney, I know that what Mas says, teaches, and writes is the best state-of-the-art knowledge you can get.

I would be remiss if I did not mention that it is essential that every gun owner make contact with a trained and gun-knowledgeable, experienced criminal defense attorney so that, if the unthinkable happens, you will have someone who knows you ready to take your call and advise you before you talk with police.

So, read and enjoy — and feel good about what you have learned. You never know when your life could depend on it. ∎

If you carry, be competent with your gun. You don't need to be able to shoot this perfect qualification score with a Glock 30 and .45 hardball, but you want to come as close as you can. Confidence and competence intertwine, says Ayoob.

CHAPTER 1:
BACKGROUND

My first book on the use of deadly force by private citizens in defense of self and others came out in 1980. The title was *In the Gravest Extreme: The Role of the Firearm in Personal Protection.* It has been a bestseller ever since. Many have been kind enough to call it "the authoritative text" in its field.

The book you now hold in your hands was not written to replace it but to augment it. Deadly force is one of the most mature bodies of law that we have, and there is relatively little in it that significantly changes over time.

Since writing *In the Gravest Extreme,* I've gathered more research and experience. I've been an expert witness in criminal and civil weapons and deadly force cases for over four decades. Any veteran attorney will tell you that law school teaches you law, but experience teaches you trial tactics. From that experience, I draw many of the lessons shared here.

That experience between books has included nineteen years as chair of the Firearms Committee of the American Society of Law Enforcement Trainers, a similar period on the Advisory Board of the International Law Enforcement Educators and Trainers Association, and presenting at regional, national, and international seminars of the International Association of Law

Enforcement Firearms Instructors. I've attended several advanced homicide and officer-involved shooting investigation courses and taught at some of both. Part of my teaching load includes Continuing Legal Education courses for practicing attorneys doing firearms and use of force cases. Since writing *In the Gravest Extreme*, I founded Lethal Force Institute in 1981. I taught there through 2009, after which I established Massad Ayoob Group (http://massadayoobgroup.com), through which I now teach nationwide on related topics. In 2017, I retired from police work after forty-some years at ranks from Patrolman through Captain, all part-time but fully sworn and empowered.

There have been changes in some jurisdictions' laws as regards the Stand Your Ground and Castle Doctrine principles. Still, while these changes have been hugely controversial, they have also been widely misunderstood. As we'll discuss in these pages, once we get past the misunderstandings,

The author, right, prepares for direct testimony by defense attorney John Colley, left. The defendant was acquitted in the criminal trial over a fatal self-defense shooting.

The author, third from the left, at the scene of a shooting involving the three policemen shown in the photo.

ANY VETERAN ATTORNEY WILL TELL YOU THAT LAW SCHOOL TEACHES YOU LAW, BUT EXPERIENCE TEACHES YOU TRIAL TACTICS."

nothing of substance has changed that much.

There certainly have been changes in gun laws (as opposed to self-defense laws). When I wrote *In the Gravest Extreme*, there were seven U.S. states with absolutely no provision at law for the private citizen to carry a concealed handgun in public legally; now, there are none. In 1980, most jurisdictions offering carry permits were "may issue," meaning that the issuing authorities could pretty much grant or deny the permits at their discretion. In many places, "may issue" was a code for "we'll issue you the permit if you're white, male, rich and politically connected." Today, most states are "shall issue." This change has come about through reform legislation that mandates the issuing authorities to grant permits to all law-abiding private

The Author has spent a substantial part of his life in law libraries absorbing and deciphering deadly force law.

citizen applicants who meet specific requirements. Back in those days, there were only two reciprocity states, Indiana and Michigan, where a permit from another state was recognized; today, reciprocity is widespread. There was only one state, Vermont, where a permit wasn't even needed to carry loaded and concealed in public; people were forbidden to do so if they had a criminal record, were adjudicated mentally incompetent or could be

IN THE GRAVEST EXTREME

The Role of the
Firearm in Personal
Protection

Massad F. Ayoob

The author's first book on this topic, *In the Gravest Extreme*, remains in print and is still considered a seminal text on the subject.

shown to be carrying for malicious purposes.

By the time of this second edition of *Deadly Force*, so-called Constitutional Carry (aka "permitless carry" or "Vermont model") has been adopted by fully half of the fifty states, with more undoubtedly to come.

The largely elitist and occasionally corrupt "may issue" model of concealed carry permit issuance appeared to come to an end in late June 2022 when the Supreme Court of the United States, in a 6-3 opinion, ruled it unconstitutional in the case of *New York State Rifle and Pistol Association v. Bruen.* Writing the long and brilliantly crafted majority opinion, Justice Clarence Thomas delineated the racist history of "may issue" permitting and put a stake in the heart of New York's infamous Sullivan Law. Justice Stephen Breyer wrote a rambling dissent, which could have been cut and pasted from a list of anti-gun shibboleths, citing mass murders and suicides, for example, which had nothing to do with law-abiding citizens being licensed to carry guns in public for self-defense. This, in turn, drew a masterfully scathing rebuttal opinion from Justice Samuel Alito.

Other pending gun restriction cases were remanded in light of the *Bruen* decision. In some of the formerly "may issue" states, attorneys general told the issuing authorities that no particular special need element could be applied any longer. In others, predictably, anti-gun officials explored ways to make the permitting process more difficult for ordinary citizens.

The decision made it clear that the old, fungible two-step "means/end" test that lower courts had applied to "gun control" laws was unacceptable and that strict scrutiny would have to apply.

The majority opinion concluded, "The constitutional right to bear arms in public for self-defense is not "a second-class right,' subject to an entirely different body of rules than the other Bill of Rights guarantees.' McDonald, 561 U. S., at 780 (plurality opinion). We know of no other constitutional right that an individual may exercise only after demonstrating to government officers some special need. That is not how the First Amendment works when it comes to unpopular speech or the free exercise of religion. It is not how the Sixth Amendment works when it comes to a defendant's right to confront the witnesses against him. And it is not how the Second Amendment works when it comes to public carry for self-defense. New York's proper-cause requirement violates the Fourteenth Amendment in that it prevents law-abiding citizens with ordinary self-defense needs from exercising their right to keep and bear arms. We therefore reverse the judgment of the Court of Appeals and remand the case for further proceedings consistent with this opinion. It is so ordered."

THE MYTH OF CHRISTIAN PACIFISM
GREG HOPKINS

For devout people troubled by the idea of using deadly force in self defense, the excellent book *A Time To Kill* explains why it is justified in the Scriptures.

> **THERE HAVE BEEN CHANGES IN SOME JURISDICTIONS' LAWS AS REGARDS THE STAND YOUR GROUND AND CASTLE DOCTRINE PRINCIPLES.**

It would be very much worth any interested citizen's time to read the entire decision, including the dissent and rebuttal. It can be found at su-premecourt.gov.

Gun laws have come a long way for armed citizens. But there have also been setbacks. I can't think of a jurisdiction with magazine capacity limits when I wrote *In the Gravest Extreme*. From 1994 through 2004, our country lived with the Clinton Assault Weapons ban, which limited new magazines to a 10-round capacity. While that decade-long exercise in futility is thankfully past at this writing, such limits remain on the books in several states. In my opinion, such restrictions can hamper the defensive capability of law-abiding armed citizens in general and the physically challenged among them, in particular.

For this second edition of *Deadly Force*, I've experienced eight more years in the courts and gathered information from other cops and private-sector instructors who teach in this area, including many more attorneys and cases in which I've been an expert witness and advisor on trial strategy. Yes, as you'll see, some things have changed in the trial strategy world in that relatively short period.

It's been a long ride and a most instructive one. I've learned a lot, and I'm honored to share some of that learning with you here. ∎

"
GUN LAWS HAVE COME
A LONG WAY FOR ARMED
CITIZENS. BUT THERE HAVE
ALSO BEEN SETBACKS. I CAN'T
THINK OF A JURISDICTION
WITH MAGAZINE CAPACITY
LIMITS WHEN I WROTE IN THE
GRAVEST EXTREME.

CHAPTER 2:
STANDARDS

f 40-some years working and teaching in the justice system has taught me anything, it is this: If you act to the standards by which you know you will be judged, you should not be found wanting in the judgment.

No two use of force incidents will be the same in every respect. There is a virtually infinite potential for branching of circumstances. Because of this, the courts will hold us to standards, a formula, if you will. For the same reasons, it behooves us to use a formula to analyze each situation we face to determine whether lethal force is justified.

Lethal force (or deadly force; the terms are interchangeable) is that degree of force that a reasonable and prudent person would consider capable of causing death or great bodily harm. Various laws use the terminology "great bodily harm," "grave bodily harm," "serious bodily harm," etc.; the easiest way to remember it in layman's terms is "crippling injury."

The set of circumstances that justifies using deadly force is a *situation of immediate danger of death or great bodily harm to oneself or other innocent persons.* Since deadly force is typically only allowed as a last resort, the danger should be otherwise unavoidable and not created by the defender himself. This brings in an element called preclusion, which can vary accord-

No matter how justified the shooting, some will mourn the slain criminal and seek revenge in court. Here is a shrine to a man from one of the author's cases who died trying to kill a cop.

ing to jurisdiction and circumstances, and will be discussed separately in this book.

That situation of immediate danger of death or crippling injury is typically determined by the simultaneous presence of three criteria. Different schools use various terminology, but the most widely used and court-proven standard has been used for decades: *Ability/Opportunity/Jeopardy*, what I'll call the AOJ triad. "Ability" means that the assailant possesses the power to kill or cripple. "Opportunity" means he is capable of immediately employing that power. "Jeopardy" means that his actions or words indicate to a reasonable, prudent person that he intends and is about to do so. We will discuss each of these in great detail in this book.

Throughout the self-defense encounter, the law-abiding armed citizen must maintain *the mantle of innocence*. Think of the mantle of innocence as a legal cloak that shields the wearer from the accusation of wrongdoing. The defender must not have provoked the encounter, must not have started the fight, or an element of guilt and wrongdoing will accrue. If it's within

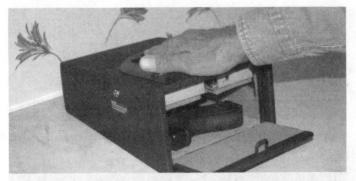

Part of your responsibility as a gun owner is keeping firearms secure from unauthorized people. However, many of today's gun safes have quick-access features so an authorized person can retrieve them quickly to prevent a home invasion.

Warren On Homicide is widely considered the standard of homicide law.

Experience in court has taught the author, "If you act to the standard by which you know you will be judged, you should not be found wanting in the judgment."

"

EACH STATE HAS ITS STATUTES AND CODES, COLLOQUIALLY KNOWN AS "BLACK LETTER LAW." THE LAWS ARE INTERPRETED THROUGH THE PRISM OF CASE LAW AND APPELLATE COURT DECISIONS THAT ESSENTIALLY NAIL DOWN THE FINE POINTS.

the defender's power to end the argument or abjure from the conflict, but instead, he "kept the ball rolling," and things predictably escalated, he may very likely be held to have been at least partially at fault.

Some states (but not all) have provisions for *excusable homicide* as well as *justifiable homicide*. In essence, a finding of excusable homicide means that the deceased probably shouldn't have been killed; however, a reasonable and prudent person would likely have made the same mistake under identical circumstances. By contrast, a finding of justifiable homicide says, in essence, that the person who killed the deceased acted correctly. In either case, the person responsible for the killing is held harmless.

You can learn much online (but not everything) about deadly force law.

Know the laws where you go. This Legal Heat app is useful for checking that on handheld electronic devices.

Lawyer, police chief, and tactician Jeff Chudwin reminds his students, "You don't have to be right, you have to be *reasonable*."

The author's former CLE teaching partner, the late Jim Fleming, was a veteran criminal defense lawyer who noted sagely, "You don't have to like reality, but you do have to face it.

(Below) The author suggests the website handgunlaw.us for up-to-date state gun laws, including concealed carry reciprocity.

Handgunlaw.us

Want to help keep www.handgunlaw.us on-line?

[Search Handgunlaw.us]

Click Here for Legislative or other important State Changes.

Site/Data Updates

St. Honoring My Lic.

Lic. My State Honors

Create License Map

RV/Car Carry

Non-Resident Permits

Right To Carry History

Site FAQs

Glossary

Gun Safety Data

Site Navigation:

Commercial Links

RKBA State Orgs

This US Map is hot-linked to the st Simply click on the states abbrevi view the All U.S. Page, click on U.

Where we have made every possi found in the top left corner of this

By using any of these links or info Solutions, Inc., Steve Aikens, Gary

You

☐ Shall Issue
☐ May Issue
☐ Right Denied
☐ Permit holder must be resident of state they honor

U.S.A.   HI

Why have this site

This site is owned by Steve Aikens and Gary Slider. We firmly believe in the Second Amendment, Concealed Carry and the fa defense. Unfortunately, we recognize there are so many variances in our state to state laws, the average individual may have di especially as they travel. Since we have the ability to research those laws and create an informative Concealed Carry specific s

Gun Sales Rise as Crime, Accident Re

We now offer T-shirts and some miscellaneous items on www.cafepress.com. You're invited to visit the store there and grab

We are a Database of Information on Carrying Firearms legally for Self-L

We must have *reasonable fear* of death or grave bodily harm when we employ this level of force. Reasonable fear is starkly distinct from what the law calls *bare fear*, which never justifies harming another. Bare fear is naked panic, a blind and unreasoning fear. It is understood that when panic comes in, reason departs. The necessary reasonable fear doesn't mean you're soiling your pants or running away screaming; reasonable fear is simply that apprehension of danger that any reasonable, prudent person would experience if they were in the same situation as you, knowing what you knew at the time.

General Rules of Engagement

Each state has its statutes and codes, colloquially known as "black letter law." The laws are interpreted through the prism of case law and appellate court decisions that essentially nail down the fine points. Some of the clearest, most easily understood legal definitions and interpretations can be found in the given state's recommended jury instructions on the various issues. All of these can be researched at a legal library. In nearly every county seat, at or near the county courthouse, you will find a legal library open to the public. The legal librarians, I've found, as a rule, are delighted to help ordinary citizens look up these things.

NO LAWYER CAN MEMORIZE THE VASTNESS OF THE LAW IN ITS ENTIRETY; THAT'S WHY EVERY LAW OFFICE HAS ITS OWN LEGAL LIBRARY. NO POLICE OFFICER CAN MEMORIZE THEM ALL; THAT'S WHY THE PATROL CAR HAS A MOBILE DATA TERMINAL CAPABLE OF LOOKING THINGS UP.

Because ours is the most mobile society on Earth, we constantly move between jurisdictions. No lawyer can memorize the vastness of The Law in its entirety; that's why every law office has its own legal library. No police officer can memorize them all; that's why the patrol car has a mobile data terminal capable of looking things up. It follows that the law-abiding armed citizen can't hold all the laws in their head, either. For that reason, in this book, as in my classes, I teach generic principles that are common to the laws of all 50 states.

Now, let's move forward and examine these matters in greater detail. ■

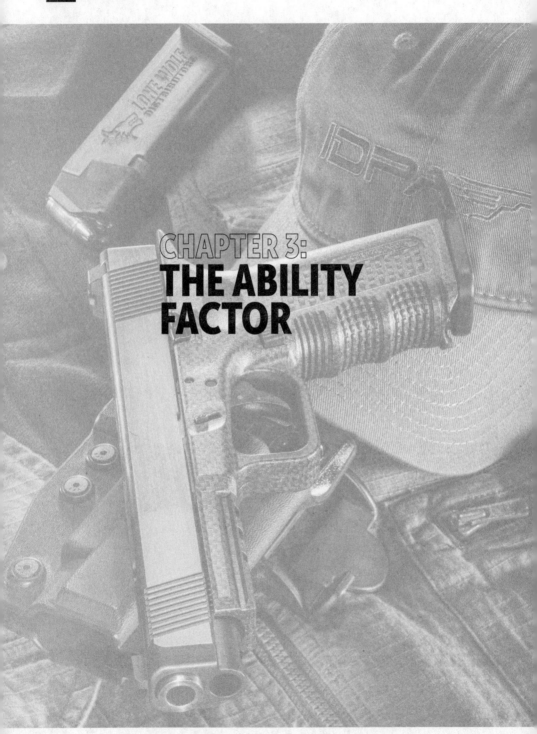

CHAPTER 3:
THE ABILITY FACTOR

n this context, *ability* means *your assailant possesses the power to kill or to inflict crippling injury.* This power most obviously takes the form of a weapon, but it also may manifest as something called disparity of force. Let's look at weapons first.

Obviously, a gun is a deadly weapon; so is a bow and arrow. So is a bludgeon, whether a club or some ordinary object used as a makeshift striking weapon, a knife, sword, icepick, razor, broken bottle or any other edged or pointed object that can be used to stab and slash.

The Opponent's Gun

How could opposing counsel ever allege that the gun your attacker was wielding or reaching for wasn't a deadly weapon? As counterintuitive as such an allegation might seem, it always crops up. "The gun wasn't loaded, so you weren't in danger; ergo, it wasn't self-defense when you shot him." "The gun in the hand of the deceased wasn't a *real* gun, so shooting him wasn't justified."

The law doesn't see it that way. The reasonable and prudent person is not Superman and doesn't have x-ray vision. They have no way of knowing whether the gun is loaded. In one case in which I testified, the defendant

Photographed in evidence, this knife was used to attempt to slash a policeman to death. Its wielder was killed, justifiably, by police gunfire.

was charged with murder for shooting a man who pulled a 9mm semi-automatic pistol on him in a state of screaming rage. The defendant drew his nine-shot 9mm and had to empty it into the attacker before the latter fell and dropped his weapon. The dead man's unfired pistol turned out to have a full magazine and an empty firing chamber. The prosecution tried mightily to use that fact to convince the jury that the defendant was not in real danger and, therefore, could not be justified in shooting.

In addition to pointing out that the defendant could not have known that his opponent's chamber was empty, the defense attorney used me as an expert witness to show the jury that the assailant could have racked the slide of his pistol and fired in a fraction of a second. Nonetheless, the defendant's exoneration took a long and arduous court battle.

AND NEVER LET THOSE WHO JUDGE YOU FORGET THAT SINCE YOU WERE CLOSE ENOUGH TO YOUR OPPONENT TO SHOOT HIM WITH YOUR GUN, HE WAS, IPSO FACTO, CLOSE ENOUGH TO SHOOT YOU WITH HIS.

The knife can be dead-lier than the gun, under some circumstances.

For a very long time now, toy guns and Airsoft guns have been manu-factured to so closely replicate real firearms that they can't be distinguished from the genuine article without detailed examination. When things happen quickly in the real world, even in broad daylight, it is no trick to show the jury or the grand jury that these realistic toys look exactly like the real thing. When the incident occurs in poor light, as is often the case, it is even more likely that no reasonable person could have been able to tell the unshoot-able "clone gun" from the real one. This does not keep clueless people and those with specific agendas from organizing protest marches and orches-trating a blizzard of letters to the prosecutor's office demanding criminal charges against the man who "shot the poor guy who only had a toy."

After the toy industry agreed to make toy guns transparent or brightly colored, or at least put a Day-Glo™ orange tip on the barrel so they wouldn't be mistaken for real ones, criminals and children alike proved adaptable. In both cases, they removed the orange tip, painted it over, or painted the whole toy gun flat black. Conversely, there are documented cases of criminals painting real guns orange, hoping that police will think they're toys and hesitate to shoot, giving the criminals time to murder them and escape.

A few years ago, I did a murder case in Baltimore. The shooting scene was a workshop that had been burgled many times. The owners were working late one night when they heard sounds indicating it was happening again, so they armed themselves. They soon found themselves facing an in-truder in dim light, suddenly turning toward them with what appeared to be a long-barreled revolver. Both shop owners opened fire simultaneously, one with a 12-gauge shotgun and the other with an HK pistol. Their 00 buckshot and .45-caliber hollowpoints killed the intruder, armed with a long-handled hammer. He had been holding it by the head with its long handle protruding as he spun toward them. I showed in court how this looked the same as a large revolver (I used a blue steel Smith & Wesson Model 29 .44 Magnum with an 8 3/8-inch barrel for the demonstration). The judge in the bench trial "got it." His verdict was not guilty for both defendants on all counts.

You may even encounter the allegation that you were out of range of the opponent you shot, even though he had a real gun fully loaded. Many years ago, the brilliant Miami attorney Jeff Weiner, who would later become president of the National Association of Criminal Defense Lawyers, hired me as an expert witness on behalf of one of his clients charged with manslaughter. The deceased had the proverbial "record as long as his arm" if you unrolled the printout showing his arrest and conviction history. On his last day on earth, he had decided to use a loaded, stolen gun to commit armed robbery on the wrong victim. He had terrorized the owner of a real estate office and his secretary, and when he fled the scene, the owner told the secretary to call the police and tell them what happened because he was going after the robber. There was a 12-gauge pump gun he kept loaded in his office; he grabbed it and sprinted out the door after the perpetrator.

A few blocks away, he caught up with the perpetrator and ordered him to halt. Instead of complying with that lawful order — the victim did, after all, have the right of citizen's arrest — he swung on his now-armed victim with

QUICK FACTS

In a typical year, more people will be murdered with bludgeons than with so-called "assault rifles" in the United States. In one recent year, the FBI listed 323 people as killed with rifles of all types, including ordinary hunting rifles as well as "assault rifles." The same study showed 496 people killed with blunt objects such as hammers, bats, etc.

the stolen gun. The victim did the logical thing: he fired. Twenty .30-caliber pellets from a 12 gauge Magnum #1 buckshot shell struck home simultaneously, and the gunman was killed instantly.

However, the shooting pushed some politically incorrect buttons. There had been a spate of killings of criminals by armed citizens in that community when this shooting went down, and the anti-gun newspaper was loudly crying for the anti-gun chief prosecutor to "do something" about this "outbreak of vigilante justice." The robber had been black (as was one of his victims, the secretary, whom the robber had called a "n****r" during the robbery), but the man who shot the robber was white. Because the gunman had been aiming over his shoulder at the robbery victim when the latter fired, the buckshot pellets had entered his body behind the lateral midline, so the prosecution characterized the armed robber as having been "shot in the back." Finally, the prosecution took the position that the victim had become the aggressor in chasing the felon.

During my sworn pre-trial deposition, it became apparent that the prosecution would make another massive issue out of the fact that some 50 feet separated the men when the fatal shot was fired. The assigned assistant state's attorney took the position that the defendant was out of range of the stolen, fully loaded snub-nose .38 with which the decedent was trying to shoot him. In the deposition, I explained that both men were within range of each other, which was how the armed robber had come to his death in the first place. The visibly skeptical prosecutor asked me how far away I would have to be to feel safe from a man armed with a short-barrel .38. I resisted the urge to say, "Oh, maybe Kenosha, Wisconsin," and instead replied that I would consider myself in deadly danger from a man so armed even at 100 yards. Noticing my examiner furiously writing on his yellow legal pad at that point, I made a "note to self" to prepare demonstrative evidence.

Upon returning home, I went to a shooting range with a notary public and four snub-nose .38 Special revolvers. I set up Colt police targets depicting a human silhouette at a hundred yards. With a Charter Arms Undercover revolver, a duplicate of the dead robber's stolen weapon, I nailed the silhouette with two of the five shots in the cylinder. I did the same with a similar five-shot .38, a Smith & Wesson Chief Special. With six-shot, 2-inch barrel revolvers, I hit with three out of six from a K-frame Smith & Wesson and all six shots from my wife's Colt Detective Special. Attorney Weiner shared this experiment with the prosecutor before trial. For this and other reasons, the prosecutor's office decided it would be inexpedient to take the case to trial.

It might be helpful, if you ever faced such a bogus allegation, for you to be able to articulate that you knew beforehand that there is a shooting sport, the International Metallic Handgun Silhouette Association, in which competitors in Production Class use handguns to shoot targets much smaller than a human being at distances up to 200 meters.

And never let those who judge you forget that since you were close enough to your opponent to shoot him with your gun, he was, *ipso facto*, close enough to shoot you with his.

If, as demonstrated above, opposing counsel can make such far-fetched arguments as "The gun you faced wasn't deadly enough," what do you suppose they'll do if your opponent's weapon can be perceived as less lethal than yours?

The Dangerous Myth of Hierarchy of Lethality

We live in a world where the entertainment and news media have demonized the firearm as a frightening, high-efficiency killing machine. A myth has arisen that I call the "hierarchy of lethality." The false belief is that the firearm represents the nuclear level of hand-held weaponry and is somehow more lethal than other deadly weapons. The general public sees

> "
> WE LIVE IN A WORLD WHERE THE ENTERTAINMENT AND NEWS MEDIA HAVE DEMONIZED THE FIREARM AS A FRIGHTENING, HIGH-EFFICIENCY KILLING MACHINE. A MYTH HAS ARISEN THAT I CALL THE "HIERARCHY OF LETHALITY." THE FALSE BELIEF IS THAT THE FIREARM REPRESENTS THE NUCLEAR LEVEL OF HAND-HELD WEAPONRY

the knife as something less. After all, they'll open their mail in the morning with something much like your opponent's knife and slice the roast at dinner tonight with something virtually identical to the blade your opponent wields. Because it's an accouterment of everyday life, they don't see the knife as a weapon, even though they know cognitively that it can be turned from culinary aid to murder weapon in a heartbeat. An impact weapon, a "club"? Well, they may see that as even less deadly.

Now, the night comes when you are attacked by a homicidal perpetrator wielding a bludgeon or blade. You are forced to shoot him in self-defense. I can almost guarantee where the subsequent attack on you is going to come from:

"He *only* had a knife!"

"He *only* had a baseball bat!"

Opposing counsel may attempt to paint you as the bully and coward who used a deadlier weapon than your assailant and will attempt to convince the jury that your shooting of a man with "a less than lethal weapon" is unfair and therefore improper. Of course, this flies in the face of the legality of the matter, which is that within their range, the club and the knife are every bit as deadly as the gun ... and, in some situations, can be deadlier.

Knife Lethality

I've been cross-trained with the knife and have had the privilege of having trained with some of the finest instructors in the field over the years. That list includes Graciela Casillas, Michael deBethancourt, Marc Denny, the late Grandmaster Jim Morell, the late Grandmaster Remy Presas, the late Hank Reinhardt, Paul Vunak, and others. The experience gave me a powerful sense of how destructive this simple, seemingly mundane tool can be.

A knife never jams. A knife never runs out of ammunition; you rarely see a gunshot murder victim who has been shot more than a few times, but any homicide investigator can tell you how common it is for the victim of a knife murder to bear twenty, thirty, or more stab and slash wounds. "A knife comes with a built-in silencer." Knives are cheap and can be bought anywhere; there used to be a cutlery store at LaGuardia Airport, not far outside the security gates. There is no prohibition at law against a knife being sold to a convicted felon. Knives can be small and flat and amazingly easy to conceal.

Anywhere on the human body where you can take a pulse, the knife only has to slice a few millimeters in to cause exsanguination or death by blood loss: it just needs to cut open an artery.

Common sense would tell you that a four-inch blade knife can only inflict a stab wound four inches deep, but knife penetration is about twice that in practical reality. Soft tissue compresses before the point of a knife: reach down to your abdomen, and see how deeply you can press in. The two-inch blade can penetrate four inches into such body parts, the four-inch blade eight inches, etc.

Having been certified to teach disarming people with various weapons — guns, knives, clubs — I am convinced that the knife is the hardest to take away from another person. The gun projects its force in only one direction, so if you can control the barrel, you can keep it from hurting you as you twist it out of another person's hands. Against the stick, if you grab it farther out than the other person is holding it, you're already ahead of the curve in taking it from him, and if you can interdict the bludgeoner's arm or wrist, you've minimized the impact he can deliver with his club. But where do you grab a knife without getting cut?

A gunshot has finite power regarding the wound it can create. The knife is limited only by the strength and range of movement of the person wielding it. In all these years of going to court in homicide cases and gradu-

> THE CLUB IS THE SIMPLEST AND CRUDEST OF DEADLY WEAPONS, BUT THAT DOES NOT MITIGATE ITS LETHALITY. IT IS ALSO THE MOST READILY AVAILABLE. IN ALMOST ANY FIGHT IN NEARLY ANY ENVIRONMENT, AN OBJECT WITHIN REACH CAN BE HASTILY GRABBED AND USED TO BASH ANOTHER HUMAN'S BRAINS OUT.

ating from many homicide investigation schools, I've never seen a human decapitated by a homicidal gunshot wound. Decapitation by knife, however, is not uncommon. Anyone who has butchered animals on the family farm or after a successful hunting trip can tell you that it takes only a matter of seconds to cut the head entirely off the body of a human-size animal, such as a whitetail deer.

Impact Weapon Lethality

The club is the simplest and crudest of deadly weapons, but that does not mitigate its lethality. It is also the most readily available. In almost any fight in nearly any environment, an object within reach can be hastily grabbed and used to bash another human's brains out. The death weapon may not have left its maker intended to be a bludgeon, but any hard object with some mass can be a makeshift bludgeon. The brick, the paperweight, and almost anything in between can be "clubbed" or turned into a striking instrument.

That seemingly harmless icon of innocent childhood, the baseball bat, is a common tool of assault and murder. Legend says notorious crime lord Al Capone used a ball bat to murder two associates he no longer trusted.

Common tools become remarkably efficient death weapons, some more readily than others. Police batons have rounded surfaces to reduce fractures to the underlying bone and minimize lacerations while delivering a stunning impact to stop the recipient's physical assault. Many standard tools and other objects have rough, irregular edges, which are *conducive* to shattering bones and splitting flesh. The ordinary claw hammer is a particularly deadly murder weapon. In blows to the head, it often punches entirely through the skull wall and into the soft, vulnerable brain tissue beneath. Hammer murderers have told in their confessions how the hammer became stuck inside the victim's skull so deeply that they had to step or even stomp on the head to break the hammer free for the next blow. Crowbars are also associated with particularly destructive blunt force injuries. The list goes on.

Anyone would recognize a broken bottle held by its neck as a deadly, edged weapon. It's easy to miss that an unbroken bottle, made of heavy glass, is more than sufficient to beat someone to death. If it is unopened and still full of liquid, it is all the more deadly once it is clubbed and turned to assaultive purpose.

Tres cervezas. What something is may be defined by what is done with it. In most settings, this is just a tasty bottle of beer...

...but held like this, it can become a deadly bludgeon...

...and in this case, a lethal edged weapon.

I took the Medico-Legal Investigation of Death class many years ago at the Metro-Dade (now Miami-Dade) Medical Examiner's Office. The legendary forensic pathologist Dr. Joe Davis was still the CME (Chief Medical Examiner) then and was the man who had created that training program. At one point, the homicide investigators and forensic pathologists taking the class were asked to look at slides of specific injuries and try to diagnose the cause.

One slide on the screen was a headless man whose neck came to a stop in a thick puddle of blood and brain matter spread flat across the kitchen floor. Hypotheticals abounded. "The stove exploded while he had his head in it?" "A hand grenade in his mouth?"

When we all gave up, Joe Davis said, "None of those things. I'll show you." He clicked the next slide up: a tiny woman about five feet tall, weighing no more than a hundred pounds, her hair and clothing covered with gore. He clicked again: a claw hammer thick with drying blood, hair and bits of brain matter. "She said she couldn't take his beatings anymore. She hit him in the head with the hammer. He fell to the floor. She was so afraid he'd get back to his feet and hurt her that she hit him again, and again, and again."

Like the knife, the bludgeon doesn't jam or run out of ammunition. The brutal blows it inflicts are louder than a knife piercing flesh but much quieter and stealthier than a gunshot. A cop or parole officer who finds a convicted felon carrying the readily available knife can arrest him for illegal possession, not so if the same convicted felon is carrying the classic heavy, ridged glass bottle of Coca-Cola.

The "Unarmed Motorist"

There are out-of-control people in our society who use their vehicles as weapons. Police run across it more than ordinary citizens, but it can happen to anyone who becomes a victim of "road rage" or finds themselves in the path of a criminal desperate to escape. It is not unknown for an angry spouse to use their vehicle as a deadly weapon and run over the partner who has incurred their rage.

If in your community tonight a violent criminal attempts to run down a police officer and is shot, it is all but guaranteed that tomorrow morning's newspaper will have a headline reading "Unarmed Motorist Shot by Police."

Unarmed? A full-size automobile traveling 50 mph generates *approximately half a million foot-pounds of energy!* Far from being unarmed, the violent man who turns his automobile into a guided missile has armed himself with the most crushingly powerful bludgeon. Deliberately driving at a person on foot is a serious crime, delineated in some jurisdictions as "assault with a deadly weapon, to wit, a motor vehicle." That angry spouse who runs over the significant other is culpable for murder in every jurisdiction.

I was in Austin, Texas, on the day in 2014 during the South by Southwest Festival when a suspect being pursued by police deliberately drove his vehicle into a large crowd of people. He killed two and injured 23 and was charged with capital murder.

The United States is the world's most motorized nation. Our vehicles become extensions of our home in daily life, complete with cushioned "armchairs" and elaborate sound systems. Indeed, the laws of some states treat the vehicle as an extension of the home. We simply don't see ourselves as armed during what may be hours a day when we hold a steering wheel. Thus, the "unarmed driver" meme is an easy sell to the general public and the jury pool. When a driver turns his car into a weapon, and someone has to shoot him to stop him and prevent the death of themselves or other innocent people, it's going to take some logical explanation to educate a jury that at the moment he was killed, that rogue driver was exerting unlawful deadly force with a destructive weapon.

There is an interesting dynamic in auto-pedestrian assaults, and perhaps to some extent, in all road rage incidents. Look to the movie "Aliens," starring Sigourney Weaver. The athletic, six-foot-tall Weaver played a female astronaut in the future, doing constant battle with a huge and almost indestructible monster from another planet. To defeat the creature, she gets inside a powerful robot designed for cargo loading, which allows her to equal the alien's great power. In the fight that followed, she flung the monster into infinite space, winning the fight and saving the day.

That movie scene is an allegory to the mentality of the angry person who turns a vehicle into a weapon. Perhaps feeling inadequate and weak on their own, the vehicle becomes their powerful exoskeleton, vastly multiplying the force they can exert and the damage they can inflict.

> "
>
> SIMILARLY, THE ANGRY PERSON WHO TURNS THEIR VEHICLE INTO A MURDER WEAPON IS MUCH LIKE SIGOURNEY WEAVER'S CHARACTER DONNING THE ROBOT EXOSKELETON TO FIGHT THE OTHERWISE UNBEATABLE SPACE MONSTER OR THE BAD GUY IN THE IRON MAN COMICS AND MOVIES WHO STEALS THAT TITLE CHARACTER'S SUPERCHARGED METAL SUIT TO BECOME INVULNERABLE AND SUPER-POWERFUL AND CRUSH HIS ENEMIES.

Life imitates art, though art more often imitates life. We've all met the person who chooses a vehicle to compensate for his perceived personal inadequacies — the man who chooses a "young" car when a mid-life crisis hits or the man who sees himself as weak and compensates with a "muscle car" or "monster truck." In the famous comic strip "Rose Is Rose," the title character is a meek and mild housewife who develops a Harley-riding biker chick persona as her alter ego to become the strong woman who takes no crap from anyone.

Similarly, the angry person who turns their vehicle into a murder weapon is much like Sigourney Weaver's character donning the robot exoskeleton to fight the otherwise unbeatable space monster or the bad guy in the Iron Man comics and movies who steals that title character's supercharged metal suit to become invulnerable and super-powerful and crush his enemies.

But in this real-life scenario, the vehicle is the powerful exoskeleton, the super-suit, and in his distorted perception, you are the enemy he is trying to crush.

The word "crush" is not an exaggeration. Any pathologist, trauma surgeon or emergency room professional, firefighter, paramedic or police officer who has seen the result of an auto-pedestrian collision can describe the sort of human wreckage that ensues.

I've seen total decapitation and heads and faces so horribly mangled that the victim's mother would not be able to identify the corpse. I remember one young man whose head and facial features were compressed into a hideously distorted egg shape by the automobile tire that went over him and fatally crushed his brain. I've seen intestines and other internal organs burst out of the body from the internal compression caused by the vehicle striking them. I've seen genitals torn away from the body by the brutal friction of the spinning tires that went over the front of the torso lengthways. The emergency services professionals cited above can tell you that the person on foot being "strained through the grille" of the car that hit them is not a figure of speech. It is not unknown to find bits of human flesh inside the grille and bumper and even the engine compartment of the vehicle that struck the hapless pedestrian.

When this kind of murder attempt goes down, I've found that often the intended victim will later say something like, "The car became a thing that was trying to kill me." The vehicle looms so large that it dominates the consciousness of the person it is rushing. If the victim cannot simply move sideways and evade, instinct takes over and tells the intended victim to fight back with the most powerful weapon available. If that weapon is a firearm, it's natural to expect the victim to resort to it.

A vehicle bearing down on you is like a huge, dangerous animal charging you. To stop it by shooting it, you can't aim for its body or legs; that won't stop it in time. Any experienced dangerous game hunter will tell you to aim for the brain. On a Cape buffalo, your hunting guide will tell you to aim into the skull just below the boss of the horns because that's where its brain is located. When the dangerous thing charging you is a motor vehicle, its "brain" — the thing guiding and controlling its charge — is located behind the steering wheel. Therefore, with the strongest logic, the intended victim of the run-down attempt shoots at the driver.

Why not simply duck to the side? This theory was the paradigm in the early 1970s when I first became a sworn police officer and law enforcement instructor in firearms and deadly force. The theory was that gunfire might kill the driver but could not stop the oncoming vehicle, so the officer should duck to the side. The theory also held that a wounded driver might go a mile away and pass out from his wounds, sending the vehicle out of control and endangering the public.

Over the years, this theory changed on both counts, based on collective experience. Vehicles are surprisingly nimble, particularly motorcycles. It's not easy to maneuver out of the path of the oncoming vehicle when its driver has the power to "track" you with a touch of the steering wheel or handlebars, but neutralizing him with gunfire prevents him from doing that. Indeed, even if the bullet only wounds the driver or misses him entirely, his instinct is often to veer away from you, the source of the pain. Moreover, in most cases, when the driver is neutralized, his vehicle comes to a halt in a relatively short distance.

Because the public, many plaintiffs' lawyers, and even some prosecutors do not see the motor vehicle as a weapon, these cases often go to trial, if only in civil court. One day in Miami, a two-time loser for drug dealing named Clement Anthony Lloyd was fleeing from the police on his high-powered motorcycle, one cargo pocket of his pants filled with the cocaine he was selling, and the other with the cash he'd received from what he had sold that day. He wound up being pursued by police through the Overtown district of the city. A Miami PD field training officer (FTO) named William Lozano was standing beside the street taking a crime report from a citizen with his rookie partner Dawn Campbell when they heard sirens approaching and what was described by multiple witnesses as the "howling sound" of a motorcycle revving at the red line. Stepping into the street to see what was going on, Officer Lozano was instantly confronted by the onrushing motorcycle, whose driver saw him and turned deliberately toward him on course to run him down.

There was no time to run. As he desperately tried to turn away, in a movement witnesses described as similar to a bullfighter's *passata soto*, Lozano reflexively drew his department issue Glock 17 and fired a single shot. The bullet struck Lloyd in the head, killing him instantly. The vehicle traveled about a hundred yards and crashed head-on into a Buick containing two felony suspects who had just been released from jail. (Welcome to Overtown.) While neither of those men was seriously injured, the crash killed a young man riding pillion behind Lloyd on the motorcycle, a tragic corollary casualty unusual for this sort of incident.

The officer had not seen the young man because he was directly behind the operator, hurtling the bike toward him. He experienced the tunnel vision effect that is so common in life-threatening encounters. The bike was a Kawasaki Ninja 600 café racer. The crashed bike was in third gear, and the 115-grain 9mm Silvertip bullet from the officer's weapon had killed Lloyd so quickly he could not have changed gears. Lozano was charged with manslaughter, and I was hired as an expert witness by his defense lawyers, Roy Black and Mark Seiden. One of the first things I did was call Kawasaki. Its engineers told me that if the Ninja 600 was "howling at red line" at the top of third gear, it would have been doing approximately 93 mph.

Florida v. Lozano went through two torturous trials. During the second, my suitcases were packed in the front hall, and I was about to drive to the airport to fly to Miami to testify when I received a noontime phone call from Mark Seiden. He told me I wouldn't be needed with an incongruously cheerful tone in his voice. When I asked why he said, "Turn on Court TV after the lunch break." That channel was broadcasting the trial live in real-time.

I watched on the tube as the lead prosecutor, a highly competent trial advocate, told the court, "The state rests." At that point, the cameras cut to

Roy Black at the defense table, who stood up and said with a big, confident smile, "Your Honor, given that the state has presented no case, the defense rests also."

It was a stunning courtroom ploy, like a jump-spinning back kick in a karate tournament. You're either going to score a spectacular knockout, or you're going to fall ignominiously on your butt.

In this case, it was a spectacular knockout. The jury soon returned with a total acquittal on all counts.

I was retained in another case of a similar nature in Sanford, Florida. A violent teenager had driven his car savagely at two private security guards, both of whom drew their 9mm pistols and fired, killing him. The cross-racial shooting of a teenager created a great furor in the community, a cry for the blood of those who pulled the trigger, and a homicide charge resulted. Attorney Chris Ray hired me as an expert witness. The prosecution objected furiously, and I had to go to Sanford for a hearing before the trial judge, where I laid out the testimony I planned to give. The judge determined

I WAS RETAINED IN ANOTHER CASE OF A SIMILAR NATURE IN SANFORD, FLORIDA. A VIOLENT TEENAGER HAD DRIVEN HIS CAR SAVAGELY AT TWO PRIVATE SECURITY GUARDS, BOTH OF WHOM DREW THEIR 9MM PISTOLS AND FIRED, KILLING HIM. THE CROSS-RACIAL SHOOTING OF A TEENAGER CREATED A GREAT FUROR IN THE COMMUNITY, A CRY FOR THE BLOOD OF THOSE WHO PULLED THE TRIGGER...

that it would be of value to the triers of the facts and ruled that I would be allowed to testify.

On the day the defense was scheduled, I was already in the courtroom. Usually, all witnesses are sequestered outside the courtroom until they have testified, but apparently, the prosecution saw no point in arguing when Ray asked if I could be present earlier. The prosecution rested. It was just before lunch. Before the court went into recess, Ray stood and performed a familiar ritual of defense attorneys: he motioned to dismiss on the grounds that the state had not proven its case. This is usually a *pro forma* gesture, done if nothing else in hopes of perhaps preserving some grounds for appeal if a conviction results. But Chris Ray didn't make it as a routine motion. He made it one of the most eloquent, heartfelt arguments I've ever heard in a courtroom, detailing every flaw in the state's theory and why the bullets fired by his client, Billy Swofford, were fired with absolute justification. The judge said he would consider it, which was surprising; as routinely as it's made, the motion to dismiss is just as routinely rejected by the bench. The judge declared a recess, and we all went to lunch.

When we returned, the courtroom and halls were *swarming* with Seminole County deputies. I heard someone ask, "Has there been a bomb threat or something?" But what went through my mind was, "Oh, my God — *he's going to grant it!*"

And he did. In a no-nonsense voice and in no uncertain terms, the judge made it clear that while the decedent was a fleeing felon, in any case, his actions in running the car toward the security officers could only be construed as an attempt to murder them, and that his death at their hands was justifiable. He then dismissed the case with prejudice, meaning that it could never be brought again.

While most such cases involve the police (or security, as the one above), it is not unknown for them to involve private citizens who fire in self-defense.

While there can always be negative outcomes, acquittal seems to be the most common outcome when the shooting of an "unarmed motorist" who attempts murder by motor vehicle meets death by defensive gunfire. Unfortunately, requiring a trial to sort out the facts and achieve this just outcome also seems to be "par for the course," if only in civil court in lieu of criminal court.

Less Lethal Weapons

When a police chief pinned my first badge on me in 1972, what we now call "intermediate force options" such as the police baton were referred to as "non-lethal weapons." If it seems unfair that such a thing would be "a deadly weapon, to wit a bludgeon" when wielded against an ostensibly unarmed man by a private citizen but was merely a tool of arrest in similar circumstances for the sworn officer, it was because there were differences in purpose and application. "Clubbing a man about the head and shoulders" constitutes potentially lethal brute force. In modern times, the police have been taught to strike at motor nerve complexes, hit the limbs to reduce mobility and "defang the snake," or thrust into the abdomen to fold the suspect, take his wind, and reduce his ability to continue fighting.

There was also the element of necessary force *vis-à-vis* equal force: the civilian was seen at law as needing only sufficient force to make an assailant stop attacking him, while the officer had a sworn duty to overpower all resistance, pursue if necessary, completely overpower and capture and manacle and transport the suspect. This being a much more difficult sequence of events to accomplish than merely convincing the opponent to abjure from the conflict, greater latitude in using that intermediate force was granted to the law enforcement officer.

Over the years, the terminology changed from "non-lethal" to "less lethal" or "less than lethal." The reason was simple: in a real-world application, intermediate force weapons weren't always non-lethal. A fight is generally a rapid swirl of movement involving at least two people. Sometimes, for example, a baton swing intended for a suspect's shoulder or upper arm might hit the rounded deltoid muscle and skid off into the head as the suspect tried to duck away from the stick. The result could be a blow to the temple with enough power to fracture the skull or cause permanent or fatal brain injury.

The same dynamic was seen with other intermediate force options as police technology advanced. Chemical Mace™ came out in the 1960s and was first seen by the public as "a magic spray that makes the bad guys go away." It was essentially tear gas delivered by aerosol, and the teaching protocol was to spray it at the offender's chest and allow the vapors to rise to his eyes or nostrils. This proved to be particularly spotty in its performance. Lawmen of the day were prone to comment bitterly that it only worked on cops and victims. In later iterations, the manufacturer issued the product with a warning to the effect of "Caution: this substance may not be effective on those under the influence of drugs, alcohol, or state of rage." (My reaction was, "Who the hell else would we ever have to Mace?")

Aerosol sprays got better, and soon we had pepper spray, known colloquially as OC for its active ingredient, oleoresin capsicum. It worked vastly better than the original tear gas sprays, but there were still some people who could resist its effects. Famed police martial arts instructor Phil Messina testified in a case in the Pacific Northwest where pepper spray failed an officer so badly that the man he sprayed beat him to death with a chunk of wood. Most police departments soon learned that since their people could be affected by the spray, they had to learn to fight through those effects, and it became a standard part of training. The cops realized that if *they* could fight through it, so could their criminal opponents on the street.

But, more to the point of the topic, there were a proportionally tiny number of deaths involving those sprays. Usually, the victim was an asthmatic or a sufferer of some other serious respiratory disease who, unknown to the officers applying the spray, could not take that level of interference with breathing. When electronic restraint devices (ERDs) typified by the super-popular TASER came out, there was the occasional death. Most commonly, medico-legal investigations have determined that the cause of such deaths was a usually-drug-induced phenomenon known as excited delirium. However, here and there, a medical examiner did attribute the death in question to the TASER. (By the way, yes, it's TASER in all caps. It's an acronym for Thomas A. Swift's Electronic Rifle, believe it or not. Never let it be said that law enforcement and the industries that serve it are totally devoid of whimsy.)

So, we see why the "non-lethal" terminology went by the board in favor of "less lethal" or "less than lethal." Which brings us to the question: *What level of force may the private citizen use against a criminal who attacks them with intermediate force weapons?*

To answer, we must first parse the weapons involved. Let's separate the striking instruments from the aerosol incapacitants and electronic restraint devices. We have already established that any club or bludgeon, even a makeshift one, is considered a deadly weapon when in the hands of a law-breaking assailant, creating the Ability factor in terms of the Ability/Opportunity/Jeopardy triad that makes deadly force justifiable in response.

Can a similar approach be taken when the robber or rapist is armed with Mace, OC spray or an electronic "stun gun"? The answer seems to be a qualified "Yes," and it comes more from Attorneys General at the state level than from case law.

Almost as soon as the incapacitating sprays came out, cops asked, "What do we do if the bad guy gets hold of our spray — or has his own — and sprays *us?*" This is a question street cops ask of their chief or department legal advisor, and it is a question that chiefs and legal advisors generally buck upstairs to their state's Attorney General. A State Attorney General is usually seen as the chief law enforcement officer of the entire state, and as far as cops are concerned, his opinion on the matter is very close to the law. If I may be forgiven for comparing the justice system with the Holy Trinity, a decision rendered by the United States Supreme Court is pretty much the word of God for practical law enforcement purposes. A Federal Court of Appeals or State Supreme Court ruling may as well have come from Jesus Christ himself. By that analogy, an official opinion by the State Attorney General's Office carries the gravitas of a determination from the Holy Ghost.

Every such State Attorney General's opinion I've seen or heard of on the matter of responding to a criminal attacking with spray or stun gun is, "You can shoot him: it's a deadly force situation." The reason is that criminal use of something intended to render the recipient helpless creates a reasonable belief that said criminal intends to do something nefarious to that recipient once the helplessness is achieved. Moreover, abuse of these tools can kill.

Yes, the incapacitating sprays are designed to be less than lethal, but they are designed to be used only until the suspect can no longer resist arrest. If the criminal sticks the spray dispenser in the victim's mouth and hoses it down his throat until it is empty, the likelihood of death or grave permanent injury is relatively high for anyone. The manufacturers and instructors of the TASER would, I'm sure, be first in line to tie the noose around the neck of the abuser who held the device against the forbidden target of a person's head or cervical spine and ran a constant series of drive stuns until the central nervous system was fried and irreparably damaged.

In 2013, at the height of public concern over group assaults on lone victims in violent flash mob attacks and a "point 'em out, knock 'em out" game of violence that became popular among inner-city youth, a teen with a stun gun attacked a victim with it. The teen suffered what I've come to call "sudden and acute failure of the victim-selection process": His intended victim, licensed to carry, drew a Smith & Wesson .40-caliber pistol and shot him down. Not only did the armed citizen go uncharged, but the teenage assailant was convicted and sentenced to a year in jail and publicly apologized to the man he had attacked.

Disparity of Force: The "Unarmed" Assailant

One of the least understood principles in deadly force law is *disparity of force*. It applies directly to the Ability factor in the Ability/Opportunity/Jeopardy equation.

Disparity of force is the principle that allows the victim, or the person defending the victim, to use lethal force against an unarmed person. It applies *only* when the ostensibly "unarmed" assailant has no "deadly weapon" *per se* but within the totality of the circumstances has a physical/tactical advantage over the victim that is so great that if the assault continues, death or great bodily harm is likely to be suffered by the said victim.

Disparity of force can take many forms. *Force of numbers* is one of the most common. A *significant disparity in size and strength* is another. *Male attacking female, adult violently attacking child*, and *able-bodied attacking the handicapped* also constitute a disparity of force. So does a *highly skilled hand-to-hand fighter attacking the less skilled*, and the *position of disadvantage*, in which the law-breaking attacker has a substantial tactical or physical advantage other than the disparity of size, strength or skill as the assault unfolds.

Because so few people among the general public, who constitute the jury pool, understand this — and because so many attorneys never hear the term "disparity of force" in law school — it's essential to discuss it here in detail.

Force of Numbers

The law has long since recognized that when two or more criminals attack a lone victim, their physical and tactical advantage is so great that their single victim is likely to suffer death or grave bodily harm if the attack is not stopped immediately. (And, of course, the innocent victim has no prudent reason to believe that the attack *will* be stopped before that point by their violent assailants.)

A classic case in this vein was *Michigan v. Ossian Sweet* in 1925. Dr.

Sweet was a black physician in Michigan when segregation was the law in the South and "practice if not law" even in the North. He and his wife Gladys purchased a home in a Detroit neighborhood that was "all-white." Hellish racial animosity ensued and rose to the level of a deadly threat. On the day in question, Dr. Sweet had been so alarmed he had bought guns for the friends and relatives who came to his home to protect him. Hostile crowds formed, at first held back by local police. When the mob began to storm the house, first throwing rocks through the windows, the defenders inside opened fire. One white man was killed, and another wounded.

Murder charges resulted. Legendary attorney Clarence Darrow took the case for the defense. In the following chain of trials, all the defenders were ultimately exonerated, either by verdicts of not guilty or by prosecutorial dismissal of charges.

Not long after this trial, the classic legal text *Warren on Homicide* appeared in 1938. This authoritative text was destined to become known as "The Bible of Homicide Law" among lawyers and judges. The author(s) made it clear that when an individual faced a mob bent on doing violence to him or his compatriots, each member shared the culpability of the entire organism of the mob. Therefore, each was equally and individually fair game for the defensive violence suffered at the hands of the lawful defender(s).

One would have thought that would have decided the issue ... and one would be wrong. It has long been a societal norm in the entertainment media, from books to "moving pictures" to the entertainment and even news media of today, that "only a cowardly murderer would shoot/stab/kill" an "unarmed man." We live in a society where media memes have so overpowered collective logic and even long-established law and case law precedent that it takes a full-blown trial for the truth to come out and for law and justice to prevail.

Significant Disparity In Size and Strength, Which Favors the Assailant

When it comes to significant disparity, the first and most obvious question is, "What exactly marks the borders of *significant?*" The answer is, in a buzzword of the courts, it depends on "the totality of the circumstances."

In February 2013, I testified in a first-degree murder case in West Virginia. I was brought in as an expert witness by Brian Abraham, a highly skilled defense attorney who had formerly been District Attorney in the jurisdiction where the shooting went down. In my continuing series "Ayoob Files" in *American Handgunner* magazine, where my article on the case is archived, at the request of the defendant, I changed the names of the participants in the deadly fight to "Mr. Phist," the now-deceased attacker, and "Mr. Gunn," the defendant who shot him in defense of his own life and the lives of his wife and two little boys. To make a long story short, Mr. Phist was six-foot-three, and Mr. Gunn had been told he weighed "300 to 350 pounds of solid muscle," and on the night in question, dressed in cold weather garb, "Phist" appeared to be all of that. "Gunn," by contrast, was an average-size man.

Phist had threatened previously to "beat the life out of" Gunn, and when he showed up on Gunn's doorstep, the latter had the presence of mind to tell his wife to take the kids into another room and tucked a Ruger P345 pistol into his waistband before he answered the door. (Arming himself would later be cited by arresting officer and prosecuting attorney alike as the "premeditation" element which justified a first-degree murder charge. In court, I explained to the jury that the bailiff had armed himself with a .40-caliber pistol and the arresting officer who sat beside the prosecutor had armed himself with a Smith & Wesson .45, not because they intended to murder someone that day, but because they knew their duties might require them to defend innocent human lives, including their own — and the defendant had armed himself for the same reason, in light of his right to protect his own life, and his ethical duty to protect his wife and children from clear and present danger.)

Stepping through the front door to talk to the man in hopes of calming his anger, Gunn was met by angry screams from his massive opponent, who soon repeated, "I'll beat the life out of you!" ... and then proceeded to start to do exactly that. Phist landed a punch to the face so brutally powerful that it knocked Gunn's teeth loose and sent him rocking back, and knowing that this was his last chance to protect himself and his family, Gunn drew his .45 and fired as fast as he could pull the trigger. Not until his pistol had run empty to slide-lock did he realize that, in the dim light of a November evening, his opponent had turned and run and then collapsed.

Several fatal bullets had entered behind the lateral midline — "shot in the back" in the common parlance, yet another dynamic that the general public has been conditioned for centuries to associate with an innocent victim murdered by a vile killer who deserved severe punishment. I was able to explain the dynamics of that, too, in the same way they are explained elsewhere in this book. Other elements were in play, but a critical factor in the case was the unarmed man being shot by a man with "a .45 automatic loaded with extra-deadly hollowpoint bullets."

When the corpse was weighed at autopsy, Mr. Phist was only in the high 200s on the scale. Close enough. Remember the yardstick of judgment: "What would a reasonable and prudent person have done, in the same situation, knowing what the defendant knew?" Seen in the light most favorable to the prosecution, the deceased was still vastly larger and more physically powerful than the man who shot him. Seen in the light most favorable to the defense — what the defendant knew at the time he drew his gun and fired the fatal shots — the attacker was all the more advantaged over the defendant by a disparity of force.

The jury came to what I consider to be the correct conclusion. They found the defendant not guilty on all charges. He went home that night to sleep in his bed in the same house as his two little boys. Sentencing guidelines in the state where it was tried would have sent him to prison for life without parole if he had been found guilty.

Male Attacking Female

It has long been understood at law that a man attacking a woman has a huge physical advantage over her. The male of our species tends, on average, to run larger and heavier than the female. Any physiologist can tell you that, even if height and weight are equal, the man has dramatically more physical strength than the woman and that this is particularly true regarding upper body strength. *Human beings kill with their hands, whether or not those hands are holding deadly weapons.* When the "personal weapon" is the kicking or stomping foot instead of the punching or strangling hand, the greater weight of the male body driving the blow causes more damage.

Moreover, it is well understood in logic and law alike that the cultural predisposition of the male is toward combat and conflict, and that of the female is toward tenderness and nurturing. Throughout history, the males of our society have been taught to hit hard and play tough and that aggressiveness is the sign of the "winner." The females of the same period were taught, "My dear, no one likes a pushy, assertive bitch." It ain't fair, it ain't right, but it is what it is, and we'd all be fools not to recognize it. In its wisdom, the law recognizes the differences between males and females in terms of physical strength and a predisposition to aggression and ferocity of attack.

I had to deal with this for the first time in the 1980s in the case of *Florida v. Mary Menucci Hopkin* in Miami, Florida. Mary was a tall, slender woman of 63 who had acute arthritis. Her common-law husband, James Yarolem, was 43 years old, weighed about 230 pounds, and liked to brag to Mary about having once murdered a man and gotten away with it. She worked; he didn't; he lived in her trailer like a parasite. He also beat her frequently and mercilessly. The day came when she told him, "Jim, you drink all my beer, you smoke all my cigarettes, you won't get a job..." and told him it was time to go. She didn't mention, "You also beat the crap out of me," because that was pretty much a given.

Jim didn't take that news well. He began to beat the hell out of her *again*. When she reached for the telephone on the wall of her trailer to call the police, he ripped it out of the wall before she could make the connection, then wrapped the cord around her neck and strangled her until she became unconscious, and he thought she was dead. Satisfied with what he had done, he left the mobile home and went to the nearest bar. While he was there, she regained consciousness and crawled out of the trailer to a nearby mobile home for help, where someone called the police. When Jim came back, the police were there and arrested him. The cops who made that arrest would testify at her trial that as they took him away, James Yarolem was screaming, "Mary, you fucking bitch, I'll kill you for this!"

Before long, James had bonded himself out of custody. Pausing only long enough to find enough booze to get him to the .18 percent blood alcohol content that autopsy would determine was in his bloodstream after he died, he made his way back to the trailer. Like the Big Bad Wolf, he yelled threateningly, "Mary, let me in!" Armed with a cheap RG-14 .22-caliber revolver made out of pot metal — thank heaven, one of the few ever made that worked — Mary answered that she knew what he was going to do, and she wasn't going to let him do it, and she begged him to stay away.

James Yarolem broke down the door — the jury saw the pictures of the shattered doorway — and came at her. Mary pulled the trigger three times. James turned and ran and got into the yard before he collapsed and died; one of the little .22 bullets had found its way into his heart.

Mary Hopkin was charged with murder in the second degree. At 63, if convicted, she would have died in prison. Living at the poverty level, she qualified for a Public Defender or, in Florida, Assigned Counsel. In a stroke of great good fortune, the Assigned Counsel she drew was Mark Seiden.

It was not the first case I would do with this gifted defense attorney and would not be the last. The time would come later when Mark and I would serve two years as co-vice chairs of the Forensic Evidence Committee of the National Association of Criminal Defense Lawyers. He called me to see if I would take the case since there was no money to pay for expert witnesses. After reviewing the evidence, I took the case.

There were other elements besides the apparent disparity of force in size, strength, gender, and predisposition to extreme physical violence. Still, the disparity of force was, in my opinion, the primary issue. Mark took his time at trial, taking me through direct testimony explaining why she couldn't effectively retreat, why there was no time for her to call the police, etc. and, perhaps most important, why the jury could believe that this time, the man who had left her for dead once before could finish the job and make sure that she was dead.

My testimony under Seiden's questioning — he has always been detail-oriented and always knew enough to leave no stone unturned and no issue on the other side still intact — took quite a while. Cross-examination, on the other hand, was a personal best for me, probably about 45 seconds.

I don't have a transcript to quote from. Transcripts are expensive, and testimony need not be transcribed when neither side appeals the issue. But just going from memory, it went like this:

Q: Mister Ayoob, you're normally paid for your testimony in cases like this, aren't you?

A: I'm paid for my time, sir. My testimony is not for sale.

Q: How much do you charge for your time?

A: (What I charged in the 1980s). (NOTE: at this point, the prosecutor was conspicuously rubbing his thumb against his forefinger in front of the jury in the age-old gesture that says, "For Money.")

Q: And how much have you already been paid in this case?

A: Nothing, sir. I took this case at no charge.

Q: Why?

A: (Going from courtroom voice to teaching voice) Because this case is an outrage.

Q: Your honor!

(Brief digression for explanation: when you are testifying on the witness stand, and lawyers on either side say "Objection," you are supposed to be silent until the judge has ruled on the objection. However, if they have *not* uttered the magic word "objection," that does not hold.)

A: (Same stern voice): I've seen injustice before, but nothing like this.

Q: (finally): Objection:

Judge: Overruled. You asked him the question!

Q: Sidebar, your honor?

Outside the hearing of the jury:

Q: (By prosecuting attorney) I didn't know he was going to say that!

A: (By attorney Seiden, for the defense) I knew he was going to say that.

Judge: I knew he was going to say that.

Back on the record, within the hearing of the jury:

Q: No further questions.

The bottom line: the jury was out for approximately two hours, including dinner, before they returned a verdict of not guilty on all counts. Some of the jurors waited outside on the courthouse steps to hug Mary Hopkin and tell her they thought her being tried was an outrage, too.

This gives you an idea of how well recognized the male attacker versus female defender disparity is, as seen by a jury in a self-defense shooting.

Skilled/Highly Trained Fighter vs. Average Person

A professional boxer against someone who has never fought except in the schoolyard is recognized at law as someone who has a considerable advantage over the ordinary person they attack. Have you ever heard, "I'm a black belt, and my hands are registered as deadly weapons"? As stated, that's total BS, but in the case law (as opposed to most of the "black letter law" of the statutes and criminal or penal codes), there's some truth to it.

The tricky part is, *how did you know your opponent had that advantage over you?* Once again, we must bear in mind the Reasonable Person standard: "What would a reasonable and prudent person have done, in the same situation, *knowing what the defendant knew?"*

In the case of *Tennessee v. Shawn Armstrong* just a few years ago, the defendant testified that she knew the violent, estranged husband who attacked her and beat her and kicked her when she was down — and was now apparently coming back toward her to "finish the job" — had been trained by the United States Army itself in advanced hand-to-hand combat to the point where he could kill adult male enemy soldiers with his bare hands. Therefore, I was able to speak to that as an expert witness for her defense. It was a cornerstone of our winning an amazingly swift acquittal thanks to the masterful lawyering of her defense attorney, John Colley.

Perhaps you, the defendant, *didn't* know your opponent was a champion fighter, a black belt in this or that martial art, or whatever. But you have just seen him sidekick a six-foot-tall security guard through a plate glass window. That's probably close enough. Remember the standard of judgment: "What would a reasonable and prudent person have done, in the same totality of the circumstances, knowing what you, the now-defendant, knew?

The attacker was where Ayoob is seen here in the foreground when the defendant opened fire. The larger assailant was unarmed, but after the disparity of force was explained to the jury, the defendant was found not guilty.

I was a consultant in a case in South Florida that began when a young man was invited to a party a beautiful young woman was holding at her home. What the young man didn't know was that the home in question belonged to her live-in boyfriend. As the night went on, the young man perceived her as playing up to him, and he responded in kind. The live-in boyfriend took this in the same hostile fashion as you might expect, and since it was his place, he roughly ordered the young man in question to leave.

After taking a while to figure out what was going on, the young man did leave, escorted out by the angry boyfriend and the boyfriend's coterie of friends. The "escorting out" became more and more hostile. In the driveway, in his pickup truck about to leave, the young man in question came under attack: a bat was slammed against his car, and then, the angry boyfriend punched his fist straight through the safety glass of the side door window at his face. Terrified, the young man came up with a .38 and opened fire, killing the assailant. He then sped away, firing a warning shot to keep the others from following, which went harmlessly into an unoccupied part of the building.

To make yet another long story short, the young man in question was acquitted for the killing of his attacker because a skilled defense team made it clear to the jury that a blow that could shatter side window safety glass was a blow that any reasonable, prudent person would conclude was likely to cause death or grave bodily harm if the same powerful fist had connected with the temple it was aimed at. (Ironically, the young man in question was still sent to prison because of the warning shot fired from his vehicle as he was fleeing, which, in the prosecution's theory, could have endangered innocent bystanders ... but that's a topic for another part of this book.)

Adult Violently Attacking Child

Here, we are not talking about the adult defender using deadly force against a large, strong teenager attacking him. We're talking about a full-size adult human attacking a small child who has not yet reached the age of maturity.

In Texas, not long ago, the father of a little girl came upon a man in the act of undeniable rape: forcing sexual intercourse upon his child. The father pulled him off his daughter, hit him with his fists, and kept hitting him — beating the child rapist to death.

In Texas, any homicide typically goes before the Grand Jury. The Grand Jury, in this case, returned a verdict of No True Bill, which says in essence, "We, the Grand Jury, do not believe that a crime has been committed here."

I see no problem with that.

Do you? I didn't think so.

I haven't spoken with any of the people involved in that case. Still, I suspect that they realized that what was going on when the father happened upon the scene was so heinous a felony that it warranted a degree of force that rendered the offender incapable of continuing his horrible crime.

This book has elsewhere addressed the difference between *malum prohibitum* and *malum in se*, the difference between "It's against the law because a law was passed prohibiting it," and "It's against the law because it is a crime so horrible that throughout the history of human society it has been rigidly prohibited and severely punished."

It's hard for any member of society, including the jury pool and the judges who stand as referees of the law, to imagine anything more heinous and worthy of deadly force response than the infliction of death or grave bodily harm (such as rape) upon a helpless young child.

Able-Bodied Attacking the Handicapped

Able-bodied attacking the disabled is an absolute example of disparity of force, *even if the handicap occurs in the conflict!*

Let's suppose that the fight began with no weapons involved except your gun, which was in your holster. For purposes of argument, let's further presume that your opponent is exactly the same height, weight, age, muscularity and gender as you. It has been fist to fist until now.

But then, the opponent lands a kick which, at least for now, cripples one of your legs or arms or makes you reasonably believe that you are about to lose consciousness. Now it is no longer a battle of equals. Your ability to block or evade kicks or punches is now severely limited. The likelihood of your being killed or crippled in the continuing assault is so high that it becomes the equivalent of a deadly weapon in your opponent's hands, war-

> " EVIDENCE AND TESTIMONY SHOWED THAT MARTIN HAD ATTACKED ZIMMERMAN, HAD HIM DOWN AND WAS STRADDLING HIM IN A "MIXED MARTIAL ARTS MOUNT," AND SMASHING HIS HEAD INTO THE SIDEWALK WHEN ZIMMERMAN DREW HIS 9MM KEL-TEC AND FIRED A SINGLE, FATAL SHOT. ZIMMERMAN WAS FOUND NOT GUILTY BY THE JURY.

ranting your recourse to a per se deadly weapon.

One such case in which I testified for the defense as an expert was *Minnick v. Shawn Joyce and Sacramento County*. Shawn was a deputy with the Sacramento County Sheriff's Department and had sustained a severe injury to his right wrist that kept him off full duty at the time of the shooting. It happened at his parents' home in the countryside, where he and his wife were visiting with their kids. There was an informal shooting range on the property, and the family was shooting .22s on a pleasant weekend after-noon. Suddenly a man came charging through the bushes from an adjacent property at the family, screaming like a maniac. Shawn grabbed for one of the target rifles, a semi-automatic .22, identifying himself as a law enforce-ment officer. Following his Pressure Point Control Tactics (PPCT) training, Shawn kicked the attacker in the common peroneal area of his thigh. The powerful blow had no effect: the assailant, who had a long and ugly history with drugs, also had a high blood-alcohol content.

Shawn drew the off-duty gun he was carrying, his wife's SIG Sauer P230 semi-automatic, and ordered the man to halt. Right-handed, he had withdrawn the pistol with his injured right hand out of habituation. When the man lunged for the gun, Shawn realized that he could not effectively retain it against a man this large and strong with his severely weakened wrist, and he opened fire. It took seven of the eight .380 hollowpoints in the little pistol to stop the forward charge. The assailant, Minnick, stopped as if pausing for breath with his hands on his knees as he glared at the deputy. Then he slowly sat down, laid down and died. All seven bullets had hit him, most of them "center mass" in the torso.

The shooting was thoroughly investigated by agencies other than his own and ruled justifiable by law enforcement and the District Attorney's office. However, that was no bar to a lawsuit by the deceased's family, against the officer personally and also against his department.

When I was called to the stand by the masterful Attorney Terry Cas-sidy, I explained the disparity of force issue pretty much as I did here. The desperate plaintiffs had even argued that it was negligence for a man who hadn't qualified on the training range with his off-duty gun to carry it at all, let alone use it, in light of the injury to the wrist of his gun hand. I was able to dispose of that with one of the shortest answers ever in my career on the witness stand: "He fired seven shots, and hit him seven times. Marksmanship is not an issue."

Our arguments succeeded, the principle of disparity of force as it applied to the handicapped attacked by the able-bodied was understood, and the result was a total defense verdict.

Position of Disadvantage

Position of disadvantage is another element of disparity of force. My friend Chris Bird, author of the excellent books *Thank God I Had A Gun* and *The Concealed Handgun Manual*, has written splendidly of the first case in Texas in which an armed citizen used a gun to save his life after shall-issue concealed carry was signed into law by then-Governor George W. Bush. It involved a man of middle years who became the victim of a large, strong, violent young man in a road rage incident. It culminated when the younger man came to the driver's door of the older man's car and began raining savage punches upon him through the open window.

The driver was trapped by his seat belt; the lap and shoulder restraints held him as if the assailant had a criminal accomplice holding him from behind for the first assailant to batter at will mercilessly. The driver could no longer roll with a punch or evade a punch. He could not generate power in counterpunches because of the trapped position. In desperation, the Texas driver drew his .40-caliber Beretta 96 pistol and shot the larger man in the chest. The attacker staggered back when the defender stopped shooting, stumbled toward his vehicle, and collapsed, dying.

As is usually the case with any homicide in Texas, the case went before the Grand Jury. Hearing the facts, the Grand Jury returned No True Bill, effectively saying there was no reason to believe a crime had been committed by the innocent motorist who had shot and killed his attacker in self-defense.

Another example of the position of disadvantage creating disparity of force is found in a case discussed in depth elsewhere in this book, the high-profile shooting death of Trayvon Martin at the hands of George Zimmerman. Evidence and testimony showed that Martin had attacked Zimmerman, had him down and was straddling him in a "mixed martial arts mount," and smashing his head into the sidewalk when Zimmerman drew his 9mm Kel-Tec and fired a single, fatal shot. Zimmerman was found not guilty by the jury.

Suggested Reading

It would be useful for any law-abiding citizen who carries a gun to own a copy of the authoritative text *Medico-Legal Investigation of Death* from Charles C. Thomas Publishers in Springfield, Illinois. Don't just buy it; read it and absorb it! It is edited by Dr. Werner Spitz, one of the all-time great forensic pathologists. I testified with Dr. Spitz in a lawsuit arising from a fatal SWAT team shooting of a suspect in Port Huron, Michigan, and I can tell you the man is simply remarkable in court.

The book explains — and, perhaps more importantly, photographically illustrates — the death of human beings by all sorts of means. Gunshot, knife, bludgeon, stomping, strangulation, automobile collision, auto-pedestrian strike, death by fire and more are thoroughly covered.

When opposing counsel says of your opponent, "He only had a knife (or stick, or bottle)"... "He was unarmed!"... "He was just driving his car!"... "He was only standing there with an ordinary can of gasoline and an ordinary Zippo lighter!"... I would like you to be able to honestly say, "Counselor, at that moment, I knew what he could do to me. My mind flashed back to pictures I had seen of someone stabbed/clubbed/stomped/run over/burned to death. I pictured my mother or my spouse having to identify me looking like that on a slab in the morgue, and I knew I had to stop him."

If you had read the book and articulated what you remember from it, there is now an excellent chance that your attorney can introduce those photos to the jury since those images you had seen were germane to your mindset. Those twelve people and their alternates will now see exactly what you were trying to prevent when you fired defensively. It would be a powerful way to get the truth of what you faced across to the jury. "What would a reasonable and prudent person have done, in the same situation, *knowing what the defendant knew....*"

Ability, the power to kill or cripple, must be readily and immediately deliverable by the attacker to warrant the defender using deadly force against him. That brings us to the next chapter, the opportunity factor. ■

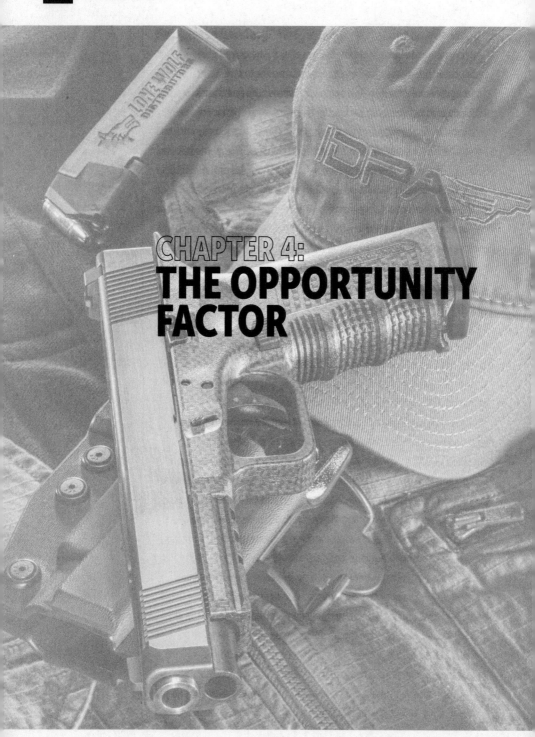

CHAPTER 4:
THE OPPORTUNITY FACTOR

A nother criterion that must be present in the AOJ triad for circumstances warranting defensive deadly force is opportunity. "Ability" means that the opponent possesses the power to kill or cripple; opportunity means that the opponent can carry out that ability in the immediate here and now.

The opportunity factor encompasses distance, obstacles, and perhaps most importantly, time.

Distance Element

The most famous research on the distance element of the opportunity factor was published in 1983 in SWAT Magazine in the article "How Close Is Too Close" by Dennis Tueller. Dennis, at that time, was a sergeant in the Salt Lake City, Utah, Police Department and an adjunct instructor at Jeff Cooper's famous shooting school, Gunsite. One of the Gunsite drills was to start at the seven-yard firing line with hands clear of the holstered weapon and, on the start signal, draw and shoot a silhouette target twice in the chest in 1.5 seconds. This drill is a good test of skill at what Gunsite founder Jeff Cooper called "pistolcraft." Gunsite students usually worked from an

The Tueller Drill in action. A student in the Attacker role runs at one in the Defender role, as a third in the Timer role wields the stopwatch.

exposed open-top holster; it is more challenging when the pistol must be drawn from concealment or a typical "snatch-resistant" police security holster.

Dennis tells me, "I was running the Firearm Training program for SLCPD at that time, and was doing the (draw and fire twice in 1.5 seconds) drill ... with a group of recruit officers. This led to a discussion of the use of deadly force when one of my recruit officers asked about shooting someone who is attacking with a knife, club or other contact weapons. He wondered how close the attacker had to be before you would be justified in shooting. I realized that I didn't have a good answer to that question, and that led to our experiments into reaction and response time."

He continues, "We actually did a role-play with an 'aggressor' and 'victim officer' with two observers with stopwatches to time the attack. I didn't have a rubber knife available, so I think we simply used a plastic pocket comb to represent a weapon."

Their average time was roughly 1.5 seconds.

Tueller adds, "I was doing a class at Gunsite shortly after conducting these experiments at the SLCPD Academy, and was sharing this information with my fellow Gunsite instructors and discussing how to incorporate this into our training. Chuck Taylor was the Operations Officer at Gunsite at that time and was also an editor for the new SWAT Magazine. It was Chuck who encouraged me to write the now famous article."

It was a stunning breakthrough. Before Tueller's revelation, self-defense shooting investigations had often presumed that a man with a contact weapon such as a knife or club had to be within touching distance for his intended victim to be justified in killing him. A police training film produced by Woroner Films and distributed by Motorola Teleprograms, Inc. titled "Shoot/Don't Shoot" was in virtual universal use at police academies. Incorporating the Ability/Opportunity/Jeopardy standard, it was seen as the moving picture equivalent of what the courts call an "authoritative text." Early in the film, officers saw a violent man grab a woman and shove her against a chain link fence while he wielded a knife in such a manner that it was obvious he was about to stab her with it. The film explained that while this scenario would undoubtedly justify deadly force, that might not be the case if the attacker was 10 feet away from his victim.

SWAT magazine had always been widely read in the training commu-nity —including John Farnam and Manny Kapelsohn, to name a few. Most people's reaction to Tueller's article was, "Twenty-one feet in a second and a half? From a standing start? It can't be that fast!" We went out and tried it ourselves and discovered that Tueller was absolutely correct.

We incorporated it into our training immediately, giving attribution. Shortly after the article was published, I taught a Lethal Threat Management for Police class at the Tacoma, Washington, Police Department range. Of course, many Tacoma training officers were in the class. The "Tueller Drill" (more about that shortly) was an eye-opener. The instructors at the depart-ment took it so seriously that they incorporated it into their training, produc-ing a training film on the topic and running every officer through the drill.

Something happened after that, which proved to be a classic example of what some in the training world call the "oil stain effect." Akin to the "rip-ples from a rock thrown in the water" metaphor, it means that if you place a tiny drop of oil in the middle of a piece of linen, the oil's stain will spread, wider and wider. One entity does the research. The result of that research is spread to several instructors. They, in turn, pass it on to far more practitio-ners, and the research saves lives in that last generation of the transmission.

Soon, an incident occurred in Tacoma. A crazed man with a knife attacked a woman and absolutely savaged her. A BOLO (Be On the Look-Out) was broadcast to Tacoma officers. Soon, the suspect was spotted. He was hard to miss: naked, covered with blood, wielding a large knife in one hand and a bludgeon in the other. The first officer who spotted him called for backup, and soon multiple officers were on the scene. They arrayed themselves in a semi-circle to prevent a crossfire, something their critics would later describe as "firing squad formation." All the cops, of course, had their guns drawn. The highest-ranking officer present, a sergeant, ordered the suspect to drop his weapons.

With a hostile expression, the suspect moved toward the sergeant, who fired one shot. The 9mm bullet struck the madman's center chest. The knife wielder paused for a second, then uttered an inchoate scream of rage and lunged at the officer.

The cops all opened fire. The assailant went down in the proverbial hail of bullets, falling virtually at the sergeant's feet, stopped barely in time by multiple gunshot wounds.

The deceased attacker was African-American. There had been allegations of racism and police brutality against the department involved. The situation flared like kerosene on a fire. "Cross-racial shooting." "He only had a knife." "Why couldn't five cops restrain one lone, nude man without killing him?" "Why did they have to shoot him so many times if malice wasn't involved?" "They shouldn't have killed him; he wasn't in his right mind, so it wasn't his fault!"

What seemed to be ignored in the whole matter was the dead criminal's victim, an African-American woman he had attacked and mangled like Jack the Ripper.

It became a major political issue in the city, and the case went before a grand jury. The proceedings of a grand jury are usually secret, but in this unusual instance, it was made public.

Each of the officers who had fired testified. All but one stated in their initial reports that it was fresh in their mind from their (Tueller Drill) training how quickly the man could have reached the sergeant with his deadly blade if he was not stopped by gunfire. They all said the same to the grand jury.

The trainers were brought in to testify. They made the speed of closure apparent to the grand jury. They demonstrated the drill live in front of the ju-rors. I was told later that, during their deliberations, the grand jury members went out into the courthouse hall and ran the drill themselves.

They returned No True Bill, which means a determination that no crime had been committed by the officers who fired the fatal shots. The foreper-son of the grand jury, a prominent African-American woman, stated publicly that there was nothing else the officers could have done at that point.

Let's review the oil stain effect. First, Tueller completes and publishes his research. Second, his peers evaluate and accept it ("peer review" at its most effective level) and begin teaching it. Third, those who receive the training share it with others who need to know it. And at the fourth level of transmission, it saves the life of one law enforcement officer and the careers of many more.

Grasping Tueller's Principle

That oil stain under discussion will always be most intense at its center. As it spreads, it can weaken. Remember VHS videotapes? People would copy and copy them, and in each stage of copying, they became fuzzier and more indistinct and harder to interpret. So it was, unfortunately, with Tueller's research.

We came to see misinterpretations. Some said, "Okay, this means that if the guy with the knife is 20 feet, 11 inches away, you can shoot him, but if he's 21 feet, 1 inch away, you can't." False! That simply is not the correct interpretation.

Suppose the man with the knife stands still, 21 feet away from you or his other victim. Suppose he is holding a knife but pointing it to the ground and standing as if in a catatonic state. Would you be justified in shooting him? Of course not, at least not at that moment.

Suppose he is half again as far away but has already attacked you twice and is lunging at you with that knife after uttering threatening words? Are you expected to wait until he crosses an invisible 21-foot line before press-ing the trigger? Of course not.

This writer had to deal with that in the 1980s, in the case of State of New York v. Frank Magliato. Magliato was attacked on a New York City street by a junkie who had threatened him with deadly force more than once earlier that night. The soon-to-be-deceased Anthony Gianni screamed, "I've been looking for you, fucker!" and, raising a two-foot police baton over his head in a ready-to-club motion, began to lunge. At that moment, Magliato — who had drawn the .38 Colt Detective Special revolver he was licensed to carry, cocked the hammer (unfortunately) and shouted for the man to stay back — unintentionally pressed the trigger. A 158-grain Winchester semi-wadcutter bullet struck Gianni in the forehead, killing him instantly.

NYPD determined that the two men were 32 feet apart when the fatal shot was fired.

Now, there were many issues in the Magliato case. One was "flight equals guilt," discussed elsewhere in this book; the panicked Magliato fled the scene, turning himself in later. Another was that the discharge was unintentional. A third was that in cocking the hammer and creating what the prosecution argued was a "hair trigger effect," the prosecution (and later, the appellate court) determined that there was an element of negligence.

But, on point to the topic, the prosecution also argued that a man with a contact weapon 32 feet away could not be considered a danger.

I was hired as an expert witness for the defense by Bob Kasanof, the original defense attorney retained by Magliato. When Magliato changed horses in midstream and hired famed defense lawyer Gerry Lefcourt to represent him, I came along with the package. I assembled a dozen or so men who fit the physical profile of the deceased and timed them as they lunged 32 feet from a standing start to strike a silhouette target in the head with a Monadnock 24-inch Monpac police baton. Their average time to "crush the skull of the target and kill the victim" was 2.08 seconds. (My friend, colleague, and past student Michael

The Texas Tower today. In 1966, when a mad sniper opened fire murderously from here, armed citizens hundreds of yards away justifiably pinned him down with return fire.

DeBethancourt, who rose to prominence as one of today's top self-defense instructors, incorporated this case into his training and calls it the "Magliato Drill.")

There is another lesson to learn from this case, which is very much on point with this book. The case was tried in Manhattan. New York is a "trial by ambush" state in that, unlike most other jurisdictions in the U.S., the defense doesn't get to see everything the prosecution has until it is about to be presented at trial. Therefore, on each side of the court-room fight, counsel voir dires the witness in court but outside the hearing of the jury, and the judge determines whether the evidence can be presented to the jury or not.

During my voir dire for Magliato's defense, I explained the Tueller research and that in preparation for the case at bar, we had determined that someone like the deceased in that case could be expected to cross those 32 feet in 2.08 seconds or so. I explained ability, opportunity and jeopardy. The question arose: Would I have fired intentionally under the circumstances Magliato faced when his Colt was discharged. I replied in the affirmative. Unfortunately, the reporter was there to hear that; the jury wasn't. The next day, one of the New York City tabloids headlined their story on the trial, "Cop: I Would Have Shot Him Myself."

Remember, that dialogue took place during voir dire of an expert wit-ness, with the jury out of the courtroom. Judge Thomas Sullivan addressed the defendant directly and asked Magliato if he had known Gianni could have reached him and clubbed him that quickly. Frank Magliato replied honestly that no, at that time, he did not. The judge ruled that he would not allow that element of my testimony to go in front of the jury.

We can never forget that the reasonable man standard encompasses "what would a reasonable and prudent person have done, in the same situa-tion, knowing what the defendant knew." If we did not know it at the time we took the action for which we are being judged, we are unlikely to be able to use it in our defense in court.

This was the first case I was ever involved in as an expert witness where the side I was testifying for lost. Magliato was convicted of depraved murder. The appellate court reduced it to manslaughter eventually, but he still served years of hard time and was branded a felon for the rest of his life.

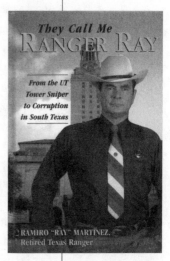

They Call Me RANGER RAY

From the UT Tower Sniper to Corruption in South Texas

RAMIRO "RAY" MARTINEZ
Retired Texas Ranger

Ramiro Martinez, one of the heroes of the Texas Tower incident, in his autobiography *They Call Me Ranger Ray*, credits return rifle fire from armed citizens on the ground for stop-ping the murderer's rampage.

Of the many lessons from this case, one is, be trained! Training is discoverable and therefore introducible to educate the jury. Magliato had not been trained in this. Had he been able to introduce this opportunity element from having been trained in it, I strongly believe he might have been acquitted.

The distance element of the opportunity factor has been widely misunderstood in other ways. I have lost count of people who claim that "if you shoot a man more than 7 yards/10 yards/25 yards/whatever yards away, you won't be justifiable." In and of itself, that statement is simply BS.

Let us go back to 1966 and the Texas Tower Massacre, the mass shooting perpetrated by Charles Whitman. His sniper's perch was 330 feet above ground level, and he murdered helpless victims from hundreds of yards away with a scoped rifle. History records that he was killed at reasonably close range atop the tower by Austin, Texas, police officers. You have to dig into history to find that the murders were cut short well before that conflagration at the pinnacle of the tower by armed citizens on the ground who returned fire with hunting rifles and at least one target rifle!

Far from being criminally charged for "shooting at a man too far away to constitute a danger," these citizens were lauded for their courage in pinning down the mad sniper and stopping the killing. While Whitman was thus held in check by armed citizens, another armed citizen named Alan Crum led Austin police officers Houston McCoy, Ramiro Martinez, and Jerry Day up through the inside of the tower to the roof where the mass murderer held forth. Finding a cluster of victims hiding from Whitman inside the tower, Day ushered them to safety. Crum guided the other two officers to the roof; they approached Whitman's position from one side and Crum from the other. Crum was the first to see Whitman, lying in wait for the cops with a sawed-off semi-automatic 12-gauge shotgun. A shot from citizen Crum's rifle, a .30-caliber Remington handed to him earlier by a law enforcement officer, was the first round of the final shootout, and it "broke the ambush," startling Whitman. This allowed the officers to open fire. A blast from McCoy's Winchester pump shotgun mortally wounded the gunman; Martinez emptied his Smith & Wesson .38/44 service revolver into the killer, then snatched McCoy's shotgun and blasted Whitman one more time. The long, terrible nightmare was over.

In his autobiography, *They Call Me Ranger Ray*, Martinez wrote, "I was and am still upset that more recognition has not been given to the citizens who pulled out their hunting rifles and returned the sniper's fire. The City of Austin and the State of Texas should be forever thankful and grateful to them because of the many lives they saved that day. The sniper did a lot of damage when he could fire freely, but when the armed citizens began to return fire the sniper had to take cover. He had to shoot out of the rainspouts and that limited his targets. I am grateful to the citizens because they made my job easier."[1]

Understanding and Interpreting the Tueller Principle

Some people lose sight of the fact that Dennis Tueller's work was geared to opponents armed with contact weapons: people who must touch their victims to kill them. This encompasses the opponent armed with a knife or some sort of bludgeon, and in a disparity of force situation, the attacker attempting to punch, strangle or kick their victim. The person attempting to grab the lawfully wielded gun of the homeowner or cop, since they must lay hands on the gun to snatch it, should also be treated as a contact weapon assailant. In all these cases, Tueller's principle will be highly relevant.

For thirty years, Tueller had to watch his work bastardized and misinterpreted by others. People began to refer to the "21-Foot Rule" and to read it as "Shoot him if he's closer, don't shoot him if he's farther." Tueller, one of the great firearms instructors of his generation, never said that. Circa 1990, he and I did a training film on the topic, using the same title as his seminal article: "How Close Is Too Close?" He has always made it clear that the purpose of the exercise was to make the trainee understand how quickly such a distance could be closed and to evaluate it as the courts would in the aftermath: in the context of "the totality of the circumstances" to determine whether defensive lethal force was or was not justified and necessary at a given moment in an encounter.

Today, Tueller adds, "We should also give credit to Calibre Press. They referenced my article in their Tactical Edge book and incorporated and demonstrated some of the principles in their 'Surviving Edged Weapons' training film, correctly using terms such as 'proxemics' and 'the reactionary gap.'"

Terminology is an issue in this discussion. The core research establishing that the average adult male can close seven yards in a second and a half from a standing start is what I refer to as the Tueller Principle. Almost immediately after reviewing and confirming Tueller's seminal work, I began teaching what I called the Tueller Drill. This exercise was experiential training geared to bring home the unforgiving speed of a potential assailant. One way to do it is to have a single person in place as the Timer and another in the role of Defender or Intended Victim. Each student begins standing still at a starting line seven yards from the latter. This student then lunges and closes the distance as fast as they can.

We learned early that the Timer should not blow a start whistle, shout "Ready, set, go," or issue a start command. The reason is that this creates a reaction time of a quarter second or so for the student in the Attacker role, which in turn falsely understates the speed at which the distance gap can be closed. In real life, the attacker does not have to deal with reaction time; they initiate the attack themselves. Accordingly, we learned to have the Attackers start at their own command. The Timer should be ready and start the time as soon as the Attacker begins to move and stop the time when the Attacker makes physical contact with the Intended Victim. Any "reactionary gap" on the part of the timer will be equalized and negated by the fact that reaction time on the start and stop buttons will be the same at the beginning and the end of the run.

I found early that the best way to implement the Tueller Drill was to break the students up into groups of three and have each take turns in each of the three roles: Timer, Attacker and Defender. They were instructed to bring their pens and notebooks to the exercise. Before taking their run in the Attacker role, each student would dictate the following for other students to write down in their notes: their height, weight, age, gender, footwear and existing injuries or medical problems. (Ground surface would also be listed, and the same for all participants.) Momentarily, after the run, the entry in the notebooks would be completed with elapsed time, announced by the Timer. Tueller comments, "Early on, we also did a variation of this exercise using toy dart pistols and rubber knives."

This meant that at the end of the exercise, each student would have a comprehensive list of students with a broad range of physical attributes, at least one of which would probably be reasonably close to the physical description of a future assailant who might be coming at them. Having acted out all three roles would allow them to say the following in court: "Counselor, I knew how fast that person could close the distance and kill me because, in my training, they made me do that to another person. I knew it because, in my training, they made another person do that to me. I knew it because, in my training, they made me stand back so I could see the forest for the trees and time another person doing it to someone else. And if need be, I can demonstrate that here in this courtroom."

Over more than thirty years of running Tueller Drills, I observed thousands of people run it. Tall and short, male and female, ectomorph and endomorph and mesomorph, the "lame and the halt," and those in the prime of life and health. I could share information with countless peers in the training world who had supervised a similar number of drills.

Many people were faster than 1.5 seconds. Very few people could complete the Tueller Drill in under a second flat, usually in the high nine-tenths of one second. These tended to be accomplished athletes and martial artists, and they would often close the final part of the gap with a leap.

I saw two men with freshly broken legs in walking casts — Jan Stevenson in a class I taught in England and Bob Smith at a class I taught in Idaho — hobble through a Tueller Drill in two seconds flat.

I saw men in wheelchairs do it at roughly the same time. Our "wheelchair record" was set by a partially quadriplegic Vietnam veteran. He did it in 1.8 seconds.

A memorable moment in the history of Tueller Drills occurred in June 1993 at an LFI-I class I was teaching for Lethal Force Institute at the Pioneer Sportsman range in Dunbarton, New Hampshire. Larry Anderson, age 43, was the participant. Larry suffered from recurring orthopedic issues in the lower limbs. I watched as he began his run; he appeared to stumble initially, then righted himself and completed the lunge. As he made contact, he fell to the ground with his next and last step.

He had suffered a spiral fracture of the tibia and fibula. Surgery involving steel bolts was the result. Larry told me later, in the Emergency Room, that he had felt a bone in his leg crack as he began the run but pressed onward.

His sacrifice was for all of us. Suppose that sometime in the future, you have shot your assailant in the leg, but he continues his attack, and you have to shoot him again. In court, opposing counsel may say, "You can't believe he was in danger from a man who only had a knife and was seven yards away because that man had a bullet in his leg and couldn't run." Thanks to

Larry Anderson's experience, it is now a matter of record that a man with a freshly broken leg, untreated, can still close that gap and deliver what would be a fatal knife thrust in the time Larry was witnessed and recorded to do it that day — 1.8 seconds!

We learned many counterintuitive lessons over the years that we've shared with law enforcement and law-abiding armed citizens. The perception that "big equals slow" is an absolute myth. Tall people with long arms and legs are deceptively fast. Their higher center of gravity may allow them to gain momentum and speed slightly faster than their shorter brethren. Their long legs allow them to cover more ground with fewer steps. Their long arms allow them to reach their victim more quickly. Even morbidly obese people are surprisingly fast. The reason is that the weight they are constantly carrying strengthens their leg muscles with every step they take in daily life, and it is leg muscles that drive a short-range anaerobic movement pattern such as a knife attack.

The attacker with the heavy crowbar would initially seem slower than the same man with a light, fast-moving knife — Au contraire. A long club-type instrument can add as much as another arm's length to the assailant's reach. This means he has one fewer step to take to harm his victim, making him that much faster, not slower.

Similarly, assailants in poor physical condition for other reasons can still move with more speed than the average person would expect. I testified in two trials on behalf of Mark Branham, an ex-cop in Virginia who shot and killed a man who was in the unprovoked act of clubbing him about the head with two weapons.

In one hand, the attacker swung a heavy miner's lantern against Branham's skull, and with the other hand, the assailant was pistol-whipping him with a loaded Smith & Wesson Model 10 .38 Special revolver. A special prosecutor hired by the family of the deceased alleged, among other things, that the assailant posed no danger to Branham because the assailant was known to Branham to suffer from coal worker's pneumoconiosis, also known as "black lung disease" or "miner's lung." When I was called to the stand as an expert witness for the defense by Branham's brilliant lawyer, Eugene Compton, I could counter this by explaining that such brief, violent movements do not require a large aerobic reserve to carry out. "This is probably why there is no Olympic event called 'the seven-yard dash.' Almost anyone can do it," I pointed out. Branham was ultimately acquitted. He returned to law enforce-ment and completed a distinguished career, culminating as Chief of Police.

Fine Points of the Tueller Drill

One thing we observed over the years was that people would disad-vantage themselves and slow themselves down by starting too far back at the beginning of the Tueller Drill. We learn to "toe the line" on the firing line at a shooting range and not to let our toes get forward of the "do not cross" line when standing in the queue at a security gate. In the real world and court, the distance between two people is generally perceived and mea-sured "torso to torso" in this writer's experience. A person preparing to run — or an attacker standing in an aggressive posture — will generally have one foot ahead of the other, with the torso centered between the spread-apart feet. Accordingly, we learned to have each student in the Attacker role begin with one foot forward of the line, the other behind, and the torso centered over the line. This gave a more accurate reading of potential speed.

Safety is critical in performing this drill. Shoes with smooth leather soles are like roller skates when attempting to run over smooth, hard surfaces. While it might be interesting to see how fast a woman in high heels could run, the likelihood of tripping and falling is so obvious and potentially dangerous that, in the interest of student safety, we chose not to explore it. We always noted ground surfaces for the record. Sand and gravel, because they slip from under the feet, slow the run. So does wet grass. So, of course, does ice and snow; this is why we do not have data on running speed upon such surfaces. We had no right to endanger the students by asking them to do that.

We constantly lectured the students beforehand: "If you have a bad back, knees, heart, high blood pressure, history of stroke, etc., do not at-tempt maximum speed! This is why we noted pre-existing injuries and medi-cal conditions. If you fit any of those medical profiles, just walk it quickly. You'll still close the distance in three seconds or less, and that isn't time for your life to flash before your eyes before you die if you don't stop the attack. You're not short-changing the other students by walking the Tueller Drill quickly instead of running it flat out. On the contrary, you are giving them the knowledge they can use in court if their attacker happens to be disabled in a future, real encounter, and opposing counsel argues that the Tueller

Principle only covers healthy athletic police academy recruits."

Additional Safety Considerations

We have always been careful to have the students take off their guns before doing a Tueller Drill, even on a "cold range" where the weapons were unloaded. In the Defender role, we didn't want them to reflex to their weapons. If they fell and rolled, we didn't want them to have guns (or other heavy things) on their belts, which could cause a hip or lower back injury in the fall.

We discovered early that there was injury potential even with dummy knives. Those who train extensively with the knife know that a blunted "drone" knife made of metal or even edgeless wood can cause severe bruising or even broken bones. Even a rubber knife can leave nasty bruises or cause damage to the eye or larynx with a hard blow.

Moreover, in the training environment, no one wants to slam full-speed into an inanimate target, let alone a human training partner. This caused the students to slow down in the instant before contact, which falsely slowed their time to make contact. In the real world, we knew the opponent would seek aggressive contact and slam into their intended victim like a charging rhino.

The best way I found to have the students replicate "real-world speed" without training injuries was to have the Attacker run full speed past the Defender, slowing only after contact had been made. Because even a light "strike" or pulled punch could unintentionally be made harder by the Attacker's forward momentum, I would have the Defender stand sideways instead of facing the Attacker. The Defender's arm would be somewhat (but not entirely) extended, with the palm facing the Attacker, who would slap the Defender's palm like a "high five" as he passed. This kept the Attacker's hand away from the face and torso of the Defender, further avoiding injury. The sideways stance of the Defender kept a hard hand-slap by a strong man from dislocating his shoulder. I also recommend that all participants wear safety glasses in case of an unintentional strike to the eye area.

When performing Tueller Drills, expect someone to take a fall. I've rarely supervised one of these where someone didn't go to the ground. It will generally be a male who has been sedentary for many years and hasn't sprinted full out since his school days. (The early warning is an awareness that your head is well forward of your feet, which are struggling to keep up.)

I remind the students that should they fall, they want to catch themselves on flat palms and forearms, with palms and forearms in a straight line. Instinct will tell them to catch themselves with just the palms, which tends to hyper-extend the wrists, resulting in sprains or fractures.

What if, after the training, the student is attacked by a knife wielder who trips and falls or perhaps goes to the ground after the student's first de-fensive shot? Instead of staying down, the assailant now tries to rise with his knife, and the student, logically, shoots him again. Expect opposing counsel to argue, "The Tueller Drill training invoked by the defendant is irrelevant! This man wasn't starting on his feet when the defendant fired the fatal shot; he was starting from flat on his face (or flat on his back)! The defendant wasn't in immediate danger!"

When time permits, I like to proactively counter this argument by taking a volunteer student and having them start supine (on their back) or prone (face down). They can generally spring to their feet and sprint seven yards to contact in three seconds or so, and I've seen it done in two by the more athletic individuals. That's still more than sufficiently "immediate" to constitute the ability factor — and now it is provably known to the student beforehand in a way that will generally be court admissible.

Dennis Tueller retired many years ago from SLCPD at the rank of Lieu-tenant and, ever since, has been teaching good people to stay alive in the face of criminal violence. His pioneering, groundbreaking work has saved countless "good guys and gals" from death on the street and from ruin and prison in the courtroom. His contributions cannot be overestimated. I am proud to count him as a friend and colleague. Much credit also goes to SWAT Magazine for publishing this critical research.

Having addressed the distance element of the opportunity factor, we'll move next to the obstacle(s) element.

Obstacles Element

Distance and the attacker's potential running/lunging speed are not the only elements of the opportunity factor. With contact weapon assaults, there is also the matter of obstacles.

The most obvious obstacles are physical barriers. Let's say that you are standing near a doorway fitted with a steel door. You are just outside the door, and a knife-wielding maniac some distance away in the parking lot walks toward you with a menacing glare. Perhaps a single step could put you through that doorway and let you quickly slam that steel door and lock it before the opponent could reach it. Taken in a vacuum, assuming no other innocent people to whom you owed a legal or ethical duty of protection, this would certainly be the tactical thing to do. In a "back to the wall" jurisdiction that requires retreat, it could be seen as legally demanded. Even in a "Stand Your Ground" jurisdiction that does not require retreat, you can expect the prosecutor, plaintiff's counsel, and jurors to question why you didn't simply close that door and block the threat without bloodshed.

In February 2014, the State v. Michael Dunn case went to trial in Jacksonville, Florida. Dunn, a 40-something white male, had been parked outside a convenience store when loud rap music emanated from a sport utility vehicle next to him. Dunn asked the four young black males in the vehicle to lower the music. The driver initially complied, but passenger Jordan Davis leaned from his position in the right rear seat and turned it back up. Davis then engaged in a heated, profanity-laden verbal exchange with Dunn. Dunn drew a Taurus PT-99 pistol from his glove box, racked a round into the firing chamber, and proceeded to open fire. The reconstruction showed that his initial burst of three shots struck Jordan Davis with three Winchester 9mm jacketed hollowpoints. After a brief pause, he fired a string of four more rapid shots. In the six seconds that followed, the SUV backed out and began to drive away, and Dunn maneuvered into a position at the back of his vehicle, from which he fired three more shots at the fleeing vehicle. This much was not in dispute.

Dunn fled the scene, but a witness noted his license tag, and he was arrested the next day. Nine of his ten bullets had gone into the Dodge Durango. Jordan Davis died of his wounds, while the other three teens emerged physically unscathed. They all testified that Davis had not been armed or stepped out of the vehicle. Dunn's story, unsupported by any other testimony or evidence, was that Davis had threatened to kill him and raised what appeared to Dunn to be a shotgun, prompting Dunn to fire in self-defense. No gun was ever found.

After several days of trial and thirty hours of deliberation, the jury unanimously found him guilty of three charges of attempted murder in shooting in the direction of the fleeing teens and one charge of firing deadly missiles into a vehicle. On the charge of murder in the first degree in the death of 17-year-old Jordan Davis, the jury hung. Their initial vote had been ten for guilty and two for not guilty on the grounds of self-defense; by the time they finally deadlocked, the vote was 9 to 3. The judge ruled a mistrial on that charge, and the prosecution announced that it would re-try Dunn on the murder charge.

Michael Dunn was convicted in his second trial and sentenced to life in prison without parole.

This case has many ramifications relevant to this book. Still, the one most on point is that the first juror to speak of the deliberations publicly said that she voted guilty because she believed Dunn could have avoided the shooting by simply backing out of the parking space and moving his vehicle — in effect, creating enough distance that there would have been no opportunity factor for Jordan Davis and therefore, no deadly danger to the defendant. This, even though the jury instructions included an explanation of Florida's then blazingly controversial Stand Your Ground law, which did not require a defendant to leave a place where he had the right to be before using deadly force in otherwise reasonably perceived self-defense.

In the Dunn case, the prosecution also raised the issue that the proximity of Davis' right-rear door to the left side of Dunn's sedan acted as an obstacle to any attempt by Davis to get out of his vehicle and approach Dunn. This argument would have been weaker had there been solid evidence of Davis being armed with a firearm, since such a remote control weapon could quickly be deployed through an opened rear window or even blast through a closed window's safety glass.

There are many obstacles that a reasonable and prudent person might recognize as capable of slowing an assailant's approach. One is as simple as uphill versus downhill. It takes longer for an assailant to travel uphill, and moving downhill, he can gain momentum and speed more rapidly.

An example of the former occurred in a case in which I was involved as an expert witness for the defense in 2011, Commonwealth of Tennessee v. Shawn Armstrong, mentioned in the discussion of disparity of force in the chapter on the ability factor. Shawn, you'll recall, had been viciously beaten and flung to the ground and kicked by her larger, stronger, Army Ranger-trained husband. She lay curled in a fetal position to shield the gun in the front of her waistband so he couldn't gain control of it and turn it against her. He strode back to his car, then turned, glared at her angrily, and began moving toward her again. At that moment, she opened fire, killing him with a single bullet that entered his chest and lodged in his spine.

Early in the case, the Tueller Principle and the 1.5 seconds to cover 21 feet had been mentioned. I could not visit the shooting scene until the week of the trial. The gunfight occurred in a partial clearing in the woods, and the movement path between the deceased when he was hit and the spot where the defendant had pushed herself upright to a sitting position was uphill. The ground in between was "rutted" and covered with tangled plant growth. Our testing determined that an athletic, prime-of-life man such as her husband and roughly the same height and weight might have taken more like 3 seconds to close the gap and "finish what he'd started."

I made that clear in my testimony. On cross-examination, the prosecutor made a big deal of how he would have taken twice as long as average Tueller Drill time to harm her again. I replied that 3 seconds still constituted an immediate danger and that it wasn't time for the victim's life to flash before her eyes before she was killed. The jury understood and acquitted Shawn Armstrong of all charges in less than half an hour of deliberation.

The Time Element: Immediate, Imminent, Inevitable and the Robinson Hypothesis

Each case must be taken on its own merits, based upon the facts in evidence and the totality of the circumstances. No deadly force case is ever exactly like any other.

Suppose you've been kidnapped and taken hostage by a person far stronger than you and highly skilled in unarmed combat. He has made it abundantly clear that he will hold you prisoner for a week, and at the end of that week, he intends to murder you. You are unarmed and have determined that you have no reasonable chance to overpower him without using a deadly weapon. However, halfway through that period of your imprisonment, you notice that each morning when he brings you a meal in the room where he keeps you captive, he turns his back on you when he sets down the food tray. You've also observed that he carries a large knife in a sheath behind his hip, and you realize that if you catch him by surprise, you can snatch that knife. You're confident that if you try to take him at knifepoint without harming him, he will unquestionably be strong enough and skillful enough to overpower and disarm you. But, if you take that knife in one smooth motion and plunge it into his heart from behind ...

With some embellishment, this scenario was postulated by Attorney Paul H. Robinson in his excellent 1984 analysis in Criminal Law Defenses. Robinson's considered expert opinion is that, with this set of facts, if you snatch the kidnapper's knife and fatally stab him in the back, it should be justifiable homicide. I have come to call it "Robinson's Hypothesis."

Other brilliant lawyers, Robinson's peers, have evaluated this hypothesis and come to the same conclusion. One such is Cynthia Lee, who had this to say about it in her excellent book Murder and the Reasonable Man:

"One way to deal with the problems caused by a strict imminence requirement is to combine the imminence and necessity elements and require the defendant to have honestly and reasonably believed that his use of force was 'immediately necessary.' This is the approach taken by the drafters of the Model Penal Code. Under the Model Penal Code, 'the use of force on or toward another person is justifiable when the actor believes that such force is immediately necessary for the purpose of protecting himself against the use of unlawful force by such other person on the present occasion.'"[2]

The reader will recall that my definition of the situation that justifies using deadly force draws from the law's wording. "Immediate, otherwise unavoidable danger of death or grave bodily harm to the innocent." As we consider that wording, note that many states use the word "immediate" in their definition of justifiability for deadly force. Some, however, use the word "imminent."

In the parlance of the public, "words mean things." However, we must never forget that the most crafty lawyers are wordsmiths who play with definitions to win their cases. Let's look to dictionary.com's definition of "imminent":

im·mi·nent [im-uh-nuhnt] adjective

1. likely to occur at any moment; impending: Her death is imminent.

2. projecting or leaning forward; overhanging.

Synonyms

1. near, at hand. Imminent, Impending, Threatening all may carry the implication of menace, misfortune, disaster, but they do so in differing degrees. Imminent may portend evil: an imminent catastrophe, but also may mean simply "about to happen": The merger is imminent. Impending has a

weaker sense of immediacy and threat than imminent: Real tax relief legislation is impending, but it too may be used in situations portending disaster: impending social upheaval; to dread the impending investigation. Threatening almost always suggests ominous warning and menace: a threatening sky just before the tornado struck.

So much for the plain English definition of "imminent." Now, let's look at the legal definition of the same word from the authoritative Black's Legal Dictionary via thelawdictionary.com:

A manslaughter defendant, right, re-enacts with the author acting the role of attacker, showing where she and her attacker were when she fired the fatal shot. Charged with manslaughter in this self-defense shooting, she was acquitted at trial.

"What is *IMMINENT DANGER*?

In relation to homicide in self-defense, this term means immediate danger, such as must be Instantly met, such as cannot be guarded against It calling for the assistance of others or the protection of the law. *U. S. v. Outerbridge*, 27 Fed. Cas. 390; *State v. West*, 45 La. Ann. 14, 12 South. 7; *State v. Smith*, 43Or. 109, 71 Pac. 973. Or, as otherwise defined, such an appearance of threatened and impending injury as would put a reasonable and prudent man to his instant defense. *State v. Fontenot*, 50 La. Ann. 537, 23 South. 034. 09 Am. St. Rep. 455; *Shorter v. People*, 2 N. Y. 201, 51 Am. Dec. 280.[3]

Let's analyze that. "Immediate danger, such as must be instantly met, such as cannot be guarded against it calling for the assistance of others or the protection of the law." Well, in Robinson's Hypothesis, we may still be a few days away from the arbitrary "deadline of our death" set by the murderous kidnapper, so that phrase might seem to rule out using deadly force on him today or tomorrow morning. However, "... such an appearance of threatened and impending injury as would put a reasonable and prudent man to his instant defense" found in the very following sentence appears to contradict the first and support Robinson and Lee in their contention that deadly force by a captive victim against criminal captor now meets the opportunity factor standard.

We return to plain English via the thesaurus, which lists the following synonyms for "imminent": at hand, on the way, forthcoming, immediate, impending, inevitable, likely, looming, possible, probable, unavoidable, about to happen, approaching, brewing, close, coming, expectant, fast-approaching, following, gathering, handwriting-on-the-wall, in store, in the air, in the cards, in the offing, in the wind, in view, ineluctable, inescapable, inevasible, menacing, near, nearing, next, nigh, on its way, on the horizon, on the verge, overhanging, see it coming, threatening, to come, unescapable.

Immediate? Check! "Overhanging," that familiar definition from Black's Legal Dictionary? Synonymous, too. "Inescapable," "unavoidable," "about to happen"? Those are all there, too.

However, when I've gone through case law on this definition of "imminent," it has become apparent that in the eyes of the courts, "imminent" is generally defined as "immediate." This explains the suggestions of Lee and the Model Penal Code that a standard of "immediately necessary" use of deadly force against danger, rather than a standard of the immediacy of the deadly danger itself, is the direction in which defense counsel should go when this element becomes an issue at trial.

Pre-Emptive Homicide and the "Ten 'til Midnight" Conundrum

What might be called "justified pre-emptive homicide" has primarily been the purview of designated police SWAT and elite military hostage rescue teams. A case in point occurred in the hijacking of the cargo ship Maersk Alabama in 2009, immortalized in the book A Captain's Duty and the movie

"Captain Phillips." Four armed Somali pirates took over a freighter that had a crew of 20 unarmed men (yes, there is a lesson there, too). Three pirates took the captain hostage aboard a lifeboat as the fourth attempted to negotiate ransom with the U.S. Navy.

The negotiations broke down. Captain Phillips was not necessarily in immediate danger of the armed pirates blowing his brains out in the next second or even the next few seconds. But the Navy SEALS arrayed on a small boat on rolling seas knew that they couldn't get onto the lifeboat and disarm the Somali gunmen physically. The latter had threatened the execution murder of the ship's captain. And it was clear to the SEALS and commanders aboard the Navy mothership, the USS Bainbridge, that it was more likely than not the captain would be murdered soon.

In one of the most exemplary and astonishing displays of tactical marksmanship and orchestrated shooting in history, the SEALS opened fire simultaneously with their sniper rifles and, despite the platform of a rolling sea, instantly killed the three armed pirates and saved Captain Phillips' life.

Far from being seen as unjustified, this incident has been viewed as a benevolent rescue from virtually certain death. The immediate necessity to end the threat, as defined by Robinson and Lee above in the Robinson Hypothesis and Attorney Lee's interpretation of the Model Penal Code, clearly prevailed over any need for the danger presented by the pirates to be measurable in mere seconds, as seen within the totality of the circumstances in the actual situation.

Third Edition
THE LAW OF
SELF
DEFENSE
The Indispensable Guide for the Armed Citizen

By Attorney
Andrew F. Branca
Foreword by
Massad Ayoob

The author recommends Andrew Branca's excellent book, *The Law of Self Defense*, now in its third edition.

If you have ever talked with a victim of a seriously committed stalker, you know the maddening helpless horror they and their loved ones experience while the stalker remains at large. Rebecca Schaeffer, an up-and-coming young actress, was murdered by Robert Bardo in 1989 after being stalked for three years; she was 21. For every famous, murdered stalking victim such as Ms. Schaeffer or John Lennon, there are countless victims from ordinary life. It is understandable, if not excusable (when the criminal justice system seems to be doing nothing to protect them), that these victims and their loved ones think desperately of killing their stalker pre-emptively. However, it's a strategy that the justice system can neither condone nor forgive, no matter how sympathetic everyone from the public to the judge might be to the person who pulls the trigger.

In teaching Lethal Force Instructor classes, one tool I use is an old (1983) Charles Bronson movie, "Ten 'til Midnight." As entertainment, it's a "B film," but it is remarkably useful as a discussion trigger for understanding lethal force law. Bronson plays a big city detective assigned to catch a particularly cunning rapist/murderer. He finds him, but the man knows how to play the system and is released. Taking the investigation personally, he stalks Bronson's daughter with obviously monstrous intent. In desperation, Bronson tries to frame him by planting false evidence and gets caught and suspended, shredding his+ "mantle of innocence" and creating an element

> "
> IF YOU HAVE EVER TALKED WITH A VICTIM OF A SERIOUSLY COMMITTED STALKER, YOU KNOW THE MADDENING HELPLESS HORROR THEY AND THEIR LOVED ONES EXPERIENCE WHILE THE STALKER REMAINS AT LARGE. REBECCA SCHAEFFER, AN UP-AND-COMING YOUNG ACTRESS, WAS MURDERED BY ROBERT BARDO IN 1989 AFTER BEING STALKED FOR THREE YEARS; SHE WAS 21.

of malice on his part. At the film's climax [Spoiler alert – Editor], he barely saves his daughter from being murdered by the suspect and chases him on foot. The killer runs into a phalanx of responding uniformed officers, who seize him. Face to face, as uniformed cops struggle to hold his arms, the killer screams at Bronson that he's going to get off on an insanity plea, come back, and take his revenge on Bronson's daughter.

Convinced after all that has occurred thus far that this is precisely what is going to happen, Bronson says coldly, "No ... you ... won't" — and shoots the killer in the forehead with a Colt Detective Special.

I present this film to the class as The Facts In Evidence, and we proceed to hold "moot court" in the case of state versus Bronson's character. If there's a real judge or at least a criminal lawyer available, they take the role of a judge; if not, I'm stuck with that. Prosecution and defense counsel are appointed. I've played both of those roles against actual attorneys taking the opposite position.

As it appears — Bronson the disgraced detective shooting the now-helpless stalker/rapist/murderer in cold blood to keep him from coming back for his daughter — the moot court jury has convicted more often than it acquits. Even though everyone in the room is sympathetic with the Bronson character, they do as juries generally do and apply the law as instructed. The law does not permit individuals (police or private citizens) to take revenge or kill to prevent possible killings in the future.

The law is complicated, however, and so is the scenario of every shooting, real or fictional. Where I've brought the likelihood of acquittal up about equal to the likelihood of conviction in the moot court case of "State v. Bronson" is when I've been in the defense counsel role and changed the nature of the argument. In the film, just before Bronson kills him, the human monster struggles with the police officers holding him and appears to break free. His hands are not clearly visible to the camera or viewer. Still, his violent body movements are not inconsistent with trying to grab one of the officers' service handguns from its holster. With that possibility in the mix, reasonable doubt is created that this was a new deadly force encounter. The Bronson character fired his revolver to keep the stalker from killing him or other officers with a snatched gun. It's a frail reed, though, inconsistent with Bronson's icy words, "No ... you ... won't." That's why, even in a moot court environment with a jury far more sympathetic to the shooter than would ever be found in a real-world courtroom, conviction for murder or lesser included manslaughter results at least half the time.

The researcher will look long and hard to find a recent case where a person was acquitted for shooting a stalker to death to prevent a future crime. We recall that the standard is "reasonable fear" versus "bare fear," and the danger must be defined as imminent by the triers of the facts.

The only case of exoneration in such an instance that comes readily to this author's mind is the death of John Wesley Hardin. Hardin was the Western gunfighter who claimed to have killed 41 men. On the night of his death, he had been threatening to kill lawman John Selman, Jr. Selman's dad, John Sr., got wind of it, walked into the Acme Saloon in El Paso, Texas, strode up behind Hardin, and put a bullet through Hardin's head, killing him instantly. Witnesses said he shot him from behind, while Selman's defenders contended that it was a face-to-face gunfight. With a hole in the back of Hardin's skull, another in his face, and little knowledge of forensic evidence yet developed in the American criminal justice community, that matter became "he said/she said." Selman was exonerated in the killing, and it was said at the time, "If he shot him from the front, he showed good marksmanship. If he shot him from behind, he showed good sense."

Selman was killed in a gunfight with U.S. Marshal George Scarborough the following year. He had killed John Wesley Hardin in the year 1895.

The reader is reminded that it has been a very long time since 1895. Things are different now.

Opportunity Factor: The Bottom Line

For the use of deadly force to be justified, the opponent must possess the power to kill or cripple and be readily capable of employing that lethal power here and now. The fear of his doing so must be not only sincere but reasonable, as measured by the yardstick of the reasonable person standard. ∎

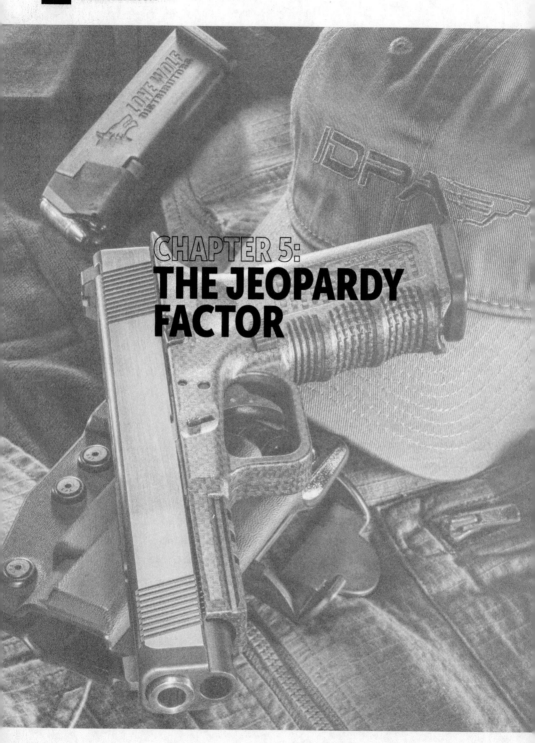

CHAPTER 5:
THE JEOPARDY FACTOR

n this discussion, the *jeopardy* factor comes into play when your assailant utters words or performs actions that a reasonable and prudent person would construe as demonstrating an *intent to kill or cripple.*

Beware of "combat semantics" when discussing this issue. I've seen some outlines for concealed carry and self-defense courses where the "jeopardy" element is called "intent." I strongly urge the instructors I teach to get away from that terminology. When you hear someone say, "words mean things," it isn't just a hackneyed old catch-phrase. It's a truth of life, particularly in court.

Let's say the prosecutor was after your scalp, cross-examining you on the witness stand. Suppose the prosecutor (or worse, your defense lawyer on direct examination) had elicited from you a statement like, "His intent was to kill me." (All he would have to do is to ask, "Did he intend to kill you?" and hear your answer in the affirmative; always remember that in legal proceedings, anything you say "yes" to is treated as if the entire statement had come out of your mouth.) If you fell into that trap, I would expect the prosecutor to pounce. "So, you say you knew his intent! Are you telepathic? Do you have the power to read minds?" Any skilled trial advocate could make a monkey out of anyone with that.

The simple fact of life — and remember, the jury's stock in trade is the common sense garnered from their collective life experience — is that none of us can honestly know the intent of another. Have you never had someone express benevolent intent to you and then, sooner or later, stick the proverbial knife in your back?

What we all *can* reasonably and prudently determine is *manifest intent,* and that's what the jeopardy element is all about. The best definition of manifest intent in understanding the jeopardy factor is: *"words and/or actions a reasonable, prudent person would construe as representing an intent to kill or cripple."*

Jeopardy is often less obvious to witnesses at the scene and the triers of the facts later because assaultive behavior cues can be subtle. In the same sense that a dog's nose can catch scents that a human will miss, the untrained observer who is not carefully watching your opponent can miss or fail to recognize signals that raise a red flag to you, the hopefully trained and competent armed citizen.

"Witness dynamics" are a function of human nature. Basic truth: If you are not looking for something, you will likely not see it. If you are not listening for something, likely, you will not hear it. *And if you do not recognize or understand what you have seen or heard, it is as if you have not seen or heard it at all!*

It's true if you witness the attack of A on B. And, if *you* are the "B" who is attacked by the "A," you may not see an attack coming until it is too late to defend against it.

Jeopardy is easier to show in some cases than in others. When Corporal Randy Willems was criminally charged for shooting his assailant, and he and his department were later sued over it, it was certainly helpful to me as one of his expert witnesses that his attacker had grabbed the cop by the throat with one hand and grabbed his holstered service Beretta with the other and screamed, "Give me your fuckin' gun! I'll blow your fuckin' brains out!" Enough verbalization *and* physical action to cause a reasonable, prudent person to believe that the attacker manifested an intent to kill or cripple? It was enough for two juries. Randy was acquitted in the criminal case, and he and his department won a total defense verdict in the civil lawsuit.

In another case I was consulted on in California, a large, strong suspect managed to get a police officer's baton away from him. Raising it like a Neanderthal as if to club him in the head, the man announced loudly and imperiously, "I *am* going to kill you!" The officer immediately drew his service sidearm and shot the man dead. The shooting was ruled a justified homicide by the criminal justice system.

They're not all as clear as that. I remember one sad case in the Midwest where two ordinary, law-abiding, average-size brothers went to a rural roadhouse to have a few drinks. One had more than a few and was suckered into a brawl by two physically huge, powerful men who had a penchant for starting fights with guys they knew they could overpower and then savagely beating them. The drunk brother agreed to "go outside" and was knocked senseless to the ground by the first punch. The other brother shouted, "He's had enough," but the two thugs then began stomping the man who was down.

With no self-defense training, knowing he could not stop the brutal stomping with his bare hands, the victim's brother sprinted to his nearby automobile and retrieved his .380 pistol from the glove box. He ordered the men at gunpoint to leave his brother alone. One did, stepping back and raising his hands. The other leered at him and moved toward him in a menacing advance. The defender fired a warning shot, which only inflamed his opponent: the big man lunged at him as if to take the gun, and the brother fired a single shot that stopped the assailant instantly and fatally.

A reportedly anti-gun prosecutor brought him to trial. When the defense lawyer called me, I was locked into another case on that trial date and referred him to Bob Houzenga in Iowa. I had known Bob for many years. A career cop who later became chief, he was a six-time national shooting champion and master instructor whose testimony had saved wrongly accused cops in court. He spent many hours with the lawyer and defendant, drafting his direct examination and explaining the importance of things they would have to get across to the jury.

The preparation time turned out to be wasted. When the lawyer brought Houzenga to the stand as an expert witness, I've been told, he rambled through a few irrelevant questions and then passed the witness. The prosecutor — who, if he had done his homework, must have been sweating bullets because he would have known by then that Houzenga was unimpeachable — wisely abjured from cross-examination. Remember, the witness can't stand up and yell in court, "Here's what you need to know!" They can only answer the questions they are asked. There was only one chance to get the reality of the self-defense shooting across to the jury: the defendant's testimony.

When his lawyer gave him direct examination on the stand, defense counsel asked the defendant, "Why did you shoot him?"

The defendant answered, "He was gonna kick my ass."

And that was it.

"He was gonna kick my ass"? That's what Moe did to Larry and Curly in "The Three Stooges." It does not sound like deadly force, and taken in a vacuum, a "kicked ass" does not justify deadly force.

Convicted of the lesser included offense of manslaughter, that man spent many years in prison. Suppose instead that the defense's expert witness had been allowed to articulate the disparity of force elements — huge size and strength advantage, multiple opponents, downed and now-disabled man being stomped by the shod feet of heavy, violent men — and shown the jury why the rescuing brother had no alternative but to fire? Suppose that man had sat on that witness stand and said, as he honestly could have, "Either of those men could have killed my brother or me with their bare hands. Now both of them had him down. He was being stomped. I knew that a man on the ground would suffer much more serious injuries from a stomping than a standing man taking a kick he could roll with to lessen the impact. I couldn't face my parents and tell them I let my brother be turned into a corpse or a vegetable. I begged them to stop. One did. The other came at me, obviously about to take my gun and shoot us both. He ignored my warning shot. I knew he could overpower me and murder us both, and I fired one shot from my small-caliber pistol."

Think that might have made a difference?

Dealing With Escalating Jeopardy

Many times, threats begin small and then escalate. The stalker. The "strange ranger" at work or in school. The crazy neighbor whose mission in life seems to be harassing everyone else in the neighborhood. It's the sort of person my friend Ron Borsch, the expert on mass murderers and how to interdict them, describes as having "Numerous Unsettling and Troubling Symptoms." In the short term, the guy who cuts you off and gives you the finger in traffic can quickly escalate into classic and deadly "road rage."

With the latter, be the first to get on the telephone: remember that the person who first calls 9-1-1 is logged into the system as the Victim/Complainant, and the guy who calls in second has already been marked as the Suspect/Perpetrator. In the other situations described above or anything like it, you probably already know that "anything that isn't in print didn't happen." You need to realize that goes at least double for such situations.

Then, there is the long-term harassment/bullying/stalking situation. It's the nature of peaceable people to think, "If I call the cops, he'll only get madder and get worse. I'll just shut up and hope it all blows over." That rarely works for battered spouses, and it rarely works for victims of harassment or stalking. Often, the lack of interdiction by authorities emboldens the perpetrator and makes them confident that they can escalate without fear of consequences.

If it continues to escalate to the point where that individual attacks you or someone within the mantle of your protection and forces you to apply deadly force to stop that violent attack, *you will want to have already established a paper trail determining who is who and what is what.* The history of modern law enforcement in this respect has been that when we get to a scene where two antagonists fought after a long period, we see it as illegal, voluntary mutual combat. Such mutual combat has been outlawed in the Western world since the principle *homicide se defendo* came into the English common law many centuries ago. The bottom line is this: *the loser goes in the meat wagon, and the winner goes in the paddy wagon.*

If there has been bad blood between you and the neighbor/relative/coworker/stalker, *and you have not reported his transgressions to the authorities,* those now-arriving authorities see it as a Hatfield-McCoy-like feud in which each party is equally culpable, and you and your defense attorneys will have a very steep uphill fight.

But if, instead, the criminal justice system's records show that you reported the other person's threats or harassment to them, perhaps repeatedly, *and they did nothing effective to stop it,* prosecutor and investigating officer alike may realize that fact will come out in court, and make them appear to be ineffectual. More to the point, your reports *establish who was the bad guy and the good guy from the beginning.* These factors are likely to come together to determine justifiable homicide early in the investigation, without the terrible ordeal of a trial.

Suggested Reading

ACLDN, the Armed Citizens Legal Defense Network, has an excellent training film by unarmed combat expert Marc MacYoung titled "Recognizing and Responding to Pre-Attack Indicators." That sort of knowledge is priceless in establishing your recognition of the jeopardy factor in court, and, more importantly, in recognizing the danger in time to save your life and other innocent lives in the first place. The video is available to ACLDN members via armedcitizensnetwork.org.

Read books on body language. Get training in it. I've seen it work; it's valid science, not New Age yuppie BS. The single best course I've seen in recognition of assaultive behavior cues is given by Major Tania Penderakis (athenatraining.net). In the meantime, check out my article on recognition of assaultive behavior indicators at the *Backwoods Home* magazine website, at backwoodshome.com. It is reprinted below from *Backwoods Home* Issue No. 87:

Body Language and Threat Recognition

By Massad Ayoob

Reader mail indicates that while some *Backwoods Home* readers turn to this column for advice on putting wild game on the table or keeping four-footed poachers out of the garden, others are more interested in firearms for self-defense in lonely places. And, of course, there are readers who are concerned with family protection but don't like guns. Let's speak in particular to the latter two groups this issue. We'll get away from firearms this trip, and look at something else related to personal safety: recognition of pre-assaultive behavior cues.

People have been hurt — sometimes by strangers, sometimes by people they knew and loved — when they failed to realize that the other person was experiencing a level of hostility that was about to boil over. Being able to recognize body language associated with imminent violent action can allow you to, in the best-case scenario, disengage and leave the scene. At worst, it can give you time to activate a plan of self-defense soon enough to effectively protect yourself and those for whose safety you are responsible.

Danger Signals

The eyes, it is said, are the windows to the soul. Often, the way in which a hostile person looks at you can be a predictor of what his plans are for you.

Cops, soldiers, and mental health professionals are all too familiar with "the thousand-yard stare." This is the person who seems to be not so much looking at you as through you. He may be unresponsive or inappropriately responsive in other ways. What this should tell you is that in this moment he is in an alternate reality of his own, a place where you are probably not welcome. When you see this, start "creating distance" unless you in fact are a law enforcement officer, health professional, or someone else who has a responsibility for containing and restraining this person's actions.

The opposite of the thousand-yard stare is the "target stare." This is the guy who narrows his eyes and glares directly at you. The narrowing of the eyelids does for our vision what shutting down the f/stop on your camera does for the lens: it enhances depth perception. It tells you that you have become a very intense focus of his attention. If the circumstances indicate that this individual is at all hostile, the target stare is not a good sign. If you're not a cop, psyche nurse, etc., Mother Nature is telling you again to start creating distance between you and him.

There is also "target glance." Cops learned the hard way over the years that if a man casts a furtive glance in a certain direction, he may well be checking his avenues of escape: his quick look has just told the officers where he is likely to run. Is he staring at your chin? In a hostile situation, he's not admiring your Kirk Douglas chin cleft and he hasn't noticed a zit you missed this morning in the mirror. More likely, he's thinking about sucker punching you right "on the button." If his eyes go down to your crotch, he's probably not a gay guy scoping out your package ... more likely, he's actively considering opening the fight with a kick to your crotch.

A brief aside to the shooters in the audience. You know how when you see a cop, you immediately look at his holster to see what sort of sidearm he's wearing? Have you noticed that every now and then when you do that, you get a dirty look from the officer, who may step back or otherwise change his physical orientation to you? The reason is, he has been taught about pre-assaultive behavior cues, too, and he has learned to interpret a look at his holster as a "target glance" that may indicate the person is thinking about snatching his service pistol.

"Fight or Flight" Indicators

When the brain perceives that we are about to be in a strenuous physical conflict, a primitive mammalian survival reflex kicks in which prepares us to do battle or to flee. Quantified in the early 20th century as "fight or flight response" by Dr. Walter Cannon at Harvard Medical School, this phenomenon may reveal itself to another person with subtle physical manifestations ... if that other person is sufficiently alert and informed to recognize what they're looking at.

When we go into a high level of "body alarm reaction," the lizard that lives in the base of our brain and controls the machinery and the thermostats decides to kick up oxygenated blood supply. The heart begins to race and the lungs begin to take in more air. Watch for rapid breathing or panting in a person who has not performed any strenuous physical activity. You may even be able to see a pulse throbbing at the neck or the temple of some individuals.

Now, let's perform a process of elimination. There is no common danger that threatens those at the scene. You have done nothing to threaten him. Neither has anyone else. He has not been exerting himself. Yet, his blood vessels are pulsing violently and he is breathing heavily. By this process of elimination, we can determine where the fight or flight thing has come from: He has already decided that he is going to fight. (Or, if you are lucky, that he is going to run.)

The adrenal system instantly releases powerful chemicals in a fight or flight state, including epinephrine ("adrenaline"). One side-effect of this is tremors, often violent ones, which will usually manifest themselves first in the non-dominant hand, almost immediately thereafter in the dominant hand, and then in the legs, particularly the knees. If you observe tremors in those locations in a situation that you perceive may turn hostile, go through that process of elimination again. Could the person be simply shivering in the cold? Do you have reason to believe he has Parkinson's disease or some other ailment of which trembling is symptomatic? If not, you know the diagnosis, and you know the first step of treatment — create distance.

The Body Language of Fight/Flight

Facial expressions and body movements can give you early warning that the person you face has gone into fighting mode. All the way back to Dr. Cannon, certain cues have been recognized as classic.

The person is likely to "quarter," that is, step back with one leg, turning his hips to something approximating a 45-degree angle. In this posture, the body is best balanced to take or deliver impact in any direction. Fighters call it the "boxer's stance." Martial artists call it the "front stance." Shooters call it the "Weaver stance." Cops are taught to stand this way, prepared immediately to react and fight, in an "interview stance."

The hands will typically be up, between hips and face, usually level with some point on the torso. The fingers may be partially closed. (The hands clenched into fists, or opening and closing into fists repeatedly, is a particularly blatant sign that the "fight" side of "fight or flight" has been internally engaged.)

The knees may flex slightly. This is the true "combat crouch." The head is likely to be slightly forward of the shoulders, and the shoulders forward of the hips. Combat trainers call this posture "nose over toes." It's what they teach their students to go into intentionally when they prepare to fight to the finish. When someone does it instinctively, it has given you what we in police work call "a clue"...

Life experience has already taught you that emotionally aroused people may not realize that their facial expression is reflecting their internal emotions outward for all to see. This happens in hostile situations too. A snarl that brings the lips back from the teeth doesn't require a professional behaviorist to interpret for you; it clearly doesn't bode well. The human is a natural carnivore, and a grimace that exposes the canine teeth is a particularly overt indication of aggressive intent.

A seemingly opposite expression can mean the same thing. Tightly clenched jaws, which may even include grinding teeth, and tightly pursed lips, can also be signs of extreme anger.

Let's go back for a moment to fight or flight basics. The heart and lungs are sending oxygenated blood through the body as fast as they can. However, if no strenuous physical activity has yet taken place, the body is now over-oxygenating, and hyperventilation can set in. Generations of medical professionals have advised hyperventilating patients to breathe into a paper bag. This causes them to inhale carbon dioxide they've just exhaled, and helps to quickly restore a normal O2/CO2 balance.

As it happens, people in actual fight or flight situations don't usually have access to paper bags. This includes both you, and your potential opponent.

If you are the one hyperventilating — at a high-risk scene or anywhere else — I and my fellow instructors will advise you to consciously perform what has been called "combat breathing," "stress breathing," or "crisis breathing." Martial artists call it "*sanchin* breathing." The breath is intentionally held, then slowly hissed out. It is the internalized version of the paper bag treatment. If you have been trained in the Lamaze Method of natural childbirth, you are familiar with a very similar version of stress breathing.

Sometimes, people do that automatically under stress without realizing it. If the person you are facing in a hostile situation is breathing like this, wake up and smell the coffee. Remember when we did the math before. If there's nothing else to cause stress, it is reasonable to deduce that he is planning something stressful and strenuous. One particularly common manifestation is what my mom used to call, with perhaps more justification than she knew, "blowing off steam." This is the person whose cheeks work like a bellows as he seems to intentionally hiss out a long, hard exhalation of air. It may help reduce over-oxygenation in his blood, but guess what: if he's in an uncontrollable state of rage, that building head of steam isn't going to just "blow off." There's a good chance that it's going to "blow up" instead. And you know the response. Say it with me: "Create distance..."

Look for meaningless movements. The guy who bounces up and down on the balls of his feet. The "walk that goes nowhere," that is, purposeless back and forth pacing. And, as noted before, hands which clench and unclench. (Sometimes, also, jaws that clench and unclench.) The body is subconsciously trying to burn off the excess oxygen, circulated through the bloodstream by the fight or flight response, to prevent hyperventilation. This doesn't mean the response is over with. The bottom line is, it means the fight or flight response is there.

Among Americans, nodding the head forward and back is a signal of "yes," and shaking the head from side to side is a cultural signal of "no." When you see your potential antagonist doing either of these things — and no one has asked him a yes or no question — you are experiencing another "create distance" moment. Whether he's thinking, "Yes, I knew they were going to come to take me away, and now I must attack them," or "No, I won't let them take me away this time," there's an excellent chance that what he is thinking does not bode well for you.

The folding of the arms can mean a lot of things in body language. Sometimes it just means, "I'm afraid and I'm drawing into my shell." Remember, though, that if they're showing they're afraid of you — whether or not it's a rational fear — it is the nature of mammals in general and humans in particular to lash out at what frightens them. If the folded arms are accompanied by a tensing of the muscles, and perhaps also by a glowering facial expression or any of the other possible assaultive behavior cues, you won't be far off if you read the statement as, "I am putting on my armor, because I am preparing to fight."

Look for changes in skin color. You already know that a Caucasian who suddenly becomes "red in the face" may be displaying what is culturally recognized as the color of anger. Be aware, however, that the opposite coloration effect can mean the same thing. When the body goes into "fight or flight," vasoconstriction occurs, redirecting blood flow away from the extremities and toward the internal viscera (to "fuel the furnace" for the strenuous activity that the primal brain anticipates) and to major muscle groups. This is why frightened Caucasians tend to "turn white." However, it is also why homicidal Caucasians are sometimes seen to "turn deathly pale" before they act out their violence.

Other Signage

Street cops watch for subtle tattoos and other "subculture signals." In the gay community, a handkerchief prominently hanging out of one hip pocket or the other indicates whether you are a "top" or a "bottom." In some neighborhoods in Los Angeles, wearing red means you're with the Bloods, and wearing blue means you're with the Crips, and innocent people have found themselves dead or horribly injured for unknowingly wearing the wrong color in the wrong place.

A decade ago, I was an expert witness on the defense team for a police officer who was tried for murder after he shot and killed a man who attacked him, beat him, and tried to snatch his gun and slay him with it. A key factor in winning his acquittal was that he was able to articulate that before he was attacked, he recognized his assailant's distinctive gang tattoos and correlated that knowledge with his remembered training, which had taught him that inner-city gang members often trained themselves how to disarm and murder police officers.

Teardrops tattooed on the face mean one to five years per teardrop of hard time served in prison, for example, depending on the given subculture and locale. The tattoo "AFFA" stands for "Angels Forever, Forever Angels," and marks either a genuine member or a wannabe member of the quintessential outlaw motorcycle club, Hell's Angels. A patch — whether motorcycle club patch, or police department shoulder patch — worn upside-down on a biker's vest signifies in the outlaw subculture that the wearer has taken it from a legitimate owner he has vanquished in combat. These things are good to know if you end up fighting someone who is "wearing the sign."

Other symbols or "signage" can give you clues to where the other person is coming from. In the photos that (originally accompanied) this article, one of the role-players is wearing a cap with a logo that reads "*Pilemos Estin Ergon*." That translates from the Latin as, roughly, "War Is Work." Could it give you a clue as to the personality of the wearer, when you face him in a hostile situation?

Perspectives

Let's keep this all in perspective. What we are talking about here is taking the above cues in context with a situation which is such that hostility can be anticipated by any reasonable and prudent person. Don't forget that the guy might be breathing heavily because he has recently exerted himself physically performing some perfectly innocent task. Always remember that the guy with the red face might simply have high blood pressure or a bad case of sunburn, or just be embarrassed, and that the person with the pale white face may come by that complexion naturally.

Let's also touch one more time on what your response should be to these "cues" we've been talking about. I cannot emphasize too strongly that "create distance" thing that has been repeated throughout this article. Any master martial artist, any role model military general, will tell you that the best battle is one you don't have to fight. The best course of action is always to avoid the conflict. The police officer, the psychiatric nurse, the professional security guard has a duty to stay at the scene and contain any violence that is threatened to those he is duty-bound to protect. For anyone else, the best thing to do is to abjure from the conflict, to back off and do everything possible to defuse the potential violence. The best fight is the one that never takes place.

In many jurisdictions within the United States, the law expressly states that there is a "retreat requirement." This means that the private citizen who is assaulted is expected to retreat or at least attempt to retreat before using physical force in self-defense. There are only two exceptions. One is an attack by a stranger in one's own home; there, under what the English Common Law called the Castle Doctrine, retreat is not required. Attacked by an intruder in one's own home, one has the right to stand his or her ground and use force immediately to repel the attack, but only equal force may be used. The other exception exists in every jurisdiction where the retreat requirement holds sway, and it says in essence, "Retreat is only demanded when it can be done with complete safety to oneself and others who are in danger."

Sometimes, the assault will come so quickly that you can't disengage, and you have no choice but to defend yourself. The law understands that. But even in that worst-case scenario, being able to read the fast-developing and fast-breaking danger signals of the other person's behavior can sometimes be sufficient to buy you just enough time to react swiftly enough to defend yourself and your loved ones effectively. If things get cut that close — and they often do — the early warning of the danger signals the opponent put off can make the difference between survival and death for you and those you love. If he's going to serve up violent assault, you want to see it coming in time to return the volley more effectively than he served it, and win the match.

But if it's avoidable, recognition of pre-assaultive behavior cues may be your key to seeing it coming, in time to avoid it by breaking off contact entirely. The best advice on this doesn't come from me, or Jeff Cooper, or any of the other people who teach self-defense in violent situations. It comes from the humorous poet Ogden Nash. Nash wrote:

"When called by a panther ... Don't anther."

Remember the bottom line of the jeopardy factor: it means that you, *as any reasonable person would have in the same circumstances, knowing what you knew,* concluded that your opponent was about to kill or cripple you or someone you had the right to protect.

We have now discussed the elements of Ability, Opportunity and Jeopardy. When the three of them are simultaneously present, they create the situation of *immediate danger of death or grave bodily harm.*

And that, in turn, is the set of circumstances that justifies the use of lethal force. ■

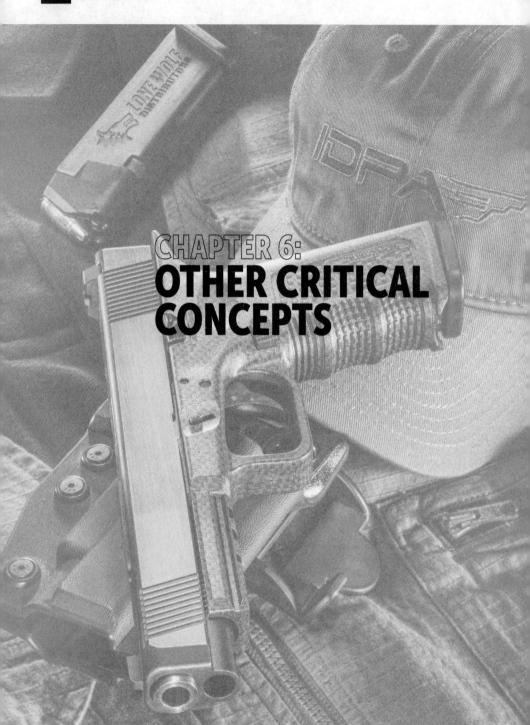

CHAPTER 6:
OTHER CRITICAL CONCEPTS

T o understand how the justified use of force in self-defense differs from criminal assault and homicide cases and legitimately-brought wrongful death or injury lawsuits, we need a firm grasp of some legal concepts not widely known among the general public. Let's start with the principle of the affirmative defense.

The Affirmative Defense

In a justified shooting in defense of self or others, the defendant would be foolish to claim that he didn't do what he did. Instead, he stipulates that he did indeed shoot his attacker but maintains that he was justified. This is an *affirmative defense*.

The affirmative defense is a two-edged sword. I've always felt that when dealing with a double-edged sword, if the edge working for your side is the sharper of the two, you'll cut yourself free of the problem. To see why that's true with the affirmative defense, let's look at both edges of the sword, the good news and the bad news.

The good news, the righteous defendant's razor-sharp edge, is that the affirmative defense is known in trial strategy as a perfect defense. The website uslegal.com defines the perfect defense thus: "Perfect defense is

P 79 Results (cont.)

e officers crouched low and fired
times with 2 hands; sometimes

lmost never fired with the "off" h
n advantageous.

Chicago street cop Bob Stasch, with well over a dozen gunfights behind him, knows when he should press the trigger and when he shouldn't. He is demonstrating with a Ring dummy gun that matches his preferred duty piece, the SIG P220 .45 pistol.

a defense that meets all legal requirements and results in the full acquittal of the accused. A defense is a denial, or answer or plea in opposition to the truth or validity of a claim by a plaintiff. For example, a perfect self-defense meets all of the generally accepted legal conditions for such a claim to be valid. It is the use of force by one who accurately appraises the necessity and the amount of force to repel an attack."

Lawyers can debate interminably what does and does not constitute a perfect defense. Still, it means this: the judge's instructions to the jury are likely to be interpretable as, "If you believe the defendant's account of the incident as a self-defense action, you must find him not guilty." Not "you may," or "you might," but – "*you **must** find him not guilty.*"

Hear the power in that! But we all know that power never comes cheaply, and here, the price is exceptionally high. That price is the other edge of the sword.

For all practical intents and purposes, the affirmative defense shifts the burden of proof. Typically that burden is upon the accuser, the prosecution in a criminal case or the plaintiff in a civil case. But, when the defendant has stipulated that he did the act — something much of the world will see as a "confession" — the burden falls upon him to convincingly show that he was indeed correct in having carried out that act. It needs to be proven to a preponderance of evidence standard, that is, a greater than fifty percent certainty, to the trier(s) of the facts.

Wikipedia explains, "In an affirmative defense the burden of proof is generally on the defendant to prove his allegations either by the preponderance of the evidence or clear and convincing evidence, as opposed to ordinary defenses (claim of right, alibi, infancy, necessity, and [in some jurisdictions, e.g., New York] self-defense [which is an affirmative defense at common law]), for which the defense has the burden of disproving beyond a reasonable doubt."

Wikipedia continues, "Because an affirmative defense requires an assertion of facts beyond those claimed by the plaintiff, generally the party who offers an affirmative defense bears the burden of proof. The standard of proof is typically lower than beyond a reasonable doubt. It can either be proved by clear and convincing evidence or by a preponderance of the evidence."

> "... THE AFFIRMATIVE DEFENSE SHIFTS THE BURDEN OF PROOF ... WHEN THE DEFENDANT HAS STIPULATED THAT HE DID THE ACT — SOMETHING MUCH OF THE WORLD WILL SEE AS A 'CONFESSION' — THE BURDEN FALLS UPON HIM TO CONVINCINGLY SHOW THAT HE WAS INDEED CORRECT IN HAVING CARRIED OUT THAT ACT. IT NEEDS TO BE PROVEN TO A PREPONDERANCE OF EVIDENCE STANDARD, THAT IS, A GREATER THAN FIFTY PERCENT CERTAINTY, TO THE TRIER(S) OF THE FACTS."

The element of the affirmative defense's shifted burden of proof is more subtle than it appears. In his excellent book *The Law of Self-Defense*, my friend and graduate Andrew Branca wrote, "While in 49 states the prosecutor must disprove self-defense beyond a reasonable doubt, in Ohio the defendant must prove he acted in self-defense by a preponderance of the evidence."[4] Ohio later updated its law, coming into line with the other 49 states, to say that once self-defense is on the table in a trial, the burden of proof shifts back to the accusing side.

So, which definition is correct: the affirmative defense shifts the burden of proof from the accuser to the defendant or Branca's observation that the state must still carry the burden of proof beyond a reasonable doubt? The answer, I believe, is that both are correct. The law and the recommended jury instructions may state that the burden of proof is upon the prosecution. However, real-world jury psychology and trial tactics tell us that when the defense itself says, "Yes, the defendant killed this man," the burden is upon the defense to show that any reasonable and prudent person would have done the same had they been in the defendant's position and known what the defendant knew. Thus, in reality, the defendant does indeed carry

"FOR A SITUATION TO EXIST THAT BRINGS THE DOCTRINE INTO PLAY, THERE IS AN INDISPENSABLE INGREDIENT CALLED AN EXIGENT CIRCUMSTANCE. AS APPLIED TO THE USE OF FORCE, THE EXIGENT CIRCUMSTANCE WOULD BE AN EXTREME EMERGENCY IN THE IMMEDIATE HERE AND NOW, WHICH CONSTITUTED A THREAT OF INJURY OR DEATH TO ONESELF OR ANOTHER INNOCENT PARTY."

a burden of showing the triers of the facts that he was correct in taking the action he did.

Why do I say the defendant's side of the sword is sharper? Because if it has been honed with the stone of knowledge and ethics, and the defendant has done the right thing, that defendant (with a good legal team!) should be able to demonstrate precisely that convincingly to those who will judge him.

The Doctrine of Necessity

The English Common Law, largely the template for law in the United States, encompasses the *doctrine of competing harms.* Some states articulate it under that terminology, but many describe it as *the doctrine of necessity.* The two are the same. As it applies to the lawful defense of self or others, this doctrine holds that you are allowed to break the law in the rare circumstance where following that law would cause more human injury than breaking it.

The legal section of freedictionary.com offers this definition:

"A defense asserted by a criminal or civil defendant that he or she had no choice but to break the law." This source continues, "The necessity defense has long been recognized as Common Law and has also been part of most states' statutory law. Although no federal statute acknowledges the defense, the Supreme Court has recognized it as part of the common law. The rationale behind the necessity defense is that sometimes, in a particular situation, a technical breach of the law is more advantageous to society than the consequence of strict adherence to the law. The defense is often used successfully in cases that involve a Trespass on property to save a person's life or property. It has also been used in cases involving more complex questions with varying degrees of success.

"Almost all common-law and statutory definitions of the necessity defense include the following elements: (1) the defendant acted to avoid a significant risk of harm; (2) no adequate lawful means could have been used to escape the harm; and (3) the harm avoided was greater than that caused by breaking the law. Some jurisdictions require in addition that the harm must have been imminent and that the action taken must have been reasonably expected to avoid the imminent danger. All these elements mirror the principles on which the defense of necessity was founded: first, that the highest social value is not always achieved by blind adherence to the law; second, that it is unjust to punish those who technically violate the letter of the law when they are acting to promote or achieve a higher social value than would be served by strict adherence to the law; and third, that it is in society's best interest to promote the greatest good and to encourage people to seek to achieve the greatest good, even if doing so necessitates a technical breach of the law.

"The defense of necessity is considered a justification defense, as compared with an excuse defense such as duress. An action that is harmful but praiseworthy is justified, whereas an action that is harmful but ought to be forgiven may be excused. Rather than focusing on the actor's state of mind, as would be done with an excuse defense, the court with a necessity defense focuses on the value of the act. No court has ever accepted a defense of necessity to justify killing a person to protect property."

For a situation to exist that brings the doctrine into play, there is an indispensable ingredient called an *exigent circumstance.* As applied to the use of force, the exigent circumstance would be an extreme emergency in the immediate here and now, which constituted a threat of injury or death to oneself or another innocent party.

If you think about it, virtually any defensive use of deadly force will fall into this category. It is simply common sense in a world that often deals in shades of gray between pure good and pure evil. We all learn as children, "If life gives you a choice between two evils, a good person is expected to choose the lesser of the two evils." The doctrine of competing harms is simply the law's recognition of that reality. I see it as proof that the Law is wise, the Law is mature and the Law understands the nuances of the human condition more than it sometimes appears. It's worth noting that in at least four states — Arkansas, Hawaii, Nebraska, and Oregon come to mind — the doctrine of competing harms is delineated in their state's law books as the "doctrine of two evils."

Some might wish to invoke the doctrine of competing harms as a defense for illegally carrying a gun. This frequently occurs when a convicted felon acting for the common good picks up a gun and shoots a violent criminal to save an innocent human life. In one case in New Hampshire, a now-law-abiding man with a felony conviction on his record witnessed the murder of a police officer. The policeman fell, shot in the back by the cop-killer. The witness snatched the SIG .45 pistol out of the murdered lawman's

holster and, as the confrontation continued, had to shoot the cop-killer to death. Technically, the witness was a felon possessing a firearm, a felony in and of itself. However, recognizing the doctrine of competing harms, the State Attorney General's office held him harmless for the act within the totality of the circumstances, and he was not charged.

The reason the doctrine of competing harms is not often invoked on a charge of illegal carry of a weapon is that, usually, no specific competing harm exists. A few years ago, I was on the defense team of a Rhode Island man licensed to carry in that state who had inadvertently crossed the state line into Massachusetts, where he did not have a non-resident carry permit before he realized he was still wearing the Glock 23 pistol he routinely carried. Within hours, that technically illegal gun had saved his life: he fired a single .40-caliber bullet, which mortally wounded a man who attacked him with a knife. He was charged with manslaughter and illegal carry of the

The author learned a lot from the late Bill Allard (right), who he knew for more than 40 years. Bill was the one man who killed more armed robbers in gunfights on NYPD Stakeout Squad than his famous partner, Jim Cirillo. The interview with Bill can be found on the ProArms Podcast YouTube channel.

firearm, a first-offense felony in that state.

We explained things to the jury, which acquitted him in the shooting. The defense attempted to invoke the doctrine of competing harms as a defense to the gun charge. The judge would not allow it, citing case law in that state which required the competing harm — the specific danger — to have been present when the defendant armed himself. Her ruling was that, since he had been carrying the gun without a Massachusetts permit before the threat presented itself, the doctrine could not apply. A jury that never heard the doctrine of competing harms argument found him guilty on the felony charge of illegal carry, triggering a minimum mandatory one year in jail. He would remain a felon, prohibited from owning firearms thereafter.

(Ironically, the defendant had been eligible for a non-resident Massachusetts carry permit, and the application had been on his desk for more than a year before the shooting, but sadly he had never applied. In retrospect, he never would have been charged with the offense for which he was convicted if he had acquired the permit for the contiguous state.)

One reason I am including the doctrine of competing harms in this book is the same reason I have included it in class ever since I began training armed citizens in 1981. If it is known to the defendant and was part of the defendant's decision process at the time of the incident, if the defendant takes the stand, there is an excellent chance that his attorney can bring it out during direct examination when he asks the defendant why he was armed in the first place. In a case like the one just cited, awareness of the doctrine would give jurors an excellent reason to hold the defendant harmless for possessing the firearm.

Obviously, the best approach is to always carry the firearm *legally*.

Jury Nullification

It is not widely known that even if a jury determines that the defendant broke the law, if the jury believes the law itself is bad or stupid or wrong, the jury can still come in with a verdict of not guilty. This is known as "jury nullification." I have never heard of a case where a judge instructed the jury that nullification was an option. Indeed, the judge's job is to instruct the jury to follow the law, not disregard it.

An organization exists called FIJA, the Fully Informed Jury Association. Its stated purpose is to educate the general public — the jury pool — about the fact that jurors have the option of nullifying laws they disagree with. People often join because there are certain laws they disagree with. Membership includes proponents of drug legalization, some who fear Draconian gun laws, etc.

While I can understand FIJA's rationale and empathize with some of its goals, I have never joined for several reasons. One reason is that I carried a badge for over four decades and was certified as a police prosecutor from 1988 to 2017. To join an organization dedicated to telling people to disregard the law would make me a hypocrite. But another reason is that it's hard for me to find a case where a person who had done the right thing *would* benefit from jury nullification and *would not achieve* the same goal if the doctrine of competing harms was injected into the case. ∎

CHAPTER 7:
FURTIVE MOVEMENT SHOOTINGS AND OTHER WIDELY MISUNDERSTOOD EVENTS

The dynamics of violent encounters are, in legalese, "beyond the ken of the jury." That's an Old English phrase still in common legal use describing matters that the average layman in the jury pool could not be expected to know without explanation by court-approved experts. Indeed, these things are seldom, if ever, discussed in law school.

If you keep or carry a firearm for defensive purposes, you are a potential victim of an unjust accusation based on legitimate actions. These actions will need expert testimony so the jury can correctly and fairly interpret the evidence to determine the facts. It will be hugely helpful in court — and to your decision-making ability at the danger scene — for the law-abiding armed citizen to understand these things beforehand. We'll look first at the "furtive movement shooting."

Furtive Movement Shootings

A furtive movement is a physical action that provokes suspicion. It often evinces stealth or secrecy, but not always. It can encompass a great many things. We're talking about a very narrow, specific subset here. In a furtive movement *shooting*, the individual who was shot has made a movement *consistent with reaching for a weapon but **not** reasonably consistent* *with anything else within the totality of the circumstances.*

A man's hand reaching to the hip or the pocket, in and of itself, is not enough to warrant whipping out a gun and shooting him. As the courts say, the situation has to be judged by *the totality of the circumstances.* I teach my students to assess the furtive movement as satisfying only one prong of the Ability/Opportunity/Jeopardy test, the *ability* element. However, *the opportunity and jeopardy elements must be separately present.*

If those other elements are present, the furtive movement may create the ability element by giving the potential victim prudent reason to believe the suspect is armed with a deadly weapon. Let's say you've just had a fender-bender auto accident. The other vehicle's driver comes boiling out of his car and approaches you rapidly, screaming, "You SOB, I'll blow your brains out," and reaches under his clothes as if going for a gun.

Well, his threat to shoot you in the head creates the element of jeopardy. Since your vehicles were close enough to make contact and he is now coming toward you, he is obviously within gunshot range: the opportunity element is present. Within the totality of the circumstances, his movement consistent with going for a weapon and not reasonably consistent with anything else now completes the triad with the element of ability.

True, you have not yet seen the gun. However, a part of the dynamics of violent encounters is understanding how rapidly an opponent can deploy a concealed weapon. Once the hand is on the hidden gun or knife, it can be brought to bear in a fraction of a second. It's true of knives or guns. Years ago, I filmed it with legendary blade master Mike Janich for the Paladin Press training film on knives and knife fighting, "Masters of Defense." Starting with my hands empty and in front of me, I reached to a start signal, drew my concealed training knife, and stopped the time by striking an electronic timer in front of me with that knife. The impact stopped the timer at *under one half of one second*. With a real knife instead of a training drone and a human abdomen instead of an electronic timer as the target, that would have produced an eviscerating, life-threatening wound. And, be assured, many people have faster hands than me.

Decades ago, I spoke in defense of a police officer charged with manslaughter for shooting a suspect who, as the cop and his partner were arresting him for illegal concealed carry, went for his gun. The suspect's gun, stolen and fully loaded, was in evidence; it was found on his person, still with its barrel barely inside his waistband, which was consistent with him starting to clear it from its hiding place to draw and shoot the cops when the police bullet short-circuited his central nervous system and killed him instantly.

Incredibly, one of the prosecution's theories was that it couldn't be justifiable because the patrolman had not yet seen the suspect's gun coming clear when he fired. When asked at the scene what he observed, the cop said he saw the man's upper right arm coming forward, consistent with a cross-draw; the dead man's gun had been butt-forward in the left side of his waistband, and he had been reaching with his dominant right hand. A detective from his police department testified that the cop was wrong to fire because he should have waited to see the other man's gun.

When I was asked about that on the witness stand after being called in the officer's defense, my answer was, "If you wait to see the gun, you're going to see what comes out of it." And then, I demonstrated it to the jury in the courtroom. They understood, and they acquitted the officer on all counts.

However, I never considered that case to be a furtive movement shooting, simply because the man who was killed had a gun, and the officer knew it! That's why he was making the arrest. Even so, since the prosecution painted it as a furtive movement shooting, we had to address it as such to defeat the unsubstantiated allegation of a bad judgment shooting.

In years past, when something like this happened, and the man who was shot *didn't* have a gun, it was common for the prosecutor to think something like this: "Let's see ... you say you shot him because you thought he had a gun. But you were wrong. I'll consider that to be bad judgment. What do my old law school notes say? It looks like 'bad judgment plus death equals manslaughter.' That's it, then; I'll charge you with manslaughter." And that ain't just theory, folks; it was happening in court. Such things led, in the old days, to the practice of officers carrying "throwdown guns" or "alibi guns."

Elsewhere in this book, we discuss why planting a weapon on the man you've shot when his actions put you in reasonable fear for your life is a hugely bad idea. The advice came from a time when legal principles of deadly force were not as well established as they are now.

One of my mentors was the great Border Patrol gunfighting trainer Bill

Jordan; he wrote the foreword to my first book, *Fundamentals of Police Impact Weapons*, in 1978. I had read and re-read his classic book on gunfighting, *No Second Place Winner*. It remains one of the timeless classics on the topic. In it, Jordan wrote:

"Let us suppose that an officer is checking freight trains at night. He receives urgent information that a man had just shot and killed two policemen in the adjoining town and was believed to have caught and be riding the freight our officer is about to check. The killer is described as 'medium height and weight, wearing a brown hat, khaki pants and shirt, and believed to be heavily armed and of course, obviously dangerous.' As the train pulls into the yard and stops, a man, answering that description in externals, steps from between two box cars. Anticipating the possibility of trouble, our officer has his gun in one hand and his flashlight in the other. Flashing the light on the suspect he says, 'I am an officer. Don't move!' Then, instead of obeying the order, the suspect reaches for his hip pocket. What would YOU do? Well, so did our hypothetical officer! But, supposing further, when he goes over to examine the remains, he finds that it was all a mistake. This man wasn't armed. Instead, he had a bad cold and had selected a particularly unfortunate time to decide he needed a handkerchief to blow his nose. Although completely sincere in his conviction that his life was in danger and despite the fact that HAD this been the man the officer believed him to be, his wife would in all probability by now be a widow if he had waited to see what came out of that hip pocket, our officer is in a bad spot. That's where the alibi gun came in. It was a small, inexpensive gun of the 'Owl Head' or 'Saturday Night Harrison' persuasion, was fully loaded and would shoot, had no fingerprints on it and all in all was a very comforting thing to have around for the 'suspect' to hold until the coroner got there! If this looks like an unethical action to you, it is suggested that you go back and again put yourself in the officer's spot. Then do a little honest soul searching before adopting a 'holier than thou' attitude.

"Well, alibi guns are no longer needed and are a thing of the past, so I am told."[5]

For all but historical purposes, Bill's last sentence above is the operative lesson of the entire passage. *"...alibi guns are no longer needed."*

Things have changed since Bill's time on the job, working mainly in violent areas during the second and third quarters of the 20th century. As is

Experienced police defense lawyers like Laura Scarry teach the fine points of what is and is not justifiable in the eyes of the law.

explained in the chapter on "myths," where we talk about "drop guns" and "throwdown weapons" and why they're a spectacularly bad idea, it has been decades since anyone could expect to get away with such a ploy. The state of forensic evidence gathering and analysis today has advanced beyond the wildest dreams of, say, an investigator in the 1950s. But, more to the point, there is a better understanding of these things now in the legal arena.

By the late 1960s and 1970s, police defense teams were winning these cases. Such great police defense lawyers as George Franscell in Los Angeles pointed out to judges and juries that the law had never demanded that the assailant's gun be loaded instead of empty, for example, or even present. All the law had ever demanded was that the opponent's actions be such that a reasonable and prudent person would believe him to be armed with a deadly weapon. If opportunity and jeopardy were separately present, that created a situation of immediate danger of death or great bodily harm, which warranted recourse to a lethal response.

Remember the words of great police trainers like Chief Jeff Chudwin and great police defense lawyers like Laura Scarry: "You don't have to be right; you have to be *reasonable*."

Fleeing Felon Shootings

Some people believe that they can shoot any fleeing felony suspect. They are wrong! On the other end of the spectrum, some people believe that the shooting of any fleeing felon is forbidden since he is not attempting to kill or cripple anyone at that moment. Hence, the shooting is no longer a righteous defense of self or other innocent persons. Those people are not quite so wrong, but they are technically incorrect. For the private citizen, a very rare confluence of circumstances can occur that may justify using deadly force on a fleeing felon.

Let me make one thing clear: if your concealed carry instructor has told you, "Don't shoot fleeing felons, period," I'm not disrespecting them in any way. Concealed carry courses tend to be short and have a great deal of ground to cover. This writer has the luxury of 40-hour courses for armed citizens, which allow greater detail, and treatment of situations that are less likely to occur but are still possible.

Another point to clarify: suppose an armed robber is running away, and you shout at him to halt. It's not the smartest thing to do, but it is legal under the principles of citizen's arrest, which exist in the black letter law of most

"

SOME PEOPLE BELIEVE THAT THEY CAN SHOOT ANY FLEEING FELONY SUSPECT. THEY ARE WRONG! ON THE OTHER END OF THE SPECTRUM, SOME PEOPLE BELIEVE THAT THE SHOOTING OF ANY FLEEING FELON IS FORBIDDEN SINCE HE IS NOT ATTEMPTING TO KILL OR CRIPPLE ANYONE AT THAT MOMENT ... FOR THE PRIVATE CITIZEN, A VERY RARE CONFLUENCE OF CIRCUMSTANCES CAN OCCUR THAT MAY JUSTIFY USING DEADLY FORCE ON A FLEEING FELON.

states. He pivots, his back still to you but swinging his gun in your direction. You fire and your instantly fatal bullet strikes him "in the back," behind the lateral midline of his body. Was that a fleeing felon shooting?

Some will say so, but in fact, it was straight-up self-defense! He was trying to kill you; you fired to stop him from killing you, not to stop him from getting away, and at the moment he swung a gun in your direction with obviously construable intent to use deadly force, the "fleeing felon" argument just became moot. At that moment, your opponent became the aggressor in a new, life-threatening assault upon you while you were acting within the law.

The pivotal U.S. Supreme Court decision on this matter is found in *Tennessee v. Garner,* decided in the mid-1980s.[6] It is recommended as useful reading for anyone who keeps or carries a gun, if only because it is one of the very few cases in which the highest court has addressed the use of lethal force. However, for purposes of this discussion, it's also a cornerstone case on using deadly force against fleeing felony suspects. The take-away lesson from this critical decision seems to be, *deadly force will only be justified if, within the totality of the circumstances, the suspect's continued freedom constitutes a clear and present danger to innocent human life and limb.* That determination is made through the prism of the reasonable person doctrine.

There are other key standards in this complicated area of deadly force law. What makes the fleeing felon a felon in the first place? He has committed a crime punishable by a year or more in prison. There are a great many offenses in that category that are not worthy of capital punishment or deadly force response by even the victim. For a fleeing felon shooting to be justified, it would have to involve a *heinous felony against the person.* In other words, a particularly atrocious crime involving death or great bodily harm to an innocent human being. A "crime against the person" involves actual or threatened serious physical harm, not theft of what the SCOTUS has called "mere property." For example, armed robbery is a serious felony but is not usually considered a heinous felony against the person. The victim of an armed robbery can certainly shoot the robber *while still in danger,* for the simple reason that they are not firing the gun to save the valuables being stolen but to save themselves and others from the explicit danger of being killed that made it an *armed* robbery in the first place. Once the offender has broken off from his deadly threat and is fleeing, that danger of being killed no longer exists, and few jurisdictions will look kindly on him being shot down as he runs away; at that point, society and the minions of the law may see shooting him as an act of revenge, or a killing undertaken to recover "mere property." Legal definitions of a heinous felony against the person vary state to state but will generally encompass murder, attempted murder, arson of occupied buildings, stranger kidnapping, and violent sexual assault.

Notice that qualifier terms are hanging on most of those definitions. Juries can take days to determine what is murder and what is manslaughter; you, the person with the gun, are expected to make that determination in an instant. Prosecutor A may define him shooting at you and missing as attempted murder. At the same time, Prosecutor B may consider it only aggravated assault — a serious felony, but one not usually seen as a *heinous* felony. A non-custodial divorced parent driving away with his child may be seen by the custodial parent as a kidnapper but very likely won't be seen that way by the courts; hooded drug cartel members kidnapping a witness against them is a different story entirely. The man who burns down an unoccupied barn he has no right to destroy is indeed a felonious arsonist, but not in the heinous felony class of the person who deliberately sets fire to an orphanage full of children. A chauvinist boss pats his employee on the buttocks; in the strict letter of the law, he may be technically guilty of simple sexual assault, but as much as his employee might want to shoot him at the moment, the law does not allow that. An actual rapist, on the other hand, is a heinous felon by every standard and "bought and paid for."

The shooter has to be sure that this fleeing person *is* the one who committed the heinous felony in question! For all practical intents and purposes, that means you've seen him do it.

Deadly force must always be a last resort. If the totality of the circumstances is such that the fleeing felon's capture is imminent, killing him to stop him now would not be a great idea. But if the totality of those circumstances indicated that he would remain at large indefinitely to commit more heinous crimes if not immediately stopped, the balance now tilts toward justifiability.

By that same "last resort" criterion, all other means of capture should either be impossible or impractical or have been tried and failed.

Another element comes not from law or case law but common sense. Suppose that within the totality of the circumstances, you realize that if you shoot this fleeing felon now after he has already committed his crime and perhaps thrown his weapon away, it will look to all the witnesses as if *he* is a helpless victim running for his life, and *you* are the cold-blooded murderer who shot him in the back? Nature is warning you that pulling the trigger will plunge yourself and your loved ones into a long legal nightmare. If you take your finger off the trigger without firing, no one has grounds to blame you. Remember, a duty to kill never arises for the private citizen, only the *right* to do so. Again ... common sense.

Reviewing the above, you can see why it is so rare for those six criteria to be simultaneously present. Heinous felony against the person, known for sure to have been committed by *this* individual, who is likely to remain at large to do it again if he is not stopped right here, right now, in a situation where you are clearly the Good Guy, and he is clearly the Bad Guy, with no other reasonable way to stop him; and, overriding everything, a situation in which his continued freedom presents a clear and present danger to in-nocent human life and limb.

Remember that this book does not give legal advice; it merely offers practical advice. The bottom line of practical advice on the use of deadly force against a fleeing felon is this:

If there is the **slightest** reasonable doubt, **Don't Shoot!**

"Shot in the Back"

Bullets in the back don't always involve fleeing felons. Again and again, the shooter says, "He was coming at me with a weapon, I fired, and I stopped shooting when he spun and fell." All well and good, total conformance with the rules of engagement. But the lead investigator says, "You're lying because the autopsy shows that one or more of your bullets *hit him in the back.*"

Is the shooter lying? Very probably not. Here, a demonstrable action/reaction paradigm is not taught in law school and often not taught in professional homicide investigation seminars.

Back in the 1970s, my friend and colleague John Farnam did tests that proved that the *average* person — not just a shooting champion — can fire four shots in one second from a double-action-only handgun with a long trigger stroke for each shot, and five shots in one second from a semi-automatic pistol with a short-reset trigger. World champions can shoot roughly twice as fast. Two men I've learned a lot from and shot with often, whom I'm proud to call my friends, are Rob Leatham and Jerry Miculek. Jerry is, almost

Being filmed for "Personal Defense TV" Season 7 on the Sportsman Channel and using Airsoft guns, Rich Nance in the bad guy role spins away as Ayoob is still firing. Note that the bad guy takes "hits" in the back while still a clear danger to the good guy.

indisputably, the finest double-action revolver shooter who has ever lived, and he is on record and video firing eight shots in one second from an eight-shot Smith & Wesson heavy-frame revolver — and getting all hits. Decades ago, at the first Single Stack National Championships, I saw Rob pump six shots from a Springfield Armory 1911 .45 automatic into a fast-turning target in what couldn't have been more than one-half of one second. Hold all those times in your mind for a moment.

We've just looked at it from the defender's side. Now, let's examine it from the attacker's side. He is lunging at his victim, probably not the first time he's done something like that, and now something unexpected happens: the victim comes up with a gun! Instinct tells him to turn away from the danger, and what we know now about human reaction time shows he can start that turn in a quarter of one second, or even less. As a rule of thumb, a human can pivot his torso *a quarter turn in a quarter of a second*. That's 90 degrees, and if his side was angled toward you, the defender — something familiar in the "body language" of human-on-human assault — the lateral midline of his body has passed your gunsights in 0.25 of one second. A human can do a half-turn, 180 degrees, in half a second. That means that even when the bad guy is square-on when you started shooting, he can have his *back* square to you in 0.50 of one second.

The third thing we have to factor in is the shooter's reaction time to the unanticipated change of events when the attacker suddenly turned away. Reaction time to *anticipated stimulus* runs plus/minus a quarter of a second. But the shooter firing in self-defense doesn't anticipate a sudden break-off of the assailant's attack; if they thought the attacker would suddenly stop attacking, they would not have fired at all.

This brings us into another range of human reactions: reaction to *unanticipated* stimulus. The brain has to analyze this change of events cognitively and respond accordingly through the OODA Loop defined long ago by Col. John Boyd, the famed master trainer of USAF fighter pilots. OODA stands for Observe, Orient, Decide, Act. The defender must OBSERVE that the assailant is turning away. They must cognitively ORIENT to this change of events and figure out what it means, which in this case is, "I may not have to shoot anymore." They must DECIDE to change actions. Finally, they must ACT and physically carry out the new game plan, which in this case is to stop

"

BACK IN THE 1970S, MY FRIEND AND COLLEAGUE JOHN FARNAM DID TESTS THAT PROVED THAT THE AVERAGE PERSON — NOT JUST A SHOOTING CHAMPION — CAN FIRE FOUR SHOTS IN ONE SECOND FROM A DOUBLE-ACTION-ONLY HANDGUN WITH A LONG TRIGGER STROKE FOR EACH SHOT, AND FIVE SHOTS IN ONE SECOND FROM A SEMI-AUTOMATIC PISTOL WITH A SHORT-RESET TRIGGER.

pulling the trigger.

Reacting to an *unanticipated stimulus*, therefore, takes far longer. In the meantime, the original justified action — in this case, firing as fast as possible to stop the threat — is still taking place. Several shots may have been fired when the finger comes off the trigger.

During this time, the attacker's body has been turning, bringing his back toward the incoming gunfire. Thus, it becomes perfectly understandable how defensively fired shots could enter behind the lateral midline.

The first case of this kind in which I was involved as an expert witness was *Florida v. Mary Menucci Hopkin,* mentioned elsewhere in this book, back in the 1980s. It involved a battered woman who shot the homicidal common-law husband who smashed his way through the door of her mobile home and came at her after already having once tried to kill her and left her for dead. She fired three shots from her double-action revolver as fast as she could and stopped shooting when she realized he had turned away and broken off the attack. Her first shot entered the front of his torso, the second from the side, and the third in the back. The "shot in the back" element was one cornerstone of the prosecution's case against her.

Her defense lawyer, Mark Seiden, led me through an explanation like what I've just described above. It got the point across. Mary was acquitted of all charges by the jury.

This turning and shooting factor was later quantified in the peer-reviewed literature by Dr. Bill Lewinski, head of the Force Science Institute, and still later rediscovered and quantified by Dr. Martin Fackler and one of his associates at the International Wound Ballistics Association in the 1990s. I documented it on film in 2001 for ALI-ABA in a CLE (Continuing Legal Education for attorneys) training film on managing deadly force cases. ALI is the American Law Institute, the "blue chip provider" of CLE training material, and ABA is the American Bar Association. It remains in the archives of ALI-ABA in its CLE-TV series. It was documented on film again in 2012, including live-fire demonstrations on turning targets, for "Personal Defense TV" on the Sportsman Channel, available in its archives as well.

I've had to demonstrate this in other court cases, most recently at this writing in *West Virginia v. Jonathan Ferrell* in 2012. The first case I know of in which it was pivotal to the defense was the *Florida v. Hopkin* mentioned above, but it's hard for me to believe that I was the first one to figure that out; if you know of any previous case where this was proven earlier, please let me know, in care of the publisher of this book.

The bottom line is simple yet comes from something complicated: things that seem impossible or wrong at first glance can be recognized as possible and justifiable when analyzed scientifically and professionally, in context and detail.

It's something all too many in the legal profession haven't grasped — the prosecutors who bring cases that shouldn't have been brought and the defense lawyers who don't know how to explain to the jury how those things happened. And the good people who fired the shots yet didn't understand how to explain what happened to those who held their lives and futures in their hands as they judged them for those acts. ∎

CHAPTER 8:
CASTLE DOCTRINE AND STAND YOUR GROUND LAWS

As this book is written, the concepts of Stand Your Ground and the separate and distinct Castle Doctrine have become widely confused and blurred in the public eye. The following is reprinted from a handout that accompanied this writer's CLE training lecture for the attorneys attending the 2012 Firearms Law Symposium sponsored by the Texas Bar Association.

Stand Your Ground and Castle Doctrine Issues Today

Presented by Massad Ayoob,
Texas Bar Association Firearms Law Symposium
September 2012

In a nation that has become a sound-bite society — with CNN Headline News almost as popular as regular CNN, and *USA Today* our second-most widely-read newspaper — we have a public and therefore a jury pool that is increasingly vulnerable to misinformed simple answers to complicated questions. This has certainly been true in recent years, with print and electronic media having disseminated false perceptions about such topics as Castle Doctrine and Stand Your Ground laws.

We are told on editorial pages that with these laws in place, anyone can kill anyone and get away with it by claiming "I was in fear for my life." We are told that this allows criminals to commit murder and get away with it by uttering the magic words, "It was self-defense." We are told that with these laws rivers of blood will run in the streets, that both malicious and negligent shootings will go unredressed in the civil courts, and that homicides will rise and already are rising as a direct result.

The author lectured on Stand Your Ground and Castle Doctrine issues at the Gun Rights Policy Conference, September 2013, in Houston, Texas.

The facts, however, show otherwise.

When Terms Get Confused

Castle Doctrine derives from the ancient principle in the English Common Law which held that the individual's home is his castle; attacked there, he need not retreat, and even the king could not enter the cottage of the most humble peasant without a warrant. While the latter element touches on Fourth Amendment issues not on point to the topic of the moment, "a man's home is his castle" is so well established that it has long since entered daily American idiom.

The doctrine speaks to home and curtilage: the house or apartment itself, and attached or adjacent buildings; actual definitions of "curtilage" may vary in case law state by state. Typically, however, it will not extend to the front lawn, the sidewalk, or the far boundaries of one's farm or ranch.

Castle Doctrine issues can be murky. In one famous case in New England in the mid-1970s, *Commonwealth of Massachusetts v.*

> CASTLE DOCTRINE DERIVES FROM THE ANCIENT PRINCIPLE IN THE ENGLISH COMMON LAW WHICH HELD THAT THE INDIVIDUAL'S HOME IS HIS CASTLE; ATTACKED THERE, HE NEED NOT RETREAT, AND EVEN THE KING COULD NOT ENTER THE COTTAGE OF THE MOST HUMBLE PEASANT WITHOUT A WARRANT.

Roberta Shaffer, a state Supreme Court held that a woman who shot her common-law husband when he attacked her in their home was not covered because the home was his too, and therefore her invocation of the Castle Doctrine was not applicable. In 2012, however, in *State of Nebraska v. Darrel White*, the Nebraska State Supreme Court upheld a man's right to, without retreat, kill the roommate who violently attacked him in the abode they both shared.

Stand Your Ground (SYG) laws are geared to confrontations that occur outside the home since they would be redundant to the Castle Doctrine, which already makes it clear that the individual need not retreat before using defensive deadly force against a home invader. SYG protects your client *only* if —

He was not the aggressor, or if he was, has attempted to break off hostilities before the second party's attack on him now necessitates your client's use of deadly force.

He was in a place where he had a right to be.

He was not committing a crime at the time.

Since the passage of the relevant Texas law authored by State Senator Jeff Wentworth, R-San Antonio, retreat has not been required before resorting to deadly force if the latter is necessary. However, even prior, retreat has NEVER been demanded UNLESS IT COULD BE ACCOMPLISHED WITH COMPLETE SAFETY TO ONESELF AND OTHERS. This is true in Texas, and has long been true in the rest of the country as well, including the so called "retreat states."

Historian Clayton Cramer explained the development of Castle Doctrine and Stand Your Ground principles over the centuries.

Ayoob spoke in favor of Stand Your Ground laws, while prosecutor Steve Jantzen spoke against them.

It is imperative that your client know the difference. As you know, self-defense is an affirmative defense which shifts the burden of proof. In most jurisdictions, for a self-defense plea to prevail, the defense will have to convince the triers of the facts to a preponderance of evidence standard that the shooting was indeed justified. This burden, vastly higher than merely creating an element of reasonable doubt as to his guilt, is far more easily met if the defendant takes the stand. After all, you are stipulating that he shot the deceased: the issue is why he did so. Was his purpose malicious, or justifiable? You can say whatever you want in opening statement, but by the time you're ready to close, you have to introduce testimony or evidence to back up any assertions you make at opening. If your client doesn't take the stand, who ELSE can testify as to what his purpose was when he pulled the trigger?

Since there is therefore a high likelihood that your client will take the stand, it is important for you to have schooled him as to the difference between Castle Doctrine and Stand Your Ground. Suppose your client was attacked by a knife-wielding mugger in a public park, and instead of attempting to retreat, drew his legally-carried gun and shot the assailant dead. During cross examination, opposing counsel may ask him, "Mr. Defendant, what do you believe justified you using a gun on him without at least attempting to just run away without bloodshed?" If your client makes the mistake of answering "Castle Doctrine," opposing counsel has your man in a very disadvantaged position.

I would expect the opposing lawyer to hand him a copy of Black's Legal Dictionary and have your client read the definition of Castle Doctrine to the jury. Then, your opposite number will pounce. "So, Mr. Defendant, it's the home that's the castle. But this shooting took place in a park. Are you telling this jury you consider the park to be your castle grounds? Who was it, exactly, who made you the king of all the rest of us?"

This is why it's important for anyone who carries a gun to know the difference between Castle Doctrine and Stand Your Ground.

Immunity to Prosecution

Since late in the first quarter of 2012, when a shooting in Sanford, Florida, captured the headlines, that state's law is the one that has received the most popular discussion. Passed in 2005, this law not only clarified Castle Doctrine in the Sunshine State, and rescinded the previous retreat requirement, but also provided for a presumption of innocence element. The defendant can request a hearing (in this case, more of a mini-trial) in which a judge who determines the act to have, more likely than not, been justified, may dismiss the case.

Immunity to Lawsuit

Texas, like Florida, has a provision in its law that if the shooting has been determined to have been justified, the shooter should be immune to civil lawsuit. It is reasonable to assume that an allegation

Master attorney Alan Gura has won multiple landmark cases for gun owners' civil rights. Here, he is speaking at the Gun Rights Policy Conference.

of negligence by the plaintiff may, if credibly presented, bypass this protection, since by definition there can be no justifiable accident. In one case now proceeding through the civil system in Florida, the State's Attorney has chosen not to pursue the matter of a young man who killed a burglar who was menacing him and his mother. However, that prosecutor's office has not yet issued a Memorandum of Closure declaring this use of deadly force to have been justified. At this point the lawsuit is still alive and well and progressing toward trial...since it has not, by definition, been "determined" to have been justified.

In Tyler, Texas, in February of 2007, rancher Terry Graham came home to catch a drug-addicted long-time felon and burglar leaving Graham's freshly looted house. When the homeowner challenged him, the burglar gunned his getaway car at Graham with his left hand on the steering wheel and his right hand reaching into a bag of stolen guns, when Graham fired a single shot. This shot killed the assailant, and undoubtedly saved Graham's life and perhaps the lives of two other people who were with the homeowner.

I spoke for him in front of the grand jury convened by a fair District Attorney, Matt Bingham. They no-billed. The family of the deceased sued. Attorney Tracy Crawford called Albert Rodriguez and me as experts for the defense at trial in July of 2009. The jury found entirely for defendant Terry Graham. By then, however, Mr. Graham had amassed substantial legal fees and been placed under tremendous stress for nearly two and a half years.

It was to prevent such obvious injustices that the Texas state legislature passed its law creating civil liability immunity for justified use of deadly physical force, authored by Texas State Senator Jeff Wentworth (R-San Antonio). However, that law did not go into effect until September of 2007, some seven months after Mr. Graham had to fire in what was later clearly shown to be legitimate self-defense. Tracy Crawford and many other Texas attorneys felt that if the law had been in place at the time of the Graham incident, much unnecessary grief might have been saved.

While the Castle Doctrine and SYG principles are mature, long-established concepts in the law, the civil immunity provisions in Texas and Florida law are fairly recent. They have not been tested all the way up through the appellate process. In Texas, it remains less than perfectly clear as to what "deems" the use of fatal force justifiable for purposes of civil immunity.

Stand Your Ground Myths

Will an increase in justifiable homicides in states with SYG laws mean that more lives are being lost? **Not necessarily.** Historian Clayton Cramer noted that when *Time* magazine did a story on every death by gunfire for one week in America, and returned a year later to follow up on the outcomes, a significant number of those fatal shootings which had originally been implied to be criminal homicides turned out to be justified self-defense incidents.

Cramer cited one study in which justifiable homicides by armed citizens had increased three-fold — *but so had justified officer-involved shootings in the same region.* The change in law as it affected citizens certainly didn't change anything from the police side. Cramer considers it logical to conclude that, within the studied population, violent activity by criminals warranting defensive use of deadly force had simply increased.

The recent Texas A&M University study on homicides as related to SYG laws notes, "This indicates that, in addition, we look at justifiable homicide, which is a separate classification available in the Supplemental Homicide Reports. One concern with these data is under-reporting; Kleck (1988) estimates that only one-fifth of legally justified homicides are classified that way by police." Many shootings which previously had to go to trial to determine justifiability — at the expense of many tax dollars, and much human suffering by the wrongly accused and their families — are now simply found justifiable earlier. Far from being A Bad Thing, early determination of justifiability reduces the cost in public treasure and private trauma, and better serves Justice in both respects.

Will criminals kill people and get away with it by claiming self-defense? **Obviously not**, as witness the jury's recent verdict in *Texas v. Raul Rodriguez.* Skilled prosecutors have been winning convictions against murderers who falsely claimed self-defense for as long as there have been murder trials. One need look no farther than the 2012 conviction for murder of Raul Rodriguez, the Houston area man who went to a loud neighbor's house with a video camera and a gun, and as the prosecutor told the jury in her opening statement, used every "CHL (Concealed Handgun License) buzzword" in an incident that escalated until he had shot three men, killing one. Despite his on-camera statements of "I am standing my ground" and "I am in fear of my life," the Houston jury saw it as a malicious set-up. Mr. Rodriguez is now serving a long prison sentence.

Will the families of men killed in SYG self-defense shootings be denied civil justice because of the civil immunity clauses? **No**. A finding of self-defense at the hearing level means that justifiability has already been proven to a preponderance of evidence. Wrongful killings are

> ❝
> THE CONSCIENTIOUS POLICE AND PROSECUTORS OF AMERICA WELL KNOW THAT THEIR DUTY IS AS MUCH TO EXONERATE THE INNOCENT AS TO PUNISH THE GUILTY. THE RECENT, THOROUGHLY-CONSIDERED CHANGES IN THE LAW FROM TEXAS TO FLORIDA TO OTHER PARTS OF THE COUNTRY SIMPLY REINFORCE THE PRINCIPLES OF JUSTIFIED USE OF LETHAL FORCE...

exempt from immunity, a fact obvious to anyone who reads actual laws instead of newspaper headlines or the catch-phrases created by people with agendas.

Will SYG laws mean that cops will slough off investigations of homicides as soon as the shooter claims self-defense? **No,** and with 38 years of carrying a badge this speaker takes personal offense at that false allegation. "The death of a citizen" is a top-tier priority for law enforcement and the prosecutorial bar alike, and it is a gross insult to both to suggest that either entity would cut corners in the investigation of any homicide.

The conscientious police and prosecutors of America well know that their duty is as much to exonerate the innocent as to punish the guilty. The recent, thoroughly-considered changes in the law from Texas to Florida to other parts of the country simply reinforce the principles of justified use of lethal force for the protection of the innocent from violent criminal assaults, principles older than American jurisprudence itself.

The bottom line is simple: sometimes, criminals are so violent that there is no way to stop them but with deadly force. It happens for cops, it happens for security professionals, and it happens with armed citizens. It is good to see responsible entities of the legal profession presenting both sides of this matter to those trial advocates who will take these cases to court, and I thank the Texas State Bar Association for the opportunity to have addressed all of you today. ■

CHAPTER 9:
DEBUNKING MYTHS OF ARMED SELF-DEFENSE

n April 2014, the expert testimony of my friend and colleague Bob Smith in Spokane helped win an acquittal for Gail Gerlach, who was charged with manslaughter. Gerlach had shot a man who, while stealing his car, had pointed a metallic object at him that appeared to be a gun, and Gerlach had fired one shot, killing the man, who turned out to have been holding shiny keys in the dimly lit vehicle. In the anti-gun Spokane newspaper, Internet comments indicated that many people had the clueless idea that Gerlach had shot the man — in the back — to stop the thief from stealing his car. One idiot wrote in defense of doing such, "That 'inert property' as you call it represents a significant part of a man's life. Stealing it is the same as stealing a part of his life. Part of my life is far more important than all of a thief's life."

Analyze that statement. The world revolves around this speaker so much that a bit of his life spent earning an expensive object is worth "all of (another man's) life." Never forget that, in this country, human life is seen by the courts as having a higher value than what those courts call "mere property," even if you're shooting the most incorrigible lifelong thief to keep him from stealing the Hope Diamond. A principle of our law is that the evil man has the same rights as a good man. Here we have yet another case of a person dangerously confusing "how he thinks things ought to be" with "how things actually are."

As a rule of thumb, American law does not justify using deadly force to protect property. In the rare jurisdiction that does appear to allow this, ask yourself how the following words would resonate with a jury when uttered by the plaintiff's counsel in a closing argument: "Ladies and gentlemen, the defendant has admitted that he killed the deceased over property. How much difference is there in your hearts between the man who kills another to steal that man's property and one who kills another to maintain possession of his own? Either way, he ended a human life for mere property!"

Why was Gerlach acquitted in this shooting? Because Bob Smith and the rest of the defense team could show the jury that he had not shot the man "for stealing his car" at all. As the car thief drove away, he turned in the front seat toward Gerlach, raised a metallic object, and pointed it at him. In the prevailing light conditions, it looked like a gun — and Gerlach fired one shot from his 9mm pistol *to keep the car thief from shooting him!* Since the man was aiming backward at him over his shoulder, the defensively fired bullet necessarily entered the offender's body behind the lateral midline. At that point, the man stopped pointing the metallic object at him, so Gerlach stopped shooting. It turned out that this object, which Gerlach reasonably presumed to be a gun, was a key holder that resembled one.

NEVER FORGET THAT, IN THIS COUNTRY, HUMAN LIFE IS SEEN BY THE COURTS AS HAVING A HIGHER VALUE THAN WHAT THOSE COURTS CALL "MERE PROPERTY," EVEN IF YOU'RE SHOOTING THE MOST INCORRIGIBLE LIFELONG THIEF TO KEEP HIM FROM STEALING THE HOPE DIAMOND.

Gerlach's belief had been reasonable, and that allowed for the acquittal. It was not a case of a man being acquitted of a homicide charge for shooting "to save mere property."

Let's look at other common myths in discussions of armed citizens' justified use of force.

The "Drag the Corpse Inside and Plant a Knife in His Hand" Myth

Sadly, the oldest and most enduring myth is "when you shoot the bad guy on your porch, drag his body inside and put a knife in his hand before you call the police." If I've learned anything in over four decades of defending shooters in court, it's that The Truth is their strongest defense, and compromising that truth will kill their case and bring a verdict against them.

The time when someone could get away with altering evidence such as this is long gone, destroyed by modern forensic investigation techniques. When a body is moved, something called Locard's Principle comes into play, the principle of "transfer." Evidence from the body — clothing fibers, hair, blood, skin cells and DNA — will transfer to the surface over which the body is dragged. Simultaneously, dirt, sand, carpet fibers, etc., from the surface will transfer to the body and the deceased's clothing. The person trying to "cover his tracks" can get on his knees with a bucket of cleanser and scrub the floor "until the cows come home," but he won't get all the evidence off the scene. Much of it will be microscopic: the person who tried to change the evidence won't have a microscope, but the CSI (Crime Scene Investigation) crew will. The floor can be scrubbed until the naked eye sees no bloodstains, but the investigative technicians need only put down some Luminol and turn on the special lamp, and what their eye could not see before will now glow clearly.

Fingerprint experts know "use patterns," the way human hands grasp particular objects. These fingerprint patterns are distinctly different from what the latent prints look like when a knife or other object is pressed into a dead man's hand. The difference shows up, to them, like a giant red flag.

In short, you could not expect to get away with this stupid "strategy" today.

Once discovered, what criminal charges would you have left yourself open for? Well, let's count...

Alteration of evidence is a crime in and of itself, sometimes coming under the umbrella of an Obstruction of Justice charge. You may as well plead because if you've done something this stupid, you're *prima facie* guilty of that crime.

Manslaughter is now very much on the table of possible indictments because what you've done is something the general public, the jury pool from which the Grand Jury is drawn, associates with someone who panicked, shot someone they shouldn't have shot and is now trying to cover up their guilt.

Premeditated murder is another possible charge on the theory that "alteration of evidence may be construed as an indication of prior planning of a crime."

Perjury, lying under oath, is a felony in most jurisdictions and is implicit in the incredibly stupid "alter the evidence" meme.

The "Shoot and Scoot" Myth

It's not uncommon to hear, "If you have to shoot someone in self-defense, look both ways for witnesses and if you don't see any, just leave. That way, you save all the hassle." I'm told there's a fellow on one of the gun-related Internet boards who claims he's a lawyer (interestingly, without giving his real name) when he posts that stupid advice.

IF I'VE LEARNED ANYTHING IN OVER FOUR DECADES OF DEFENDING SHOOTERS IN COURT, IT'S THAT THE TRUTH IS THEIR STRONGEST DEFENSE, AND COMPROMISING THAT TRUTH WILL KILL THEIR CASE AND BRING A VERDICT AGAINST THEM.

Think about it: The prisons are full of people who looked around for witnesses and didn't see any until they appeared to testify against them at trial. When an innocent person who did the right thing takes this terrible advice, they fall into an ancient trap called "flight equals guilt." It's the assumption that the cause for leaving the scene was "consciousness of guilt." In the classic U.S. Supreme Court case *Illinois v. Wardlow*, SCOTUS upheld the actions of police who chased a man, caught him, and found inculpatory evidence upon search. They had chased him solely because he ran when he saw them coming. The majority opinion stated, "Headlong flight — wherever it occurs — is the consummate act of evasion: it is not necessarily indicative of wrongdoing, but it is certainly suggestive of such."[7]

Suppose you are a careful driver, and one night a drunken pedestrian lunges in front of your car faster than it was possible to stop. You remain at the scene and call 9-1-1. You can expect responding and investigating authorities to be sympathetic to you; after all, you went through something horrible that wasn't your fault. But suppose that instead of staying and calling in, you fled the scene. That turns it into a "hit and run," and you can expect neither sympathy nor mercy when the weight of the criminal justice system comes down on you full force, soon followed by a massive civil suit.

The same effect kicks in on the person who leaves the scene without calling the authorities after having had to use a gun in defense of self or others. For decades, I've told my students that after their gun comes out, they're in a race to the telephone. The justice system generally perceives the first participant to call in the incident as the "Victim/Complainant." The participant who is *not* the first to call in becomes, by default, the "Suspect." Many thugs have been going through the revolving doors of the criminal justice machine since they were juvenile offenders and know how things work; they'll ditch their weapon, call 9-1-1, and claim that you assaulted them with a gun for no good reason. Your subsequent claim of self-defense will ring hollow in a world where cops and prosecutors expect the victim to be the first caller.

Failing to call in immediately, and instead leaving the scene, is the single most common mistake I've seen armed citizens make after they've otherwise properly used their gun to lawfully manage a dangerous incident instigated by a criminal. Once the "flight equals guilt" factor kicks in, you and your attorney will have a steep uphill fight to prove your innocence.

The "I Can Shoot Anyone I Find in My House" Myth

A legal doctrine says, "Your home is your castle," but that doesn't include an execution chamber. In virtually every state, the fine print of the law and case law requires a reasonably perceived threat within the totality of the circumstances.

There are any number of situations where you might come home to find someone there whom you do not immediately recognize, even if you live alone. Most people have a key to their home out to *someone:* a landlord, a cleaning lady, a relative, a friend who comes by to feed the cat when they're gone. Perhaps another family member has called a plumber or electrician without bothering to notify you. We see case after case of the trusted person with the key coming unexpectedly to that house when they experience something traumatic at their own home and can't think of any-place else to go, or the guest who already has a key and arrives unexpect-edly early. Such things can make for particularly ugly tragedies if the home defender doesn't consider that possibility when seeing an unexpected figure in the shadows.

The "I Was in Fear for My Life" Myth

Opponents of Stand Your Ground laws claimed that such laws allow anyone to kill anyone and get away with it by claiming they were in fear for their life. That assertion was blatantly false, but it was claimed so many

> "
>
> FAILING TO CALL IN IMMEDIATELY AND INSTEAD LEAVING THE SCENE IS THE SINGLE MOST COMMON MISTAKE I'VE SEEN ARMED CITIZENS MAKE AFTER THEY'VE OTHERWISE PROPERLY USED THEIR GUN TO LAWFULLY MANAGE A DANGEROUS INCIDENT INSTIGATED BY A CRIMINAL.

times in many newspapers and television programs that some gun owners came to believe it. *It's simply not true.* As written in Florida at the time of this writing, for example, a successful Stand Your Ground defense requires the shooter to prove that, more likely than not, they did indeed fire in self-defense.

Earlier, we mentioned that one Raul Rodriguez strapped on a pistol, shouldered a camcorder, and marched to a nearby home where a neighbor he disliked was holding an outdoor party that was louder than Mr. Rodriguez liked. Walking onto the other man's property and ostentatiously complaining (all the while recording), he started and escalated an argument. When people became angry and frightened by his gun, he said loudly for the benefit of the camera, "I am in fear of my life" and "I will stand my ground." The situation ended when Rodriguez shot and killed the neighbor he despised and wounded two other persons present. Charged with murder, he claimed self-defense.

It did him no good. The prosecutor's opening statement contemptuously noted that Rodriguez had "used every CHL (concealed handgun license) buzzword in the book." The state presented a damning witness who testified that before the shooting, Rodriguez had told her he could kill anyone he wanted and get away with it by uttering the magic words "I was in fear for my life."

There are no magic words, and Raul Rodriguez was convicted of murder and given a lengthy prison sentence.

The "In My State, I Can't Be Sued for a Self-Defense Shooting" Myth

That's a vast oversimplification. The old saying still holds: "anyone can file suit against anyone for anything." As noted in the Castle Doctrine/Stand Your Ground chapter, the civil suit preemption provisions found under the umbrella of some SYG laws at most provide for the judge to throw out the case if it has already been determined to be an act of self-defense. However, merely not being criminally charged may not be enough. That's because the decision not to charge may have been motivated by the prosecuting authority's assessment that it could not gain a conviction by proving the act to have been criminal beyond a reasonable doubt; for a lawsuit, the plaintiff need only meet the much lower standard of preponderance of the evidence.

The same is true if the defendant in the lawsuit has been tried and acquitted in criminal court. These things fall well short of a "determination" that it was self-defense.

In the states that have protection against civil suits for shootings ruled to be in self-defense, the question is, who makes that ruling? A ruling by the judge to the effect that the court has determined the act to have been in self-defense may do it. A memorandum of closure by the prosecuting authority stating that their investigation has determined the act to have been in legitimate defense of self or others may do it. The mere fact that the case was not prosecuted, or even a trial that resulted in an acquittal in criminal court, may not be enough.

And if the plaintiff's theory of the case is that the incident occurred by accident or through negligence, the protection against a lawsuit will most likely be bypassed also.

The defendant's belief that the shooting was justified carries little weight in and of itself.

The "I'm Having a Heart Attack, Call an Ambulance" Myth

The recommendation that the shooter should pretend to be having a heart attack has been propounded widely, sometimes by people who should have been expected to know better. The theory is that the police will stop questioning the shooter for fear of civil liability and rush him to the hospital, where emergency room doctors and nurses won't let an interrogator near them. What's wrong with that theory?

Lots of things.

The hospital examination will show that you're not having a heart attack. At best, you are now seen as the panicky sort who exaggerates and overreacts — not the profile of the responsible person who effectively and properly managed an emergency. Or, worse, you are recognized as a liar at a time when your credibility will probably be more critical than at any other time in your life.

In many jurisdictions, making false pretenses to emergency services personnel (police, fire, emergency medical services) is a crime in and of itself.

Those who judge you will learn that you tied up limited emergency rescue resources that an actual heart attack or trauma victim might have needed in a life-or-death situation. Why? For the nefarious purpose of misleading and delaying a law enforcement investigation of an act for which you are responsible. What sort of impression do you think that will make on the judge and jury?

Finally, you'll get a big ambulance/ER bill for no good reason since you could have forestalled questioning simply by asking for an attorney.

The "Fire Warning Shots" Myth

You know a myth is widespread when it emanates from the White House. In 2013 while campaigning for a ban on so-called "assault rifles," Vice-President Joseph Biden told the public he had advised his wife that if there was a home invasion, she was to take a double-barrel shotgun and fire both barrels upwards. One can only imagine how the Secret Service Vice-Presidential detail felt when they heard that. I can tell you that lawyers, cops, and gun-wise people rolled their eyes and shook their heads across the nation.

The fact is, warning shots have long been prohibited by most American police departments. This is for several reasons:

What goes up must come down. The stereotyped warning shot is fired skyward. Shooting live ammunition into the sky is a practice associated with Third World countries where respect for human life is not as great as in the United States. There are many cases where such bullets "fell from the sky" and killed innocent people. In one New England case, a man carelessly fired a warning shot upward in the state's largest city; the bullet struck and killed an innocent bystander who was on the upper porch of a tenement building.

To fire the warning shot safely, the shooter must aim it into something

MURPHY'S LAW IS IMMUTABLE: IF YOUR WEAPON IS GOING TO JAM, EXPECT IT TO JAM ON THE WARNING SHOT AND LEAVE YOU HELPLESS WHEN THE OPPONENT COMES UP WITH HIS GUN.

that could safely absorb the projectile. This would force the shooter to take his eyes off of the potentially dangerous criminal opponent he was trying to intimidate — always a poor idea tactically.

What appears to be a safe place to plant the warning bullet may not be. I know a police officer who, trying to break up a riot, fired a warning shot from his 12-gauge shotgun downward from the upper floor walkway of a hotel into what appeared in the dark to be a soft patch of earth. It was, instead, darkened pavement. Double-ought buckshot pellets caromed off the hard surface, one striking a young woman in the eye.

Suppose the person who caused you to fire the warning shot runs around a corner. Another gunshot rings out; someone else shot the man at a moment when deadly force was not warranted. The bullet goes through and through fatally and is not recovered. The man who wrongfully shot him claims he fired the warning shot, and your bullet caused the wrongful death. It's your word against his unless you can say, "Officer, you'll find the bullet from *my* gun in the friendly oak tree right over there." But it would have been better in these circumstances if you had not fired at all.

Warning shots can lead to misunderstandings with deadly unintended consequences. Years ago, in the Great Lakes area, two police officers searched opposite ends of a commercial greenhouse where a burglar alarm had just gone off. One confronted the burglar, who ran. The officer raised his arm skyward for the traditional silver screen warning shot. As is often the case, the blast just made the suspect run faster. On the other end of the building, the other officer heard the shot and shouted to his partner, asking if he was all right. But the powerful handgun had gone off so close to the first officer's unprotected ear that his ears were ringing, and he didn't hear the shout. The second officer then saw the suspect running. Concluding that the man must have killed the partner who didn't answer, that second officer shot and killed a man who was guilty only of burglary and running from the police.

A single gunshot sounds to earwitnesses (and, depending on the circumstances, even eyewitnesses) as if you tried to kill a man you were only trying to warn. Did you yell the standard movie line, "Stop, or I'll shoot"? It could sound to an earwitness as if you threatened to kill a man for not obeying you and then tried to do that. Don't make threats you don't have a right to carry out, and as noted in this book, the confluence of circumstances that warrant the shooting of a fleeing felon is extremely rare. (Remember that there are usually more earwitnesses than eyewitnesses; sound generally travels farther than the line of sight, especially in the dark. Remember the infamous case of Kitty Genovese, who was murdered as 38 New York witnesses supposedly watched and did nothing. A study of the incident shows that only two witnesses saw the knife go into her body. However, more than 38 heard her scream, "He stabbed me!")

Even if there are no witnesses and the man claims you shot at him and missed, evidence will show that you did fire your gun. If he claims you attempted to murder him, it's his word against yours.

Murphy's law is immutable: if your weapon is going to jam, expect it to jam on the warning shot and leave you helpless when the opponent comes up with his gun.

The firing of a gun, even in another person's "general direction," is an act of deadly force. If deadly force was warranted, well, "warning shot, hell!" You would have shot directly at him. The warning shot can tell the judge and jury that the fact that you didn't aim the shot at him is a tacit admission that even by your own lights, you knew deadly force was not justified when you fired the shot.

If the man turns on you the next moment and you have to shoot him or die, you've wasted precious ammunition. With the still-popular five-shot revolver, you've just thrown away 20 percent of your potentially life-saving firepower. In one case in the Philippines, a man went berserk in a crowded open-air market and began stabbing and slashing people with a knife in each hand. In a nearby home, an off-duty Filipino police officer heard the screams, grabbed his six-shot service revolver (with no spare ammunition), and ran to the scene. When he confronted the madman, the latter turned on him. The officer fired three warning shots into the air, sending half of all he had to protect himself and the public into the stratosphere. He turned and ran, trying to shoot over his shoulder, and missed with his last three shots. He tripped and fell, and the pursuing knife-wielder ripped him apart. Responding officers shot and killed the madman, but their off-duty partner was dead by then.

I've come to call a subset of the warning shot the "chaser shot." This sort of warning shot sends the message, "and keep running and don't come back!" This, too, can backfire in multiple ways. I worked on one case where a burglar attacked a retired physician. The physician fired a shot at him and missed; the criminal turned and ran. In the grip of fear, untrained, the physician fired a "chaser shot;" he didn't intend for it to hit the suspect, but it did. The criminal ran a considerable distance and then collapsed, dying, from the wound. The doctor was charged with manslaughter. His lawyer was able to keep him out of jail, but it took a lot of legal fees to do that. I consulted in another where multiple people attacked a man in a driveway. He shot and killed his primary assailant and then drove away. As he did so, he raised his .38 and fired one shot over the heads of the attacker's accomplices to keep them from running toward his vehicle and dragging him out. The bullet went harmlessly over their heads and buried itself in a roof. The jury acquitted him entirely on the homicide charge, understanding that it was self-defense. However, an obscure law in that state intended to combat drive-by shootings convicted him on the lesser included charge of firing a gun from a moving vehicle. It was a felony-level conviction, and he ended up serving prison time for it.

It's clear why most law enforcement agencies forbid warning shots and why most private sector instructors, including this writer, recommend against firing them. For many years, however, I have taught Ayoob's Law of Necessary Hypocrisy, which holds this: "If I have told you, 'Do not do this, it is incredibly stupid,' and you reply, 'Well, I might be in some situation you haven't foreseen where I may feel a need to do it anyway,' I want you to know the *least* incredibly stupid way of doing the incredibly stupid thing." That applies to things like trying to do a building search alone, for example. Applied to the warning shot, if I felt some unique set of circumstances fit the doctrine of competing harms and compelled me to fire a warning shot, I would shout "Final warning!" (*not* "Stop or I'll shoot"), and would take care to fire the bullet into something that could safely and retrievably absorb the projectile. Safely, for all the reasons stated above, and retrievably because if someone else shoots, I'd want to prove that my warning shot wasn't the one that caused death or crippling injury.

But the takeaway lesson is *DON'T FIRE WARNING SHOTS!*

The "Make Sure Your Opponent is Dead" Myth

This theory says that if you ever have to shoot someone, make sure he's dead before you call the police. It's born in the public fear of liars and lawyers and a legal system most people don't fully understand. It's the old "dead men tell no tales" theory. If he's dead, he can't lie, right?

There is a great deal wrong with that sort of thinking. We shoot to stop, not to kill; if he drops his weapon and ceases hostility after a minor wound, he has been stopped. Hell, if you shoot at him and *miss* and he throws his weapon away and screams, "I give up," your right to continue shooting has just come to a screeching halt.

Can he lie? Sure. But just as smart homicide detectives and forensic pathologists can truly reconstruct events from their examination of the scene and the silent dead, a cunning and unscrupulous lawyer can craft a "theory of the case" around a criminal's corpse better than he could from the testimony of a wounded member of the underworld.

Why? Because Mark Twain was right when he said the best thing about telling the truth was that it's easy to remember. If it were me and not fate that determined whether or not my opponent died from my gunfire, I'd rather he survive. Not only because it spares his innocent family grief, but because the decades have shown me that the criminal himself can usually be caught in his lies — caught by good detectives, and caught by your attorney. If he's dead, a crafty attorney who has put his ethics in his wallet can come up with any BS theory he wants and be much harder to trip up than a live criminal. On the other hand, if your opponent has survived to give false testimony about what happened, skilled questioning by everyone from police detectives to your defense lawyer can reveal him for the lying SOB he is.

Finally, the "make sure he's dead" meme implies that you can look at an opponent who's now out of the fight, *hors de combat*, and execute him to keep him from lying about you. There's a word for that: Murder.

Anyone who thinks he can do that, I'd rather not be reading one of my books. I'd rather he take his eyes off this page, instead, and look in a mirror and ask himself what kind of human being he has become.

Given the advanced state of evidence analysis and homicide investigation today, I can tell you what kind of person he is *going* to become: a convicted murderer spending his life in prison.

The "You'll Never Have to Take the Stand" Myth

This one comes from the lawyers. It's no big secret that the great majority of people charged with criminal offenses are guilty, either of the crime with which they are charged or at least some lesser included offense. These people become the mainstream, meat-and-potatoes clientele of defense lawyers. If guilty men get on the stand under oath, one of two things will happen during competent cross-examination by skilled prosecutors: they will tell the truth and convict themselves, or they will lie and get caught in the lie and still convict themselves. If they choose the latter path, the defense attorney is in the line of fire for an accusation that he suborned their client's perjury: a low-level felony in and of itself in certain jurisdictions and certainly grounds for the attorney to be disbarred. Therefore, it's not surprising that they advise their clients not to take the stand.

This is a classic example of why defense lawyers' strategies to guard the Constitutional rights of their often-guilty clients do not work for the innocent person falsely accused. If it were indeed self-defense, you'd be employing the affirmative defense discussed at length elsewhere in this book. You'll stipulate that you did indeed fire the shot(s) that killed the deceased but that you acted correctly.

The prosecution has the burden of establishing *mens rea*, "the guilty mind." They have to show that you either intended to commit a crime or acted with negligence so gross that it rose to a culpable standard. Your only defense against that is your "mindset": what was in your mind when you took that action. *Why did you do it?*

If you *don't* go on the witness stand to testify why you did it, *who else on earth can?*

Oh, sure, your attorney can state in the opening argument that you did it in lawful defense of self or other innocent parties but whatever your lawyer says has to be backed up by facts, evidence, and testimony. The critical testimony will be yours.

I've had a few cases where we couldn't put the defendant on the stand. In one, the defendant's doctor flatly told the lawyer that if he went on the stand, he'd win the case but lose the patient because the defendant's heart condition was so precarious the physician didn't think he would survive the stress of the experience. Fortunately, the evidence in favor of self-defense was so strong that the attorney — Jeff Weiner, who wrote the foreword for this book — made that evidence clear to the judge and prosecution alike before trial. The result was a withhold of adjudication, meaning that if the defendant kept his nose clean for a certain period, the charge would go away. He did, and it did, and the client was a free man who soon had his concealed carry permit back.

Another was a battered woman so beaten down throughout her life that we knew she'd be putty in the hands of an alpha male lawyer cross-examining her. Mark Seiden tried the case brilliantly without putting her on the stand, and the evidence and testimony of other witnesses were so strong that the jury "got it." They acquitted her on all charges after about two hours of deliberation.

Those were exceptions, in my experience. The "keep the defendant off the stand" strategy is used primarily for guilty clients. Here's what I whimsically call "Ayoob's Laws": "If you hire a guilty man's lawyer who gives you a guilty man's defense, you can expect a guilty man's verdict."

Think about it. Why would your attorney tell you not to take the stand?

Perhaps he thinks you're guilty, like so many of the rest of his clients. If you are genuinely innocent, do you really want your life in the hands of someone who thinks you're guilty?

Maybe he thinks you're so stupid that you can be easily led down the primrose path in cross-examination by opposing counsel. Maybe he thinks you're too weak to withstand cross-examination. Maybe he thinks you're a lunatic gun nut who will say something stupid on the witness stand and turn the jury against you.

Whatever his rationale, I can only tell you this: If I was the defendant in a righteous shooting case that had turned into a false accusation, and my lawyer told me, "Don't worry, you'll never have to take the stand," I know what I would do.

I would ask that lawyer, "How much do I owe you for your time so far?" I would write a check for that amount, put it on their desk, and say, "You're fired."

Because that lawyer will have just told me that they have no clue how to deliver an affirmative defense for a person who has used a weapon in honest defense of self or other innocents. ■

CHAPTER 10:
CASE STUDY STATE OF FLORIDA V. GEORGE ZIMMERMAN

O n a dark, rainy, unseasonably cold February night in 2012 in Sanford, Florida, George Zimmerman was driving to the supermarket when he saw an unfamiliar figure skulking around people's windows in a housing development not far from his home. As elected captain of the neighborhood watch, Zimmerman called police dispatch to report it. The dispatcher asked for the exact location, and Zimmerman obligingly got out of his car to look for a street sign. The man he'd seen, who by now had disappeared from his view, suddenly emerged from the darkness to confront him, and without warning, delivered a powerful punch to his face. Zimmerman staggered backward and fell, with the assailant on top of him, raining blows in a mixed martial arts "ground and pound" fashion. He grabbed Zimmerman's head and banged it on the sidewalk — and then spotted the licensed, concealed 9mm pistol holstered inside Zimmerman's waistband and reached for it, saying, "You're going to die tonight." Zimmerman stated that he was able to slap the man's hand away, draw, and fire one shot.

The single Sellier & Bellot 115-grain jacketed hollowpoint bullet found the heart of 17-year-old Trayvon Martin, killing him. Seasoned police investigators, despite their initial professional skepticism, quickly determined that all the physical evidence exactly fit Zimmerman's account of the incident. He was not arrested, and the prosecutorial authority, the State's Attorney's Office, did not even see a need to bring this clear-cut self-defense shooting in front of a grand jury. However, the understandably grieving parents of the slain teen hired a lawyer, who in turn reached out to a public relations firm with powerful connections in the mass media. Soon, the "murder of little Trayvon" had become a national, even worldwide *cause celebre,* with such celebrities as CNN's Nancy Grace leading the lynch mob that howled for the head of George Zimmerman. The case passed from the hands of the highly respected State's Attorney who had jurisdiction and into the purview of appointed Special Prosecutor Angela Corey. Rather than put it before a grand jury, she indicted him for murder on her authority under an offer of information.

The trial began on June 10 and ended with a verdict of total acquittal on July 13, 2013. His life ruined, George Zimmerman remained perhaps "the most hated man in America," thanks to the unrelenting mass media attack on him that continued with little abatement. The Zimmerman case was clear-cut proof that the mantra "a good shoot is a good shoot" is a myth born of wishful thinking.

The day the verdict came in, I began a 20-part series analyzing the case and the issues at trial in my blog at *Backwoods Home Magazine*, a publication where I've served as firearms editor since the mid-1990s (backwoodshome.com/blogs/massadayoob.). It is reprinted here with the publication's permission, edited only to remove outdated links, for brevity, and for stylistic consistency. It begins with my blog post of 7/13/13.

The Zimmerman Verdict, Part 1

Minutes ago, as I write this, justice has triumphed in a courtroom in Sanford, Florida. I wish to congratulate six brave, honest, intelligent jurors. And two fine defense lawyers. And the honest cops and witnesses who testified, and the many who contributed to the defense fund for a wrongfully accused armed citizen.

Several blog followers have asked me why I haven't written here (or spoken anywhere) on this, the most important armed citizen case of our time. The answer is this:

I did write on it once, on Friday, March 23, 2012. The following day, I received a phone call from Craig Sonner, George Zimmerman's original legal counsel, to retain me on the case as an expert witness for the defense.

The weeks wore on. Attorney and client parted ways. I was subsequently contacted by Mark O'Mara, the new defense lawyer. Late in May 2012, I met with him in his office, along with his co-counsel Don West. I also attended the bail hearing in which Zimmerman's bond was revoked. During the hearing, TV cameras swept the courtroom. Some folks saw that, recognized me, and apparently assumed I was involved with the case.

A security camera photo from the convenience store Trayvon Martin patronized shortly before his death. Note that Martin, right, is markedly taller than the clerk at left, who is known to be 5' 10" tall.

In fact, I don't take expert witness cases until I've seen all the evidence, and the prosecution was extremely slow in providing that. I wound up not being involved. However, having been retained by one of the defendant's lawyers and consulted with another, I felt bound by confidentiality and did not think it would be professional to comment directly on the matter from then on.

I've been biting my tongue ever since because there was much that I wanted to say.

The verdict is now in, and I'm gonna smooth those teeth marks off my tongue, and in the next few entries here will discuss some elements of the Zimmerman case that have been widely and profoundly misunderstood.

In the meantime, to get the commentary and analysis of the case that most of the mainstream media denied you, go to the excellent day-by-day writing of Andrew Branca, an attorney who specializes in this sort of case, at legalinsurrection.com.

Your commentary is more than welcome here.

Zimmerman Verdict, Part 2: The "Unarmed Teen"

It seems that the verdict of a sworn jury in our criminal justice system means little to the haters, who are still screaming that George Zimmerman killed "an unarmed seventeen-year-old." Given that seventeen is old enough to enlist in the Marine Corps and to be tried as an adult — the *Gainesville Sun* recently headlined that a "sixteen-year-old man" was to be charged with murder in the selfsame Florida criminal justice system — the age issue doesn't hold a lot of water when seen through a clear glass.

"Unarmed?" Actually, *no*. The history of adjudicating deadly force actions shows that Trayvon Martin was "armed" two or three times over.

First, the haters (like the prosecution) assiduously ignored George Zimmerman's statement that while Martin was "ground-and-pounding" him, Martin saw Zimmerman's gun in its now exposed holster, told Zimmerman that he was going to die tonight, and reached for his victim's pistol.

If I'm your criminal attacker, you don't have to wait for me to shoot you before you can shoot me to defend your life, and you don't even need to wait until the gun is in my hand. If I announce my intent to murder you and reach for a gun, I'm bought and paid for right there. *And it doesn't matter whether the gun I'm reaching for is in my holster, or yours.* That's why every year in America, when thugs try to grab policemen's guns and are shot, the shootings are ruled justifiable.

Even before Martin's reach for Zimmerman's still-holstered pistol, the circumstances that were proven to the satisfaction of the jury showed that Zimmerman was justified in shooting his attacker. Remember when defense attorney Don West said in the defense's opening statement that Martin was

> IF I'M YOUR CRIMINAL ATTACKER, YOU DON'T HAVE TO WAIT FOR ME TO SHOOT YOU BEFORE YOU CAN SHOOT ME TO DEFEND YOUR LIFE, AND YOU DON'T EVEN NEED TO WAIT UNTIL THE GUN IS IN MY HAND. IF I ANNOUNCE MY INTENT TO MURDER YOU AND REACH FOR A GUN, I'M BOUGHT AND PAID FOR RIGHT THERE.

armed with the sidewalk? That sounded ludicrous to lay people, and I would have phrased it differently myself, but professionals understood exactly what he was talking about.

The operative principle at law is called "disparity of force." It means that while your opponent(s) may not be armed with a deadly weapon *per se*, their physical advantage over you is so great that if their ostensibly unarmed assault continues, you are likely to die or suffer grave bodily harm. That disparity of force may take the form of a much larger and stronger assailant, a male attacking a female, force of numbers, able-bodied attacking the handicapped, skilled fighter attacking the unskilled, or — in this case — position of disadvantage.

Position of disadvantage means that the opponent has full range and freedom of movement, and you don't. You're seat-belted behind your steering wheel while he rains punches onto your skull through the open window ... or you are down and helpless in a martial arts "mount" while your opponent pounds you at will.

Finally, we have the clearly proven element of Martin smashing Zimmerman's head into the sidewalk. If I picked up a chunk of concrete or cement and tried to smash your skull with it, you would certainly realize that you were about to die or be horribly brain-damaged if you didn't stop me. It would be what the statutes call "a deadly weapon, to wit a bludgeon." *There just isn't a whole hell of a lot of difference between cement being smashed into the head and the head being smashed into cement.*

Clearly, Trayvon Martin possessed the power to kill or cripple Zimmerman. That is why, under law, Zimmerman was justified in defending himself with a *per se* deadly weapon.

The jury got it. Too bad the haters didn't understand ... or didn't want to understand.

Zimmerman Verdict, Part 3: "Who Started It?"

Welcome to the new commentators here, many of whom seem to feel that Zimmerman started the encounter, a concept that concerns many of our regulars as well. Whenever there's a fight, no matter the degree of consequences, the first question is always "who started it?"

Zimmerman took the first action, calling the police when he observed Martin. He said that he was concerned because the man in the hoodie appeared to be wandering slowly and aimlessly in heavy rain. This is more consistent with what might be called "casing the joint" than with someone in a hurry to get somewhere dry. He didn't mention Martin's skin color until expressly asked about it by the call center operator.

The evidence indicates that Zimmerman didn't get out of his car until the operator asked where the suspicious person was and where the police should meet Zimmerman, the complainant. Taking that as a request for information, Zimmerman obligingly got out of the car to gather the intelligence that seemed to have been implicitly requested of him. He was, after all, the elected (not self-appointed) captain of Neighborhood Watch, and his function as Eyes and Ears of the Police had been drilled into him and the other Watch members through the police department itself. When the call-taker asked if he was following the man, Zimmerman replied in the affirmative. He was then told, "We don't need you to do that."

The evidence indicates that he stopped following Martin at that moment. His former rapid breathing returned to normal, and the wind noise from his phone stopped, consistent with his testimony that he stopped following and had lost sight of Martin. The dispatcher did not "order" him to stop following and later admitted in court that he had no authority to do so. Nonetheless, it was clear that Zimmerman was simply following Martin to keep him in sight and report his whereabouts, not "pursuing" with any intent to "confront."

Put together the timelines of the calls — hard evidence — and the testimony of the prosecution's "star witness," Rachel Jeantel. When Zimmerman lost sight of Martin, the latter was a very short distance from home. Yet, four minutes thereafter, he had to have left that location and gone toward Zimmerman's. Even Jeantel admits that the first words of the confrontation she heard were from Martin before the phone went dead.

Keeping an eye on someone from a distance is not against the law. Leaving the safety and mobility of your vehicle when suspicious unknown people are around may not be the best tactical move, but is no evidence of wrongdoing or intent to confront.

Who struck the first blow? Virtually all the evidence supports Zimmerman's account; no evidence contradicts it, and no evidence supports the theory that Zimmerman assaulted Martin first in any way. If, as some conjecture, Zimmerman had drawn the gun at the first, why did he wait until his scalp had been split open on the sidewalk and his nose smashed before he pulled the trigger? And if Martin really believed he was in danger from the man watching him, why didn't he simply call the police from the phone he was already speaking on?

Within the totality of the circumstances presented in court by the prosecution itself, it would seem that saying "Zimmerman started it" is like saying that a woman was raped "because she asked for it."

It's about evidence, not about "what-ifs." The simple fact is, no matter what some want to believe and no matter how much the brainwashers of the media have twisted the facts, there is no solid evidence to support any theory other than that Martin didn't like being watched, attacked Zimmerman violently, and was shot in self-defense by the man whose head he had been smashing against the sidewalk with potentially lethal effect.

There are more issues, of course, and we'll explore them here shortly.

Zimmerman Verdict, Part 4: The Stand Your Ground Element

Few elements of this case have been more widely misunderstood than the "stand your ground" (SYG) element. Quite simply, Florida's SYG law, statute 776.012, simply rescinded a previous requirement that one had to retreat if possible before using deadly force in self-defense. This did not particularly change the rules of engagement. The previous law had demanded retreat only if it could be accomplished in complete safety to oneself and other innocent people present. It is hard to imagine a situation in which one *would* kill another person if they could have simply walked away unscathed.

The evidence showed incontrovertibly that Zimmerman, straddled by his attacker in the MMA mount and being savagely beaten while supine, could not possibly have retreated or otherwise escaped at the time he pulled the trigger. His wise lawyers knew that from the beginning, Craig Sonner when I spoke with him in March 2012, and Mark O'Mara and Don West when I discussed it with them a couple of months later.

The media is largely either confused or deceptive about this, and so I'm afraid are many lawyers, including the Attorney General of the United States, who has called for an end to SYG laws. Florida Governor Rick Scott empanelled a blue-ribbon committee to study the law last year, which included some vociferous anti-gunners. Nonetheless, their collective recommendation was to leave SYG in place. The Governor now stands up in defense of it as well.

Sanford PD evidence photo of George Zimmerman's 9mm Kel-Tec PF9 and holster.

Stevie Wonder has announced that he won't perform in Florida until SYG is done away with. Stevie Wonder, through no fault of his own, is blind. He has my sympathy for that.

But the other opponents of SYG seem to be willfully blind, and for that, there is no excuse.

Zimmerman Verdict, Part 5: The Gun Stuff

The firearms and ballistics evidence in this case was very important, one reason why the Kel-Tec PF9 9mm death weapon was first and foremost in the minds of journalists reporting on Eric Holder's recent decision to have all evidence in this case held pending Federal investigation (again). One of the area newspapers reported in March that the death weapon was found with a spent casing still in the chamber. This would have been consistent with someone's hand grabbing the gun and retarding the slide mechanism at the moment of the shot, and I surmised as much in the one blog entry I made on it at that time, prior to being contacted by the then-defense team and confidentiality issues kicking in from then on.

It turned out that this was not the case. The officers who recovered the evidence unloaded the death weapon. The spent casing from the one shot fired in the incident was recovered from the ground on which it had ejected,

THE TAKEAWAY IS NOT TO AVOID SUCH UNMERITORIOUS COURTROOM ATTACKS BY CARRYING A .25 AUTO WITH AN EMPTY CHAMBER. THE TAKEAWAY IS, BE ABLE TO LOGICALLY EXPLAIN YOUR CHOICE OF GUN AND METHOD OF CARRY. THE DEFENSE DID EXACTLY THIS, TO THEIR CREDIT.

and another live round was ejected from the firing chamber after the officer removed the magazine. All eight cartridges, the gun's full capacity, were accounted for. The pistol had functioned normally, as designed.

Prosecutor John Guy, in his dramatic opening statement, made a big deal out of the fact that Zimmerman carried the Kel-Tec with a live round in the chamber as if this implied malice and a man looking to kill someone. Over in CNN Headline News Land, Nancy Grace took up the same cry. Zimmerman's after-the-assault attackers even made a big deal out of the fact that he had a pistol with no dedicated manual safety. Ms. Grace claimed that he carried it with the safety off, and when a friend of Zimmerman's was on her show and told her the gun *had no* safety catch *per se*, she yelled at him that he was wrong, she knew all about Kel-Tec PF9s and implied that Zimmerman must have flicked the safety off beforehand. (Premeditation, don't 'cha know?)

Of course, the PF9 pistol *doesn't* have a safety catch. Ms. Grace apparently Googled "Kel-Tec PF9" and mistook the slide lock lever for a safety lever. Did any of you folks ever hear her apologize to Zimmerman's friend, who was right when she was wrong? Let me know, 'cause I must have missed it if she did.

For perspective, very few American police officers carry guns with manual safety levers. The most popular police pistols don't have them, including the Glock and the SIG, the two most widely used. The Smith & Wesson Military & Police has an *optional* ambidextrous thumb safety, but most police departments order those guns without that feature, and the same is true for the majority of defensive pistols bought these days by America's armed citizens. The old-style service revolver didn't come with a safety either.

Like those revolvers, semi-automatics such as the Kel-Tec are normally carried ready to fire with a simple pull of the trigger, i.e., with a round chambered.

Another element I warned O'Mara and West about back in the second quarter of 2012 was that they could expect the prosecution to attribute malice to Zimmerman for loading with hollowpoints. Such ammunition is standard in virtually every police department in our nation and is the overwhelming (and logical) choice of armed citizens. The expanding bullet is less likely to ricochet, and it is more likely to stop inside the body of the offender instead of passing through to strike an unseen bystander. It also, historically, stops gunfights faster, saving the lives endangered by the attacker who had to be shot. Finally, for that latter reason, it reduces the number of wounds the offender must suffer before he stops forcing good people to shoot him. Except for the ricochet factor, all those elements were present in the Zimmerman-Martin shooting. The prosecution didn't harp on this as much as I expected, but prosecutor Richard Mantei did bring it up.[8]

Fortunately, the defense covered this superbly. They did so with the testimony of material witness Mark Osterman, the Federal Air Marshal who trained Zimmerman, and told him to get a double-action-only pistol with no manual safety and carry it with a round in the chamber. His personal knowledge carried more weight than any outside expert could ever have brought to the game, but defense expert Dennis Root did a good job of batting clean-up and filling in other points. Together, they tanked the bogus allegations of the prosecution in this case insofar as guns, ammunition, and malice or premeditation that could be ascribed to either.

The takeaway is not to avoid such unmeritorious courtroom attacks by carrying a .25 auto with an empty chamber. The takeaway is, be able to logically explain your choice of gun and method of carry. The defense did exactly this, to their credit.

This case, of course, was about much more than guns, and we'll continue with that in the next entry.

Zimmerman Verdict, Part 6: "What If" vs. "What Is"

Much of this case came down to speculation versus fact. We saw it in the trial, we saw it in the prosecution's case, we see it even in comments on this blog. In spring 2012, in the question/answer session that followed the CATO Institute "Stand Your Ground Symposium," a sincere young man who happened to be African-American asked me if SYG protection would have been in effect for Trayvon Martin if he had been violently attacked by George Zimmerman, and had killed Zimmerman in self-defense. My answer was, "Yes, of course." And I would give the same answer now.

The only problem with that hypothetical is that there is nothing to substantiate it, and there is a large body of facts in evidence to support the jury's verdict that Zimmerman was not guilty of murder or any lesser included offense. A large body of collective evidence showing that it was

Martin who attacked Zimmerman and not vice-versa.

"*What if* Zimmerman hadn't gotten out of his car and just driven on to his destination, the Target store?" Well, certainly, the confrontation would not have occurred. But that pales in comparison to *what if* Trayvon Martin had not attacked him and smashed his head into the sidewalk? In following a strange man looking into windows in a community riven by burglaries and even a home invasion, Zimmerman never broke the law. Indeed, had it not ended in death, most would have appreciated him taking notice and calling the authorities ... as people had done earlier when the head of the home-owner's association in that community had chased down and captured a burglary suspect.

"*What if* Zimmerman had avoided any danger by not getting involved at all?" Well, if the nineteen firefighters killed last month in Arizona hadn't "gotten involved," they wouldn't have died either. Does that make them responsible for their own deaths? Review the case of Kitty Genovese, and then get back to me with your "Don't get involved" argument. But take a long look in the mirror, first, and ask yourself how long you'd want to live with looking in the mirror at the face of someone who "didn't get involved" enough to pick up a phone to help Kitty Genovese, and didn't do what a reasonable and prudent person would construe the voice of authority on that phone asked you to do.

"*What if* Zimmerman hadn't carried that evil gun?" Well, with Zimmerman having his head smashed against the sidewalk and being unable to escape, Trayvon Martin would probably have stood trial for the murder of George Zimmerman. The evidence and testimony are consistent with Zimmerman's account of what happened. So is something the jury never learned of during trial: the lie detector test (voice stress analysis), which Zimmerman passed shortly after the shooting and confirmed that he was telling the truth. He also passed the "bullshit detector test" of not one but two veteran police officers who expertly and vigorously interrogated him without defense counsel present.

"*What if* it turned out that Zimmerman had made the first confrontation and pulled his gun on Martin, causing Martin to jump him and beat him in self-defense?" That *would* have been justifiable for Martin ... but there is *absolutely no evidence to indicate that it did happen*. Stop and think: would a man hungry to kill, with a loaded gun already in his hand, have taken the savage beating Zimmerman did, for at least 40 seconds, before firing?

"What if" is not the standard of the law nor the standard of logic. "*What is*" remains the standard for both. The evidence, not a hypothetical "theory of the case," is what counts in every aspect of the real world ... the real world of the courts and the real world of the streets.

A duly empanelled jury determined the truth from the facts in evidence and the testimony presented. Even the testimony of the *prosecution's* witnesses overwhelmingly favored the defense.

And that was only the evidence the jury was allowed to see. There was much more evidence that was confirmatory to Zimmerman's account of a clear-cut self-defense shooting. We'll get to that soon in this space ... and why the jury was not allowed to see it.

Zimmerman Verdict, Part 7: Why the Jury Didn't Learn About Trayvon Martin

The discovery materials the defense finally received from the prosecution after a long and arduous fight revealed Trayvon Martin to be deeply into drugs, a young man who reveled in street fighting, and more. (He didn't seem to have much respect for women, either.) None of that was allowed in.

The reason tracks to something found in the Federal Rules of Evidence in the Rule 404 series, particularly Rule 404(b). Among other things, it means that prior bad acts of the person you harmed, *if they were not known to you at the time you harmed him*, cannot be used by you to defend inflicting that harm. This is because, being unknown to you, they had no part in your decision to act as you did, and it is that act and that decision for which you are being judged at trial.

Some courts have disagreed with that. The Massachusetts State Supreme Court, in two precedent cases and the Arizona State Supreme Court in one, has ruled that if the deceased had attacked people previously in a manner similar to how the defendant described being attacked by him, the jury *should* be allowed to know. (There was a reference in the discovery materials to Martin having punched out a school bus driver.) There is no such precedent in Florida that I know of. State Supreme Court decisions from other jurisdictions do not bind other states but can be used as a persuasive argument during a pre-trial *motion in limine* to allow such evidence.

Back in 1984, I was on the defense team as an expert witness called by two of the finest attorneys I've ever worked with, the great Roy Black and the brilliant Mark Seiden. Mark and I later served two years together as co-vice chairs of the forensic evidence committee of the National Association of Criminal Defense Attorneys, and Roy's courtroom accomplishments are legend. It would be worth your time to read Roy's autobiography "Black's Law." In the 1984 trial, Roy and Mark defended Miami Police Officer Luis Alvarez against Manslaughter charges in the shooting death of one Nevell "Snake" Johnson. (There were interesting parallels between that case and Zimmerman's. An officer of Hispanic descent had shot a 20-year-old black man who was reaching for a gun as that officer and another attempted to arrest him. The shooting triggered a race riot. A scapegoat was needed. Janet Reno, then State's Attorney there, indicted the cop.)

In that case, the state had portrayed the late Mr. Johnson as a perfect specimen of innocent young manhood, and this is what opened the door for the judge to consider the 40-page memorandum of law that Black and his team put before the bench. The judge set aside 404(b) to allow the defense to rebut that characterization, and the jury got to hear an elderly black woman describe the terror she had experienced when Nevell Johnson had made her the victim of an armed robbery. To make a long story short, Alvarez was acquitted. (Which triggered another race riot, but that's another story.)

The lead prosecutor in *Zimmerman,* Bernie de la Rionda, was too smart to open that door. I understand why Judge Nelson did not allow evidence of prior bad acts by Trayvon Martin to go in front of the jury. Interestingly, though — at the very end of the trial, when it was too late for the defense to do much of anything about it — second-seat prosecutor John Guy made the state's final argument to the jury, a soliloquy rife with references to Martin, who was much taller than the man he attacked, as a "child." "Child" was also used in this respect by New York City Mayor Michael Bloomberg after the verdict and was Martin family lawyer Ben Crump's refrain from the beginning.

Yet the Trayvon Martin who emerged from the state's reluctantly provided evidence, the evidence the jury didn't see, was something else entirely.

If Guy, Bloomberg, or Crump had ever met 17-year-old Trayvon Martin in life and called him a helpless "child" to his face, I strongly suspect Martin would have kicked them in the balls.

Zimmerman Verdict, Part 8: The Quantity of Injury Argument

Professionals in the justice system knew that the prosecution was desperately scraping the bottom of the barrel when they tried to make it look as if George Zimmerman wasn't justified in shooting Trayvon Martin because Martin hadn't hurt him badly enough yet.

Anyone smart enough to pass a bar exam and research the laws of self-defense and use of force would know that you don't have to sustain a gunshot wound before you shoot the criminal gunman pointing his weapon at you. Similarly, you don't have to let the guy fracture your skull or spill your brains onto the sidewalk before you are justified in stopping him with lethal force.

Photos taken immediately after the shooting, along with eyewitness testimony, confirm that Zimmerman's nose was smashed into a swollen mess, and there was blood all over the back of his head from the lacerations there. Whether or not the physician's assistant who saw him later could confirm that the nose was broken, the evidence supports not only the violent sucker punch to Zimmerman's face that he said began the encounter but also his contention of his head being smashed against the hard surface of the sidewalk. It doesn't much matter whether your opponent is banging a chunk of hard sidewalk into your head or banging your head into that part of the sidewalk. Either way, profound or fatal brain injury is the likely result if it continues.

Why wasn't he killed or knocked unconscious by the first few such strikes? The neck muscles are among the strongest in the body. A few months after birth, they become involuntary muscles that hold your head up without having to think about it. When you instinctively resist the hands that are smashing your head into the pavement, those muscles help you mitigate the force to some degree. But with each blow of the back of your head against that unforgiving surface, you become less and less able to resist. Soon, the inevitable happens, and fatal or crippling brain damage ensues.

From what the evidence shows us, deadly force was indeed warranted at the time Zimmerman pulled the trigger and fired the single shot of the encounter. The lay jurors, even the one who couldn't quite distinguish between homicide and murder when she talked about it on TV Wednesday, understood that.

The argument that Zimmerman didn't sustain enough injury to warrant using deadly force in self-defense is simply a false argument. An argument so blatantly bogus that the knowledgeable observer can't help but wonder what motivated the lawyers who raised it in the first place.

Zimmerman Verdict, Part 9: The Propaganda Factor

Can someone spoon-feed BS to the media and sucker them into believing it? Well, TV newscasters in California were pranked after the recent crash of a Korean airliner in San Francisco. They dutifully read on the air from their Teleprompter that the plane's crew was named Sum Ting Wong, Wee Tu Lo, Ho Lee Fuk, and Bang Ting Ow.

MURDERED in Cold BLOOD
Trayvon Martin

16 YEAR OLD ACADEMIC SCHOLAR was MURDERED - EXECUTED in cold blood. Trayvon Martin had dreams of being an aviation mechanic. However, the 16-year-old Black teen is dead, the murderer George Zimmerman has not been charged or arrested. The parents Tracy Martin and Sybrina Fulton stated " We're not getting any closure, any answers, it's very disturbing. As a Father I'm hurt..."

Child killer of Trayvon Martin

WANTED DEAD or ALIVE

GEORGE ZIMMERMAN   GEORGE ZIMMERMAN

BLACK POWER MOVEMENT- TOPS The Ordinary Peopl **Society and NEW BLACK PANTHER PARTY** For Information Contact National Education Minister James J Evans Muhammad 904 613-0729 Email:jamesteacher@att.net or Minister Mikhail S. Muhammad Chairman Southern Region New Black Panther Party Call 904-705- 8556 Email: mikhail45@live.com
designed By JEM

Something similar happened in the Zimmerman case. The family of the deceased, understandably filled with grief and anger that their unarmed son had been shot to death by a man never arrested for it, hired Attorney Benjamin Crump. Crump, in turn, brought in a high-powered public relations firm associated with left-wing political causes, as reported by the *Washington Post*.[9]

The story fed to the press would outrage anyone ... and, predictably, it outraged everyone. The family provided a picture of Trayvon at age 12 or 13, which the media ran with the ugliest picture of Zimmerman they could find. The meme of a huge armed adult "stalking" a "helpless child" was born fully grown, to a Godzilla-like size. It loomed over America unopposed. The investigating officers and the State's Attorney's Office knew that the evidence showed something else: Zimmerman was attacked by Martin, who towered over him, beat him to the ground, clearly smacked his head into the concrete, and might have even gone for his gun. But cops and good lawyers don't try their cases in the press, and no voice rose loud enough with the facts to drown out the roar of the fantasy.

We can only imagine Zimmerman's emotional turmoil at that time. Like

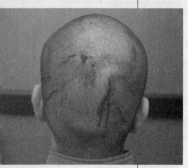

NEWS **EXCLUSIVE**

many Americans in their twenties, he was not yet fixed on a career and far from his peak earning years: the cost of hiring attorneys must have been terribly intimidating. He did not stay in touch with his original attorney, Craig Sonner — who, I thought, had an excellent grasp of the case and would have done very well for him — and Sonner and his co-counsel had nothing to work with. By the time Zimmerman had retained Mark O'Mara, the false perception had become a national reality. While O'Mara did an excellent job of trying to get the truth to the public, it was too late: his voice was simply drowned out by the media's "all Trayvon, all the time" crusade against his client.

The egregious editing of the dispatch tape by one major network, and the false report by another claiming that Zimmerman's clearly visible, well-documented head injuries were non-existent, will be taught as warnings in journalism school for evermore. I expect that legal settlements by those networks in the suits brought by Zimmerman will be huge.

One function of the grand jury is to reassure the public that a case has been investigated and the evidence evaluated. The State's Attorney of jurisdiction, Norm Wolfinger, had a reputation for being both tough and fair and had already scheduled this matter to go before the grand jury in the next session when he stepped away from the case, apparently at the request of Governor Rick Scott, who appointed Angela Corey as special prosecutor. It was necessary to show an outraged public that their anger had found receptive ears.

When Ms. Corey announced that she would bypass the grand jury, it was clear to any criminal justice professional that she was going to indict him on her own via an offer of information. There is generally one reason why a chief prosecutor will take a case away from a grand jury: the prosecutor wants an indictment and doesn't think a grand jury that has heard the evidence will deliver one.

At this point, the die was cast. The show trial was inevitable, and America had experienced a triumph of propaganda that would have been worthy of Joseph Goebbels or Josef Stalin. Even today, after the opportunity to watch three weeks of intensive trial broadcast live minute by minute, which brought much of the truth to light, a majority of Americans seem to be ignorant of the facts and still convinced that a self-appointed vigilante racially profiled a black child and murdered him. Never mind that the facts in evidence clearly showed otherwise.

When that TV station in California realized they had been pranked on the "Sum Ting Wong" broadcast, they admitted it and apologized. The mass media, sadly, has not done the same in the Zimmerman matter.

Zimmerman Verdict, Part 10: The Semantics

Anyone who has trained with me in the last few years has heard me talk about "combat semantics." Smart debaters know that many words in our language have multiple shades of meaning, and they'll often try to tell people that one of those words meant "B" when you used it when in fact, you meant "A." We saw this in more ways than one in the Zimmerman case. At a bail hearing in April 2012, George Zimmerman told the family of the deceased Trayvon Martin that he was "sorry." The next morning, newspapers all over the country ran headlines like "Killer Apologizes."

We all speak English here. You apologize for having done something wrong. When you say "I'm sorry" in any number of contexts, such as this one, you're probably trying to convey, "I'm sad for your loss, and I feel compassion for you, and I wish this bad thing had never happened." But another connotation of "sorry" is "I apologize," and "apologize," in turn, carries the connotation of guilt. At the risk of cliché, "Self-defense is never having to say you're sorry."

Another example in the commentary sections is "pursue" versus "follow." It is clear from the evidence that for a brief period of time, Zimmerman followed Martin — indeed, he answered "Yeah" when the dispatcher asked him if he was following the other person. Those who wanted to pillory Zimmerman turned that into an imperfect synonym: "He pursued him!"

To "pursue" carries the connotation of intent to seize and control. A police pursuit is intended to end with the laying on of hands which takes the pursued into custody. The pursuit of wild game implies the intent to turn the animal into a carcass that will be butchered and devoured. Even "pursuit of happiness" implies that when you succeed, you will possess that happiness. There is absolutely nothing in evidence to indicate that Zimmerman ever did, or even ever intended to, lay hands on Martin and take control of him. But this simple choice of words — by those who indeed did "pursue" Zimmerman in their way — helped to convince much of a nation that Zimmerman's actions were not what the evidence now shows them to be.

"Combat semantics" is a debater's game. Trial lawyers, if you think about it, are debaters playing for much higher stakes than the high school Debate Society.

And clearly, many of those who were out to hang Zimmerman were, uh, master debaters.

Zimmerman Verdict, Part 11: Rating the Lawyers (Defense)

Watching the Zimmerman trial in 2013 was like watching the OJ Simpson trial in 1995: while the general public got a hell of an education on how these things work thanks to live TV trial coverage, those "in the business" were assessing the skills and strategies of the key players.

The face of the defense was that of a two-man team, Mark O'Mara and Don West. The general consensus was that they did a *helluva* good job and that O'Mara was the best lawyer in the courtroom during that trial. Some criticized him for not being harsher on some witnesses; I respectfully disagree. When the jurors finally tell their stories in full detail, I think you'll find that his gentility scored big points with them. The jury figures out early in the trial that the lawyers are the Alphas and the witnesses are the Betas in the cross-examination dialogue ... they tend to identify more with the "ordinary people" witnesses than with the "power-figure" lawyers ... and they consciously or subconsciously resent those who bully the witnesses called by the opposing side. O'Mara got his points across without brutalizing anyone called by the state.

Don West was co-counsel in the truest sense of the term: he was O'Mara's partner in the battle, not his sidekick. West's long career in criminal defense practice has made him a master of caselaw and rules of evidence. But he also knows how to handle witnesses. Those who wanted a conviction complained that he was hard on Rachel Jeantel, the inarticulately angry young woman who had been speaking on the cell phone with Trayvon Martin just before the fight in which he was shot. I must profoundly disagree. He could have gone   harder ... and come across as a bully. He came across, instead, as the avuncular older man who just couldn't get what she was saying and let the jury come to their own conclusion that she was confessing to multiple lies.

West got a lot of crap about the "knock-knock" joke he used early in the defense's opening statement, and clueless talking heads will mention that for as long as the case is discussed. The lightweights also said that he spent too much time on details of the defense case in that opening. But for as long as people like me teach Continuing Legal Education courses on trial tactics in self-defense cases, West will be better remembered for laying out the defense's key elements in detail at the beginning of the trial so that each time one of the state's witnesses spouted BS from the stand, the jury had the defense's theory of the case to compare it to, and could recognize the BS when they heard it.

Of course, when you rate the players, you have to look at both teams ... and we'll discuss the other team next. (Spoiler alert: they were more skilled than the trial made them appear.)

Zimmerman Verdict, Part 12: Rating the Lawyers (Prosecution)

While there were two lawyers at the defense table, there were three at the State's: Bernie de la Rionda, John Guy, and Richard Mantei. With about a hundred lawyers to pick from, knowing her office would be in the spotlight, State's Attorney Angela Corey wouldn't have put anyone on the team she thought would make her look bad.

Mantei was third chair, and the lowest guy on the totem pole gets the scut work in any organization. For instance, he was the one they sent in to argue that the state had proven its case when it hadn't during the argument for judgment of acquittal. Perhaps the two senior guys didn't want to be on film forever BS-ing the judge. I suspect Mantei is a good prosecutor when he actually has a case.

The lead prosecutor in the courtroom was de la Rionda. He's the only one of the three I've seen live in a courtroom, and I can tell you that he knows the law and presents himself with articulate confidence. De la Rionda is said to have an extraordinarily high conviction rate. Why he accepted a case like this, as close as he is to retirement age, I cannot understand. His frustration was obvious throughout the Zimmerman trial; I can't imagine a man with his skill and experience being so abrasive in front of a jury for any other reason.

In the second seat was Guy, by far the best orator on that prosecution team. My students have heard me warn them about attorneys who seem to have majored in drama and minored in law, and Guy certainly fit that mold in *Zimmerman.* Remember his "Fucking punks" opening and his breathless assertion that the defendant killed the deceased "because he wanted to"? If he is as good a prosecutor as I hope when he has a case, he may be disgusted enough after this trial to quit. If so, he'll have a future in theater. I would suggest something Shakespearean, because the *Zimmerman* case gave him experience in things that were "full of sound and fury, signifying nothing."

I've seen other cases, more than one in Florida, where assistant prosecutors flatly refused to argue a case for conviction when the evidence showed the defendant wasn't guilty. That didn't happen here. Perhaps they truly believed Zimmerman was guilty, though it's hard for me to believe that, given the evidence they must have studied at great length. On the other hand, they worked for Angela Corey, who does not have a public history of treating kindly those employees who go against her wishes.

I've seen many people on many a forum and blog call these prosecutors incompetent. I don't think they were. They simply had no case. If you hired the greatest chefs in the world to cook for you and stocked the larder with feces, the best you could hope for them to put on the table would be a big, steaming pile of shit. And in the end, through no lack of argumentation skills on their end, that's how these three prosecutors' case ended up.

Now, forevermore among their peers, they're stuck with the blemish of this case and the accusations of withholding evidence that have come along with it and which don't seem to have been fully resolved at this writing. When retirement comes to each, I doubt that any will consider trying this case to have been their best career move.

Before you blame the team, blame the coach who sent them into a game that never should have been played. We'll discuss their coach later.

Zimmerman Verdict, Part 13: Angela Corey

In the last installment, I said that it was the coach who sent the prosecution team in to try to win a game that never should have been played. The police had determined they didn't have probable cause. The highly respected state's attorney who had responsibility for the case, Norman Wolfinger, apparently agreed. When the plaintiff-orchestrated *cause celebre* created a public outcry, Wolfinger scheduled the matter for the grand jury. But Florida Governor Rick Scott turned it over to Angela Corey, the state's attorney for the Jacksonville area, to act as special prosecutor.

Some have blamed Scott for this. I can't, at least not at this time. "The perception is the reality," it's said, and when the people who elected them cry out for a deeper investigation, those in charge have a duty to act. This is, in part, what the grand jury is for. While I think it should have been left in Wolfinger's capable hands, I can understand Scott's decision. His choice of Ms. Corey, however, is open to question in hindsight.

I gave Ms. Corey the benefit of the doubt as I watched this case unfold. I had hoped she would simply present the evidence to the grand jury. When she didn't, instead indicting on her own, it was inescapably obvious why: she had to have known that the grand jury would refuse to indict once they had seen the evidence.

The job of the defense is to be a zealous advocate for the defendant. The prosecutor's role is different. She is supposed to be the minister of justice, every bit as responsible for exonerating the innocent as for aggressively prosecuting the guilty. It is an egregious breach of prosecutorial ethics to, for example, prosecute for murder a man who the evidence shows is telling the truth about acting in self-defense. And, of course, there is the very serious breach of both rules and ethics encompassed in withholding evidence from the defense, a matter which in this case is still hanging in the air.

The right is unhappy with the special prosecutor.[10] The left apparently isn't too thrilled with her either, as seen in the *Daily Beast*.[11] Her fellow attorneys seem, for the most part, to be aghast at how she has handled the Zimmerman case, as seen in law professor Jonathan Turley's blog.[12]

The most damning moment for Ms. Corey, in this case, was her commentary to the press after the acquittal. A prosecutor should respect the system and the jury's verdict. The man she assigned to spearhead the state's case, Bernie de la Rionda, obviously understood that. One journalist asked both of them to describe the defendant and the deceased in a single word.

De la Rionda chose the words "lucky" for defendant George Zimmerman and "victim" for the deceased Trayvon Martin. He knew how to straddle the line. Despite Zimmerman's ordeal, a lot of people think anyone who is facing life in prison and gets set free is "lucky." And "victim" *is* the term that is generally and automatically used for someone who is killed.

But Corey described the young man shown by the evidence as the one who started the fatal battle as "prey" and the man the jury had just found not guilty of murder as a "murderer."

The difference is profound. It doesn't just show her to be a bad loser; it shows her to be utterly contemptuous of the jury and the system she is sworn to serve. Her answer was simply egregious.

There are those who believe that Ms. Corey took the case and tried to destroy Zimmerman's life because she had lost voter support in the African-American community and thought that prosecuting Zimmerman would be a good political move. If one accepts that, it begs the question, "How did that work for ya, Ms. Corey?"

What some call "the next Trayvon Martin case" — a white guy who wound up shooting a black teen in Jacksonville after an argument that began with the latter and his friends playing loud music in an adjacent vehicle — falls into Ms. Corey's jurisdiction. The Florida Civil Rights Association has called for the case to be taken out of Angela Corey's hands, because they think after the Zimmerman case, she doesn't have enough credibility to prosecute this one.

Zimmerman Verdict, Part 14: The Judge

Of all the key figures in the courtroom during the Zimmerman trial, I found Judge Debra Nelson the most enigmatic.

Some of Zimmerman's advocates called her the fourth prosecutor. It's true that she granted more approaches to the bench to the prosecution than to the defense, and those who kept count said she sustained far more objections from the prosecution than from the defense. Her insistent questioning of the defendant himself as to whether he chose not to testify is something I haven't seen before in more than 40 years in the criminal justice system.

I would have liked it if she had allowed prior bad acts by the late Trayvon Martin to come in to the jury. At the same time, as I've explained earlier in this blog series, she was well within judicial prerogative to make the decision to keep that material out.

The trial lasted a month, and it's been more than a month since the jury delivered a verdict. I'm still waiting to hear how she will rule on the requests the defense made for sanctions against the prosecution for the prosecution's failure to provide discovery material — evidence — in a timely manner.

But, hey: did you watch Judge Nelson when the jury verdict was read? Is it my imagination, or was she wearing a very slight smile, a smile as inscrutable as the Mona Lisa's?

Zimmerman Verdict, Part 15: Talk at the Scene, Talk on the Stand?

Many advise people involved in shootings to say nothing to the police. I'm not among them. I've seen too many cases where declining to speak is heard as "I ain't sayin' nuttin' 'til my mouthpiece gets here," and only the bad guy's side of the story gets told or assumed. I recommend that people caught up in these things tell the responding officers the nature of the attack on them, which forced them to fire, and indicate that they'll sign a complaint on the perpetrator. I recommend pointing out evidence and witnesses because both tend to disappear otherwise. From there on, I strongly suggest that they advise the police that they'll fully cooperate after they've spoken with counsel.

Zimmerman did otherwise, answering all questions that night and in the time that followed, and he prevailed at trial. He convinced the investigators that he was telling the truth about being a victim, not a murderer. He even passed a lie detector test (voice stress analysis) administered by the police shortly after the shooting. When defense lawyer Mark O'Mara got lead investigator Chris Serino to say that he believed Zimmerman was telling the truth, it was crushingly powerful for his client. Even though the judge ordered the jury to disregard that statement the next morning in court, it was a bell that simply could not be unrung. It turned out that his having done a videotaped walk-through of the scene was also critical to his acquittal: it allowed the jury to see the complicated layout of the scene, all the more important since Judge Nelson denied the defense's request to have the jury visit that scene.

I also advise my students to expect to take the stand on their behalf after a self-defense shooting. Since both sides are going to stipulate who shot who, it's going to come down to why you shot him ... and, in the last analysis, that's something the defendant can answer better than anyone else. Sometimes, *only* the defendant can really answer that question.

Why didn't Zimmerman take the stand? When I talked to Mark O'Mara a year before the trial, I got the impression he was expecting Zimmerman to testify, that Zimmerman *wanted* to testify, and that O'Mara thought his client would handle it well. After the trial was over, O'Mara confirmed that Zimmerman wanted to take the stand.

I personally think he would have done well. He certainly did when he was talking to the cops. If he's as articulate as his brother Robert, he would have done fine. Shortly after the acquittal, Robert Zimmerman went into the lion's den in an interview by hostile Piers Morgan on CNN, and the young man absolutely handed Morgan's pompous, prejudiced ass back to him on a silver platter.

Only Zimmerman and his defense lawyers can tell you why he didn't take the stand, but I can give you an educated guess: *He didn't have to.* The state's case had imploded even before the defense began theirs, with virtually every prosecution witness turning into a defense witness. *Zimmerman's walk-through at the scene, when everything was fresh in his mind, was already in to the jury ... and it was the best evidence.* There was simply nothing important enough to add.

I will continue to recommend that people involved in these confusing, high-stress incidents not submit themselves to detailed questioning and re-enactment in the immediate aftermath. That said, it worked for George Zimmerman. I will continue to warn my students that they can expect to take the stand to explain why they shot their attacker ... but in this case, George Zimmerman had already done that very well during police interrogation and had nothing to gain by repeating himself.

Zimmerman Verdict, Part 16:
The Impact on the Black Community

When propagandizing media made this case out to be something other than what the evidence showed it was, a hoax had been played on the whole country. It was a particularly cruel hoax on the African-American community.

Look at it this way. Suppose the mass media — whether through gullibility or complicity — had told a false story of a cancer victim being horribly wronged. Any of us would have been outraged and hurt ... but genuine cancer survivors would have been put through more unnecessary pain by the story than anyone else. Basically, that's what happened here.

Look back to the days of slavery. Fast forward to the Emancipation

Proclamation, and another century forward to the time of Martin Luther King when desegregation finally became law. Another half-century since, and African-Americans are still disproportionately burdened by poverty and crime.

Is it any wonder that this group felt more pain from what their country, from the White House on down, seemed to tell them was a threatening, potentially homicidal slap in their face?

A few days after the Zimmerman acquittal, I attended a meeting at an African-American church in the deep South, sponsored by the local chapter of the NAACP and focusing on Stand Your Ground laws. The discussion panel included the local police chief, undersheriff, chief prosecutor, and public defender. It became apparent that many of the mostly black attendees believed what the media had told them: that SYG laws had allowed a racist vigilante to murder a helpless young black man and get away with it. The professionals explained how things worked. The audience understood. Before long, talk from the almost entirely African-American audience had turned toward black-on-black crime, their real concern. While in the distant past, their community had been preyed upon by the Klan and suffered lynchings, they understood that past was buried, and their real concern was present crime from within their own community.

In the weeks that followed, I was a guest on Tracey and Friends, an African-American-centric radio show headquartered in Ohio.[13]

You'll get a better understanding of how bitter people are when they're singled out as suspects for their color and followed suspiciously for that reason and why some are angry enough about it to think that Trayvon Martin was right to physically confront and assault the man he perceived to be following him. I did another interview with an old friend and stalwart of the gun owners' civil rights movement, Kenn Blanchard, on his podcast *Black Man With A Gun*.

We have recently celebrated the memory of Martin Luther King, the march on Washington, and the "I have a dream" speech. It reminds us all that Dr. King made it clear that the civil rights movement was about healing, not about wounding.

The way the media — and, yes, the criminal justice system — distorted this case did a disservice to all of us. The facts in evidence clearly showed that it had nothing to do with race, and making it look as if it did plunged a knife into our consciousness as Americans.

But the way they made it look, often comparing it to the lynching of Emmett Till, the media twisted that knife into our African-American citizens with particular cruelty.

Zimmerman Verdict, Part 17: The Cops

In the first installment of this series, I mentioned that the cops were among those to thank for justice having been done in this case. Let's look at that.

Every commentator has noted that it was the police witnesses called by the state — civilian dispatcher and community watch coordinator and evidence technicians, as well as the responding and investigating officers — who cut the legs out from under the prosecution's weak case before it could ever get to its feet. Fewer commentators have spoken of the price paid by many of those honest members of the criminal justice system.

Sanford Police Chief Bill Lee, a highly respected CLEO (chief law en-forcement officer), resisted powerful demands from elected officials to file a case even though he knew there was nothing there. He did his duty and did the right thing. He was fired for that.

Detective Chris Serino was the lead detective in the case. He took a lot of heat for not wanting to file a case because he knew he didn't have prob-able cause. He wound up as a patrolman back in uniform.

Doris Singleton was in the role of the investigator on the night of the shooting. She handled things competently. She comforted Zimmerman

> "
> THE NEXT TIME SOMEONE SAYS, "NEVER TALK TO THE POLICE; THEY'RE YOUR ENEMY," REMEMBER EACH AND EVERY ONE OF THOSE HONEST MEMBERS OF THE CRIMINAL JUSTICE SYSTEM WHO STOOD UP, TOLD THE TRUTH AND DID THEIR DUTY.

when she saw he was emotionally devastated by having had to end a young man's life. And she was at the rank of patrol officer at the time she testified almost a year and a half later.

Ben Kruidbos, IT director in the office of the special prosecutor, realized that the office had failed in its duty to turn over full discovery material to the defense. He fulfilled the office's duty and got that information to Zimmerman's defense team. As soon as the trial was over, special prosecutor Angela Corey fired him for doing what she should have done.

Norman Wolfinger, the designated State's Attorney (chief prosecutor) for the district, apparently realized that there was no probable cause to arrest Zimmerman but nonetheless scheduled the case for the next session of the grand jury. This is a normal procedure. It wasn't enough to placate the media-fueled lynch mob, and the case was basically taken away from him by the governor and given to special prosecutor Angela Corey. Wolfinger retired shortly thereafter. He may have been due for retirement anyway, but it was a lousy note on which to end a long and stellar career as one of Florida's most respected prosecutors.

The next time someone says, "Never talk to the police; they're your enemy," remember each and every one of those honest members of the criminal justice system who stood up, told the truth and did their duty. The next time someone tells you that the police are the mindless minions of the Gestapo/Leviathan/The Zionist Occupation Government/The Man (pick one as suits the given agenda), remember the ones who were severely and unmeritoriously punished for having fulfilled their oath and hewed to the truth. And remember the role they all played in getting that truth across to the jury and helping to acquit an innocent man who, by every objective analysis of the evidence, was wrongly accused.

Interviewed later about his firing, Chief Lee wistfully told the reporter that at least, at the end of the day, he had kept his integrity.

That's more than some involved in the prosecution can say.

Zimmerman Verdict, Part 18: Aftershocks

There was no winner of the fight that dark, rainy night in Sanford. Only degrees of losing. When the President and the galaxy of movie stars extended their condolences to the Martin family after the verdict, we heard from them no sympathy for the defendant and his family. George Zimmerman's life has been horribly and irreparably changed. We learn that a divorce is in progress, something not uncommon after traumas like what he and his family were put through. His loved ones, at various times, have been in hiding, subjected to the same death threats as George Zimmerman. The guy gets a warning for speeding in Texas and a ticket for 15 MPH over in Florida, and each time it's national news. When I heard of the latter on CNN radio, they thought it important enough to announce it ahead of the suicide of Ariel Castro, a genuine monster of our time, which occurred in the same news period.

Trayvon Martin's family has suffered the loss of a seventeen-year-old, his life wasted twice over. He threw it away himself on that February night — dealing drugs, planning beatings, and negotiating to illegally buy guns according to his digital records, his liver damaged already at seventeen by his drug abuse according to the autopsy — when he suffered a sudden, acute, and fatal failure of his victim-selection process.

His father had supposedly put an association with the Crips street gang behind him and was gainfully employed as a truck driver, and his mother was a government employee with a Master's degree. The dad loved him enough to take him in when the mom had enough tough love for him to kick him out, and the stepmother for most of his life (who was, for the most

"

DON'T BELIEVE EVERYTHING YOU SEE IN THE PAPERS OR ON TV WHEN THE NEWS IN QUESTION IS A SELF-DEFENSE ACT. FOR DECADES AS AN EXPERT WITNESS IN THESE CASES, I'D GET BACK TO THE HOTEL AFTER TESTIFYING, WATCH THE NEWS REPORT ON THE DAY'S EVENTS IN COURT, AND WONDER WHAT THE HELL TRIAL THE REPORTER WAS WATCHING.

part, excluded from the media narrative) loved him too. Supervision and intervention did not come in time to save Trayvon Martin from his violent tendencies.

The second waste of his life is being witnessed now. His mom is on the talk circuit calling for an end to Stand Your Ground laws, which any honest and competent legal analyst could tell her had nothing to do with her son's death. It would do much more good, and perhaps save the lives of young men across the spectrum of the color lines, to hear this woman speak of the importance of seeing what's in your son's cell phone and on his Facebook page before homicide investigators have to do it.

Will there be a civil suit? Very probably. I would expect the plaintiff's counsel to wait to file it until there's some money there. I predict substantial settlements of George Zimmerman's lawsuits against the networks whose minions deliberately libeled him, whether or not he ever signs a lucrative book contract, but as soon as deep pockets are there, I expect to see vultures circling. Perhaps a Florida Statute 776.032 hearing will ward that off if it takes place in front of a judge with the courage to do the right thing. Time will tell.

The much-ballyhooed Federal investigation under Eric Holder to see if Zimmerman violated Martin's civil rights? Inconveniently for both the media and the Administration, that has already been done by a horde of specially-assigned FBI agents, all of whom reported absolutely no indication of racism or malice on Zimmerman's part. If you'll forgive vernacular, "they got nothin'." But, of course, that was true of the case Angela Corey brought against him, and it didn't stop that travesty from taking place.

Zimmerman Verdict, Part 19: Lessons

There was much for us all to learn from this case.

In this society, the person who moves toward danger in any respect is seen as "having gone looking for trouble" and widely blamed accordingly if it does not end well. I've explained earlier why I don't think anything Zimmerman did within the totality of the circumstances was the proximate cause of the death, but there's a reason for the saying, "It's not about fault, it's about blame."

When you're on trial, you aren't the player; you're the stakes. The players are your lawyers, and you want the best. Zimmerman had that, and it saved him. The evidence dealt them a powerful hand of cards. I think their two highest cards were Ace of Experts Dr. Vincent DiMaio, Jr. and Ace of Eyewitnesses John Good. The master forensic pathologist tied it all together and proved from the hard evidence what Good, the closest eyewitness, testified: it was Martin on top brutally beating Zimmerman until the shot. I did a murder case with Dr. DiMaio in Texas years ago, also resulting in an acquittal, and DiMaio was extraordinary there, too. If anyone still has the fantasy that you'll always be treated as a hero after a clean shoot, this case teaches us the reality. It's often an ordeal of lies, misunderstandings, and false accusations … and, as seen here, your family will go through that ordeal with you.

It's not something you want to face alone. Kudos to those who donated to Zimmerman's legal defense fund: you helped enormously to do justice. O'Mara establishing a website to show the actual evidence *(GZlegal-case.com)* was powerful and effective, and I think we'll see other defense lawyers modeling this strategy in the future. One useful ally would be the Armed Citizens Legal Defense Network, which I'm involved with and have seen do good work. *(armedcitizensnetwork.net)*. Mark O'Mara consulted with ACLDN head Marty Hayes on the case and appears to have put some of his advice to good use.[15]

Don't believe everything you see in the papers or on TV when the news in question is a self-defense act. For decades as an expert witness in these cases, I'd get back to the hotel after testifying, watch the news report on the day's events in court, and wonder what the hell trial the reporter was watching. We saw that classically here. The honest reporting was more in the blogosphere than in the mainstream media.

The gun prohibition subculture in this country is powerful, abetted heavily by the MSM, and you can expect them to seize on incidents like this and demonize the shooter. Zimmerman has become the poster person for this venomous trend. Even those who grudgingly accept the verdict still mutter aloud, "If Zimmerman hadn't had a gun, Trayvon Martin would still be alive."

That's probably true, but the final lesson is the flip side, which those commentators sometimes blindly and sometimes studiously ignore: If George Zimmerman hadn't been carrying a gun routinely on a night he wasn't expecting trouble, he would probably be dead.

Zimmerman Verdict, Part 20: ... And into the Future

Today is two months exactly since the day of the Zimmerman verdict, which I started blogging on that same day. Two months, and 20 entries, are nice round numbers to end upon. That's right at twice as long as the trial took, including the week of jury selection.

The strangeness continues, with the prosecution's medical examiner Dr. Shiping Bao being fired for his egregious performance in this case, and suing for a hundred-million dollars over that.

The divorce proceeding of Mr. and Mrs. George Zimmerman grows weirder. A key player in the case has decided that he doesn't want to play anymore and has a new gig.

The story will continue. It's been about 20 years since the O.J. Simpson trial, and *he's* still in the news. But I won't discuss that case until I've walked a mile in O.J.'s blood-stained, "ugly-ass" Bruno Magli shoes.

There will be books. Damn near everyone associated with the Simpson case eventually wrote one. I'll be interested in hearing from the *Zimmerman* prosecutors, from the defense lawyers, and from the judge (from whom I'm still waiting to hear a ruling as to the allegations of the prosecution withholding evidence from the defense). I'll be particularly interested to read George Zimmerman's account. Earlier in this blog, I mentioned that he had reportedly wanted to testify, that I thought he handled himself well talking to the investigators and would have done well on the witness stand if he was as articulate as his brother Robert, who tore Piers Morgan a new one on CNN. Robert Zimmerman later sent a tweet in which he said he thought his brother George would have been more articulate than he.

There already *are* books. *"Florida v. Zimmerman: Uncovering the Malicious Prosecution of My Son, George"* by the defendant's father, Robert Zimmerman, Sr., and *"Defending Our Friend: The Most Hated Man In America"* by Mark Osterman, the close friend who trained him with a gun and testified so well on his behalf, are available. The co-author of the latter was Sondra Osterman, who also helped show Zimmerman's human face when she testified at trial. I've mentioned in this series that when the mainstream media dismally failed to tell the truth, the blogosphere picked up the ball they dropped. A classic example of that was the work of *Conservative Treehouse*, the "Treepers" who told the truth about the case in all its dimensions. The best digest I've seen of that good work is *"If I Had a Son: Race, Guns, and the Railroading of George Zimmerman"* by Jack Cashill. There is also good reading on the topic to be found in *"The Lynching of George Zimmerman"* by Hunter Billings III. Those are just the ones I've read; there are more.

> ## THIS NATIONALLY DIVISIVE CASE BROUGHT OUT TRIBALISM AT A DISTURBINGLY HIGH LEVEL. BLACK VERSUS WHITE. ANTI-GUN VERSUS PRO-GUN. I, FOR ONE, DIDN'T COME FROM THAT ANGLE. AS AN ADVOCATE FOR ARMED CITIZENS, IT'S AS IMPORTANT TO ME TO STEP ON THE ONES WHO SCREW UP AS TO CELEBRATE THE MANY MORE WHO SAVE INNOCENT LIVES.

The titles of the dad's book and that of the friends show that they're obviously advocates for one side. The Cashill and Billings books clearly have advocacy in them, but that doesn't distract from the truth if the advocates are on the side of that truth, and the evidence showed that these advocates were.

I hope another book on the trial will be forthcoming from my friend and former student, Andrew Branca. His reporting from right there in the courtroom was, I think, the gold standard for commentary on the trial as it unfolded. It can be found day by day for the trial, which went from June 10 to July 13, 2013, at *legalinsurrection.com*. When you go there, budget some time to read the huge volume of commentary on each day's blog. Legal Insurrection draws an audience very heavily populated by lawyers and other criminal justice professionals, and there is gold in their assessment of the strategy and execution of the tactics seen in this trial. Branca is a lawyer who specializes in self-defense (get his excellent book on *that* topic at *lawof-selfdefense.com)*. His commentary and that of the readers will *sound* like advocacy for Zimmerman, but if you read it carefully, you'll see that he and most of the commentators are really advocating for law and reality...which just happened to favor Zimmerman.

This nationally divisive case brought out tribalism at a disturbingly high level. Black versus white. Anti-gun versus pro-gun. I, for one, didn't come from that angle. As an advocate for armed citizens, it's as important to me to step on the ones who screw up as to celebrate the many more who save innocent lives. The history of it is that any community that does not police itself will be policed from the outside. If I thought Zimmerman had done wrong, I would have said so.

Had I been going with tribes, I would have sided with special prosecutor Angela Corey. We have a lot in common. We've both made our careers in the justice system, we've both prosecuted, and we both have Arabic-American ancestry. Sorry, homegirl, I just can't side with you on this one. My career has taught me to go with the evidence to find out who's on the side of the angels, and in this case, Angela, you were on the wrong side. Simple as that.

When John Guy did his dramatic opening statement for the prosecution, he ended with his now-famous line, "We are confident that at the end of this trial you will know in your head, in your heart, in your stomach that

George Zimmerman did not shoot Trayvon Martin because he had to. He shot him for the worst of all reasons, because he wanted to."

Under the prosecutorial duty to be a minister of justice, this writer believes that Ms. Corey should have simply brought the evidence before a grand jury and given them the option to indict. Instead, she bypassed that key element of the criminal justice system and set the stage for a cruel show trial. I suspect that historians will write of it more as "Angela Corey did not put George Zimmerman and his family through this ordeal because she had to. She did it for the worst of all possible reasons ... because she wanted to."

Previously published on Backwoods Home *Magazine's blog by Massad Ayoob at backwoodshome.com.* Also, check out the blog "Ayoob on Firearms": backwoodshome.com/blogs/massadayoob. ■

CHAPTER 11:
CASE STUDY STATE OF ARIZONA V. LARRY HICKEY

T*he Larry Hickey case was a classic in terms of teaching points for law-abiding armed citizens. Having testified in his second trial, I can tell you that the following account is spot on. It was written by Gila Hayes of the Armed Citizens Legal Defense Network, which came to his aid and earned kudos from the extraordinary able team of public defenders who carried him through both trials. It is reprinted here with ACLDN's permission.*
– Mas Ayoob

Analysis of the Larry Hickey Case
By Gila Hayes

Western states like Arizona are generally friendly to ideas of firearms and self-defense, but we may forget that any state can harbor a city in which the population leans toward liberal social politics and buys into the flawed theory of gun control for public safety. Anti-self-defense attitudes, cloaked in good intentions, can intrude when a self-defense shooting entails factors that are not always clear cut, such as when one man shoots several unarmed assailants and must argue disparity of force as a justification for his actions. This is at the heart of an ordeal that ran from late November 2008 through May 2010 in Tucson, Arizona.

Larry Hickey, his wife and young son lived on a cul-de-sac in a modest Tucson neighborhood. Across the street lived three adults — two 30-something sisters and the 26-year-old boyfriend of one — along with the women's two children. The households were only peripherally acquainted through limited contact between Hickey's seven-year-old son and the two boys, ages four and 11. Mr. and Mrs. Hickey both had demanding jobs, Mrs. Hickey worked shift work in the telemetry room in a local hospital, and Mr. Hickey was employed by the Union Pacific Railroad, a job that took him away from home for several days at a time. At 37 years of age, Hickey's previous employment history included working as a safety trainer for a big chain store and a stint as a corrections officer in a high-risk facility where he dealt with violent behavior.

Hickey owned guns and had a concealed carry permit, having carried a defensive pistol for 14 years. For 10 years, he'd been an avid student of defensive weaponcraft. He took classes from local instructors, as well as a number of courses from James Yeager of Tactical Response in Camden, Tenessee. He became one of Yeager's instructors, and he also taught pre-deployment military personnel about foreign weaponry for a local firm, C&T Enterprises. When he ran into trouble, his day job with the Union Pacific Railroad was on temporary hiatus, as he had just been furloughed pending an uptick in economic conditions.

The Incident

On Monday, November 17, 2008, day faded into night as the Hickey family returned home from a bicycle ride. Trying out a headlamp he had just mounted on his new bicycle, Larry Hickey remained in the street in front of their home, riding for a little longer while his wife went into their garage and brought the trashcans to the street for collection. He pedaled over to his wife, and they stood near the trashcans discussing the dinner menu, how to dispose of some bulky trash and the other minutiae of daily living. The sisters sat in their garage smoking with the doors open, when one called out aggressively to Mrs. Hickey, then jumped up and barged across the street to confront the Hickeys.

On the 15th, the women had argued — not in person but by cell phone texts that included nasty name-calling. Mrs. Hickey filed a police report alleging harassment and threats. When the enraged woman rushed up, Hickey got between the two women to protect his wife. He will later testify that he said, "Hey, no one has to get hurt over this ... could you please go back to your side of the street?" though he had to raise his voice to be heard over the woman.

As an older woman who lives nearby drove past, she saw the other sister stride across the street and join the fray in Hickey's driveway. This neighbor will later testify that the second woman approached with her fist raised, and another woman, also driving home on the street, will testify to similar aspects of the fight.

The woman flicked a lit cigarette at Mrs. Hickey and then darted around the garbage cans toward her, saying, "I'm going to kill you, bitch," according to Hickey's testimony in court.

Mr. Hickey pushed his bike away and tried to intercede as he saw one of the neighbor women with a raised fist rushing toward where he thought his wife stood. He moved between them, trying to intercept her, and the sisters begin hitting him. Blows from both sisters rained down on the crown of his head and arms as he attempted to block their fists. Hickey ducked down, and while blocking the blows with his arms, he tried unsuccessfully to activate a remote control to open the garage door so the couple could run to safety. The front door to the Hickeys' home was securely locked, limiting their options.

From his experience and training as a corrections officer, Hickey knew about force options for various situations and, in court, will describe his control of the sisters as using "soft hands."

Nearly two years later, pondering his decisions that night, Hickey would wonder if the fight could have been aborted had he initially used more decisive physical force. "I was just trying to block the blows and keep them pushed away from me. I did not want to hit anybody," he says now. "Looking back, I wish I had been more forceful in trying to discourage them from attacking us. It almost seemed like the fact that I wasn't hitting them emboldened them. It made them attack more. They claimed that I struck them numerous times. They claimed that I grabbed their hair and beat their faces in, but there was no physical evidence of it, no black eyes, no swollen or split lips, nothing."

Hickey managed to grab the first woman by her arms and push her away. Her feet became tangled and she fell. He pushed away the second woman, who was also hitting him, and she fell. "I got them pushed away, and we were trying to get back up the driveway, and they were just up like a shot; there was no time at all, and they were back and attacking us again," Hickey recalls.

As the neighbor women renewed their attack, screaming at Mr. Hickey and hitting him with their fists, he heard the sound of running feet and glass breaking in the street. Through the narrowed field of tunnel vision, Hickey sensed only a flash of movement and then felt a staggering impact to the side of his head.

Loud voices and Hickey's struggle to fend off the women drew the attention of the boyfriend, who had recently returned home from work, removed his dress shirt, and poured a glass of wine in the house across the street. Hearing the fracas, the man ran across the street, dropping the wine glass en route, and jumped into the fight, slugging Hickey hard on the left temple. That blow changed Hickey's decision to try to get through the beating by just blocking the blows. When the other man nailed his temple, Hickey's vision blurred to white, his legs buckled, and he staggered back, nearly passing out. In court, Hickey will testify that when "the new attacker

Gila Hayes of Armed Citizens Legal Defense Network – at right, talking to a prospective member – wrote this synopsis of *Arizona v. Larry Hickey*. ACLDN provided substantial assistance to the defense.

showed up, then it went from scary to terrifying, just like that the whole dynamic changed in a split second."

Hickey's mind flashed back to a video clip his CCW instructor showed in which a Texas police constable is attacked, disarmed and shot by three smaller assailants during a drug investigation (see Lunsford murder[16]). While this flashed through his mind, Hickey simultaneously tried to confirm the location of his wife and son to be sure they were not endangered.

The mind can process a lot of things at one time, Hickey later commented, and his mind was racing as he fell backward from the blow to his temple. Trying to shake off the onset of unconsciousness from the impact, Hickey drew his Glock 19 from an IWB holster. From the retention shooting position, he fired three shots at the attackers pressing up against him, hitting the male in the abdomen and hand and striking one of the women in the lower leg.

As his attackers backed away, Hickey desperately scanned the area as he has been taught to avoid being blindsided by another attacker. He described tunnel vision as looking down the tube of the paper towel roll. The man who hit Hickey's temple and one of the women return to their home; the other woman screamed loudly that she had been shot. At the same time, Hickey feared that his wife and son may not be safe. It turns out that the 7-year-old boy opened the front door, and probably witnessed the final portion of the fight. Mrs. Hickey sent him back inside.

The Immediate Aftermath

While trying to dial his cell phone to summon medical aid and police assistance, Hickey went into his garage and grabbed his trauma kit, then closed the garage door behind him as he rushed to the injured woman's side. He had already removed the magazine from his Glock, shucked the live round out of the chamber, and placed the gun and magazine on his yard's retaining wall.

In the darkness, Hickey could not see the screaming woman's wound, but he applied a compression bandage where she was holding her leg and ankle. Finding blood, he also applied a tourniquet higher up on her leg to stop the blood loss. As he tended to the woman (who, a moment earlier, was hitting him), he looked up and saw that neighbors had circled around, drawn by the gunshots and screams. Many had dialed their own 9-1-1 emergency calls.

As a female neighbor took over tending the bleeding woman, an off-duty male police officer drew Hickey away and sat him down. This neighbor ascertained the location of Hickey's gun, and in answer to his inquiries, Hickey said, "I shot." Feeling the blood and sweat running down him, Hickey asked, "Am I bleeding?" But the neighbor told him, "Don't say anything; just hang tight." When the police arrived, the neighbor called out that he had the shooter and turned Hickey over to responding officers. Worried that he had not taken time to put on gloves before treating the woman's wounds, Hickey asked if he could wash his hands, but the request was denied. He was not allowed to wash them for several hours, not until after he was taken to the police station and photographed.

Hickey related that the first officer on the scene took him to the patrol car and cuffed him. As he was escorted to the patrol car, Mr. Hickey was taken past the injured woman lying on the ground. As the officer escorting him asked, "What happened? Did they come across the street?" Hickey responded, "Yes, they ran over here and attacked us." Not part of a formal interview, those words are forever lost and appear nowhere in the police reports from that night.

After Hickey sat for some time in the police cruiser, an officer returned and told him that he would take him to the station where detectives will interview him. While waiting in the car, Hickey thought about the case of Harold Fish, the Arizona schoolteacher imprisoned after a self-defense shooting. He'd read that as Fish's memories cleared, he gave statements that contained minor variations, leading the prosecution to accuse him of lying. Worried that he, too, may say the wrong thing, Hickey invoked his

IN COURT, HICKEY WILL TESTIFY THAT WHEN "THE NEW ATTACKER SHOWED UP, THEN IT WENT FROM SCARY TO TERRIFYING, JUST LIKE THAT THE WHOLE DYNAMIC CHANGED IN A SPLIT SECOND."

right to have an attorney present during questioning when an officer later approached him and asked if he would like to make a statement. "I was very, very brief," Hickey related. "I said, 'Other than the fact that these people ran over and attacked us, I would rather wait to give a full statement until I have a lawyer present,' or something to that effect."

All three attackers recited versions of the incident that differed from the one told by Mrs. Hickey, which differed from the report eventually given by Larry Hickey when he described the incident to his attorneys and legal defense team. All but one of the uninvolved witnesses told similar stories, but most of their recollections began after the shots were fired and contributed little to explaining what precipitated the shooting.

"As far as the State was concerned, I was completely silent because there was no record of me making those brief statements. I just said, 'They ran over and attacked us,' and I didn't get into any detail beyond that. I was trying to put the responding officers on notice about who was really the aggressors, but it didn't get noticed," he said. To this day, Hickey refuses to believe overlooking his statements was intentional, surmising, "They just got lost in the whole shuffle."

Hickey estimated that he had been handcuffed in the back of the patrol car for about half an hour when the arresting officer transported him to the police substation. "What do I need to do to press charges against these people?" Larry asked, and later, he asked the same question of officers at the jail. There, he was told that he must put that question to his lawyer. In the car riding to the substation, the officer explained that Hickey would meet with detectives at the station, but once there, he was placed in an interview room, where he remained for five or six hours. His only human contact came when he asked for water and a bathroom break.

Eventually, the arresting officer returned and announced that he needed to take Larry to the jail for booking. "What for?" Hickey asked, and the officer responded that he thought the charge was aggravated assault.

"Well, don't the detectives want to talk to me?" Hickey asked.

"I guess they got all they needed," the officer responded.

The result? Larry Hickey never made a statement to the police about what happened in his driveway the night of November 17, 2008. His assailants gave plenty of other statements, and though they were at odds with the physical evidence, the State prosecuted Hickey for aggravated assault. "I'm sure it was nothing malicious, but I don't know. There were hard questions that just were not asked," Hickey muses.

Later, when Hickey reviewed transcripts from the grand jury hearing at which he was indicted, he was surprised to read statements from the lead detective that did not concur with physical evidence from the shooting scene about which he must surely have known. In this case, the defendant was not allowed to testify to the grand jury, and Hickey found it unnerving to read the unrefuted allegations against him. "When I read this, I thought, but the evidence was in my driveway, not in the middle of the street! This is kind of a big deal! They're saying I ran out into the middle of the street, and we got into mutual combat. That is different from them running 100-plus feet across a street to attack us in our driveway. I said we attempted to retreat and were forced to use deadly force to defend ourselves. That is a big difference."

71 Days In Jail

After waiting hours to speak with detectives, Hickey was booked and placed in a cell. He told the medical technician taking down his information during booking that he was hit in the head. Most of the marks from the fight were hidden by Hickey's hair, landing as they had on the crown of his head. The blow to his temple left some swelling, and Hickey had headaches for about a week after the attack. Later, when Hickey reported headaches, the jail doctor made a simple examination of his eyes and reflexes, telling him that his symptoms were consistent with a concussion and telling him to watch out for warning signs of complications. He gave him Ibuprofen for the pain.

When the case went to trial, asking the jail doctor to testify was deemed too risky because when Hickey's attorney interviewed him, his attitude so worried the lawyer that he would not risk calling him to the witness stand. "This guy had some sort of an agenda. In my view, his attitude was that everyone lies in the jail, so they just give them stuff to shut them up," said the attorney. Although Hickey could have hired a different doctor to testify to the different types of concussions and compare those with Hickey's symptoms, Hickey's lawyer feared that doing so would not end well since the prosecutor would wonder why Hickey chose not to bring in the jail doctor, and would probably call that doctor on behalf of the prosecution.

On November 18, Hickey attended his arraignment by videoconference. During the hearing, one of the women who attacked him repeated her story that he went crazy and shot them. The bail was set at $200,000. With no attorney beyond a public defender who was present to advise all of the prisoners that day, Hickey was hit with a half-dozen charges of aggravated assault with a deadly weapon, two for each of the three attackers.

On the outside, Hickey's mother took charge. "I'll tell you who rallied everybody together," Hickey declared. "It is my mother, Callie Anderson. She is quite a fighter. She left no stone unturned. I probably wouldn't be in the position I am in today if it wasn't for her. It is kind of difficult to work on your case when you have to do it with leg irons on during a once-a-week visit with a lawyer!"

Within 24 hours, Mrs. Anderson obtained an attorney for her son. "I tell him I'd like to make a statement," Hickey recalled. "Obviously, these guys [police investigators] aren't seeing what really happened." That lawyer called the detective sergeant, leaving a voice mail message asking to set up a meeting in which Hickey will make a full statement. The call was never returned. The lawyer also represented Hickey at a bail reduction hearing, and the cash bail was cut to $100,000.

Two weeks later, during another videoconference from the jail, Hickey spoke with Pima County assistant public defender Matthew Messmer and was immediately impressed. About 10 years out of law school, Messmer impressed Hickey as someone with "fire in his belly" who would fight for Hickey's freedom. "He is really switched on. You could just see the spark when you talked to him," Hickey remembered. He was so impressed by Messmer from their videoconference that he immediately told his family he wanted Messmer to represent him.

During his initial meeting with Messmer, Hickey drew a map, diagramming the incident step by step. "Messmer said, 'OK, well, I'll get back to you,'" Hickey recalled. "This was before any statements, or any photos had started trickling in," Hickey explained. "I think I saw him a week later, and he had stated getting reports and photos showing where the evidence was located. I met with him, and he said, 'Well, the evidence is starting to come in, and you know what? You're telling the truth!'"

Matthew Messmer explained, "I really like my job, and I don't care who the person is, I have a job to do and I fight for everyone the same, but there was something about Larry's case. From the first time I saw him on that videoconference, nothing changed about his story; it was always exactly as he said. It was very easy to work on Larry's case just because he is such a polite person. He was honest from day one; nothing in his story ever changed."

"When we got the police reports," Messmer continued, "we compared the evidence that they had with what Larry had, and everything matched up to what the real evidence was. They [the assailants] were all lying. There were different stories, and I remember seeing that this was not all in the middle of the street the way they said. This was all on the edge of the Hickey property. This did not happen on the street! It was all on the Hickey property! It just bewildered us that no one was seeing that besides our team!"

Still, Messmer was frank with Hickey, outlining the challenges they faced defending his shooting. "I told him from Day One, 'I believe you, but we are going to have to figure out how to get over this hurdle because there are a lot of people out there that do not believe you can use a gun even if you are being attacked.'"

Raising Bail

As the Thanksgiving, Christmas and New Year's holidays passed, Hickey remained in jail while his family scrambled to raise $100,000 for bail. With a collapsing housing market, there was little equity in the family's homes against which to borrow, so Mrs. Anderson arranged private loans. She also reached out to Hickey's peers — fellow gun owners who communicate on James Yeager's Tactical Response forum, Get Off The X. "People would offer $1,000 saying, 'Just send it back when you're done,' and even those who put $5 in my mother's hands helped," Hickey related. "One individual put us over the top at the very end. He sent my mother a cashier's check for $20,000," he says, awe evident in his voice. "It is humbling and brings emotion out of me."

In late November, Armed Citizens Network member William Aprill telephoned Network President Marty Hayes to ask if he had heard about the Larry Hickey incident. "Mr. Aprill has a lot of contact with the folks from the training business, Tactical Response, and he related this incident to me," Hayes recalled. "He wanted to make us aware of this and see if we could help. Unfortunately, Mr. Hickey had not joined the Network; though, interestingly, Tactical Response, which he teaches for, is one of our affiliated training schools to which we give complimentary memberships in exchange for their help promoting Network membership. So I felt a little bit of moral responsibility to see what I could do to help Larry Hickey in his defense."

Hayes called James Yeager, president of Tactical Response, who confirmed the report. Yaeger referred Hayes to the Get Off the X forum, in which details and updates in Hickey's case were being discussed. Topics included both short- and long-term worries — concerns about obtaining the best possible legal defense for Hickey and the more immediate need of raising bail to get him out of jail.

"Typically, with $100,000 bail, they could raise $10,000 cash, pay a bondsman and get him released, but the prosecutor requested a cash bail," said Hayes. "I guess he thought Larry was a dangerous guy he couldn't see running loose in the streets of Tucson, so they imposed that restriction. Owing to that, it took two or three months to raise money to get Larry released. They had to bring in $100,000 in cash and hand it over to the court. For most people, it is pretty difficult to raise that kind of cash. But they got some loans and worked hard at it and eventually came in with $100,000 cash."

Since it was not appropriate to draw funds from the Network members' legal defense foundation to help a nonmember, Hayes turned his efforts to raise funds elsewhere. "Larry needed to raise some serious money, so I got involved in that fundraising, not realizing that later I would be as intrinsically involved in the case as I was," he recalls. "I went to my students at The Firearms Academy of Seattle and the membership of the Armed Citizens' Legal Defense Network, and I explained through email that I was convinced this was a legitimate case of self-defense and that this guy was one of us, an armed citizen, and, in fact, he was an instructor. Now he was being railroaded by the system, and he *was* going to be found guilty unless we did something. I don't know how much money was raised, but it was a considerable amount.

"In the meantime, the discussion was going on between contributors to the fundraiser about whether this money should be used for bail or his legal defense. It was a cordial discussion, but nonetheless, there were passionate arguments on both sides. I fell in with the camp that funds raised should be legal defense money, not bail money, and I think everybody pretty much agreed with that, and so Larry sat in jail for a few months because the money we had raised was not going to bail him out, it was to fight the legal claim."

Though Hickey had complete confidence in his public defender, Hayes was deeply concerned whether a public defender's office could put on an adequate defense for such a complicated case. "Usually, a public defender would not have enough resources for this kind of case," Hayes explained. "They needed an investigator hot on the trail of this situation, talking to all of the witnesses, getting photographs of the wounds, etcetera, and they didn't have one. This happens all the time. Because many times public defenders don't have the resources to do their own investigation, they may rely on the prosecution's investigation.

"When the train is going down the tracks toward a conviction, the prosecution doesn't always look at all the evidence. They only look at the evidence that tends to help convict the person, as opposed to possibly showing that he was justified."

In the end, some of the money raised was used to put on a mock trial for Hickey's attorneys to test defense strategies before going to court. Additional expenditures covered travel expenses of expert witnesses for the trial, including instructors under whom Hickey had trained and Hayes, who gave testimony to explain the ballistics evidence, including bullet trajectories and the retention position from which Hickey fired, to prove the extremely close proximity of Hickey's attackers at the moment that he drew and fired. This testimony stood in stark contrast to the testimony of Hickey's assailants. Hayes advised on the case *pro bono*, accepting only travel expenses, and freely contributing his time and expertise.

Hickey Set Free

On January 27, 2009, Hickey was bailed out of jail. Within a week, he went to work full-time for a friend who owns a manufacturing business in Tucson and was later called back to his regular job at the railroad. Under his bail conditions, Hickey was prohibited from coming within a five-mile radius of his assailants (and thus needed to avoid his own home), so the family moved into a spare room offered by one of Hickey's friends, a retired law enforcement officer who lives on the other side of town.

As the public defender's office was ramping up to defend Hickey in court, a second public defender, Matt Rosenbluth, joined the team, owing to the seriousness of the charges. Hickey calls both "stellar lawyers" and praises the efforts of their support staff.

Because the Public Defender's office rarely deals with self-defense cases, Hickey became immediately immersed in forwarding information from all his prior training, as well as researching principles including justifiable use of deadly force to defend against a mob attack and other disparity of force issues. "I had a completely legitimate self-defense claim owing to disparity of force but we all know that is the toughest thing to show," he said

Wisely, the defense team reached out to a leading expert on the subject, internationally renowned Massad Ayoob, who advised on Hickey's case along with Hayes. Neither Ayoob nor Hayes is sure who went to work on the case first, though both remember that in May 2009, while Ayoob was teaching at Hayes' school, The Firearms Academy of Seattle, both men participated in a phone conference with Hickey and his lawyers.

"After the phone conference, Massad was on board to serve as an expert to explain the issues to the jury," Hayes says. "A problem arose early after he accepted this case when Massad discovered he had another trial scheduled for the same time, a previous commitment that he couldn't back out of, so I was basically the pinch hitter. I substituted for Mas and got involved early on as the expert to go down and testify in court," Hayes recounted, adding that during the preparatory phases, Ayoob continued to offer advice, though he was not able to participate in the trial.

Instead, Hayes testified, focusing primarily on ballistics evidence.

"My role was to look at the ballistics evidence and see if I could make sense of it by comparing it to Larry's account of the incident versus the other people's account," Hayes explained. "When I studied the evidence, I was convinced that Larry's account was consistent with the evidence and that the other accounts were not.

"My testimony was to counter some of the claims made by the people who had the altercation with Larry. Their first claim was that after Larry shot two people, he turned his gun toward the third, and as she was running away, he fired a shot at her. I thought that was pretty ludicrous, based on what I had heard. It just didn't make sense to me. I got all the discovery, including the photographs, looked through it and determined there were three shots fired and those three bullets struck two of the people. There was no way Larry fired at a third person as she was running away," he said.

Character Assassination

In addition to the struggle to match up limited evidence with all the different stories being told, Attorney Messmer faced several more hurdles.

The first was prejudice about men fighting women.

"Even in our own office, we were very divided," Messmer admitted. "A lot of people couldn't get over the fact that Larry shot one female. That [reaction] just dumbfounded us: the aggressor coming toward you doesn't have anything to do with gender. What we knew from talking to Marty [Hayes], and Ayoob was that … being able to convince the jury that this was a disparity of force situation was really the key. We had to make them see that these people were acting in concert and that they were one force. I think it was always hard for some people to grasp that concept."

In addition, the defense team needed to counter the picture that Hickey's accusers painted of him as a crazed gun nut. Initially, hoping to discourage prosecution, the defense team disclosed all the information they had about firearms classes he had completed. "From day one, we wanted to avoid trial, so we disclosed all of Larry's training, that he's an instructor who has taught all these people, he has been training all these years, and he knows when it is proper and when it is not. We disclosed all that to the prosecutor," Messmer stressed.

They learned early on that they would have to take care to explain how Hickey's training led to the tactical decisions he made during the attack. In an effort to find the best strategies for Hickey's defense, Messmer, Rosenbluth, and their team hired a Phoenix firm that puts on mock trials in which attorneys practice their presentations and watch the reactions of a test jury to their arguments.

"The practice jury said that Larry had too much training, and he should have known better. So how much we were going to get into [his training] was always very difficult to figure out because it was absolutely important to show Larry as this person that isn't just out there with a gun and doesn't know how to handle it."

Even if the defense had chosen to give only cursory mention to Hickey's training, the prosecutor would have forced their hand at trial. He harped endlessly on the various shooting classes Hickey had completed.

"It worked to our advantage in both trials because we disclosed all that to the prosecutor from Day One," Messmer stated. "In trial, the prosecutor went overboard with that, and he really disgusted the jury because he wasted their time."

Messmer explained how, like a broken record, the prosecutor asked each expert and material witness about each class Hickey had completed, what it covered, challenging why a private citizen would need that knowledge.

Messmer believed the jury eventually thought, "Get to the point. We know that!" He adds, "It made the prosecution look bad because Larry was getting training and doing his job, and they were attacking him for that. It blew up on them in the first trial, and they went back to it, and it blew again in the second trial. We knew they were going to bring it up, but it actually helped us out."

Hard Evidence

Having prepared to confront these and other issues, on September 30, 2009, Larry Hickey, represented by Matthew Messmer and Michael Rosenbluth, went to trial in the Superior Court of the State of Arizona in and for the County of Pima, defending his case before Judge Teresa Godoy. On the other side of the aisle sat the deputy county attorney, Daniel Nicolini.

On the third day of the first trial, Marty Hayes presented ballistics evidence, identifying the most likely bullet trajectories and explaining how that proved that Hickey's attackers were right on top of him when he fired from the retention position. Using a Crimson Trace aiming laser on a plastic molding of a gun, he demonstrated how the bullets traveled at trajectories that would have made the wounds only if the attackers were extremely close.

These wounds, he testified, were consistent with shooting a handgun from what is sometimes called a retention position. He gave the history of the technique and then explained that it exists for use in circumstances under which it is impossible to bring the gun to eye level and use the sights to take aim.

Messmer clarified that the shooting method would be for use "...when the attacker is right on top of you?" and Hayes concurred, "Absolutely, yes." "...In close proximity?" Messmer pressed. "Yes," Hayes averred.

Hayes later explained that the court recognized his expertise because, "In order to be considered an expert or give expert testimony and expert opinion in court, the court requires that the individual has gained a knowledge of the specific discipline you are testifying to considerably beyond the average layman's knowledge of that discipline and that is done through formal training, formal education or simply hands-on experience. Because

I've had all three, I met the criteria of a ballistics expert very easily, and the judge allowed me to give that testimony."

Still, Nicolini challenged Hayes' testimony, asking if he was a forensic pathologist or had medical experience. Did the prosecutor's aspersions diminish the effect of his testimony? "Not that I saw because I'd never claimed to be a pathologist or doctor. He was trying to discredit me as much as possible, but it didn't seem to bother the jury. It was just basically smoke and mirrors to try to attack the credibility of the witness somehow, and that is all he could do, I guess," Hayes suggested.

There was considerable difficulty conclusively establishing the assailant's exact location because gunshot residue swabs were not taken, nor were stippling patterns recorded from the abdomen of the male, exculpatory evidence that could have scientifically proven how close the attackers were when Hickey fired. Instead, the lack of evidence created a situation in which Hickey's sole testimony had to be weighed against the stories of all three attackers. This made Hayes' interpretation of the available evidence all the more crucial. He had to work from crime scene photos, depositions and statements to police and a set of photos made by family members of the persons who were shot.

Did he have sufficient detail to draw conclusions? "You are never 100 percent sure, and you never say you are in court, but you say there is a very high probability based on what you saw to testify in court to what you believe occurred," he said.

In addition, Hayes had to give his testimony out of the regular trial sequence because he, too, had a prior commitment and was only available to testify on the third day of the trial while the prosecution was still presenting its case. He testified, after which he departed.

The next day, Dr. Julie Wynne, the physician who treated the male assailant, was called to describe the gunshot injuries and her treatment of them. Attorney Rosenbluth asked if she observed any stippling on the man's torso, but her answers were inconclusive. Driving home afterward, the physician felt concerned about her answers and decided to look in her patient's files to verify her accuracy. Opening the files, she discovered photographs taken prior to his treatment.

"Instead of blowing it off, she called the prosecutor that night and told him, 'I have photos that I don't think you ever saw, and I think you guys need to see them. I think they could answer that question about ranges and things of that nature,'" Messmer related.

"It was an honest error, I think, on the prosecutor's part," said Messmer. "I don't think he even knew they had the photos. The prosecutor has done numerous cases where people have gone to the hospital, and we have never seen photos like this before. Now we see them all the time because we know to ask for them."

Messmer and the rest of Hickey's defense team found the late introduction of the photographs surprising, as well. "That was really a unique situation," he said. "I've been doing this for nine years; my legal assistant has been doing it for 18 years, and Mike Rosenbluth has been doing this for 18 years, and that is the first time any of us has seen anything like that happen."

The newly discovered pictures were brought into court after Hayes testified to his best estimates of how close the male assailant was standing when he was shot. "I testified to the best of my ability based on the physical damage done to the hand and the lack of photographs of all the wounds on his body. There were three gunshot wounds to his body: two in the torso, one in the hand."

Did the new photos change Hayes' opinion? "Yes, we later found out through looking at these photographs that I was probably off base on how the male assailant's hand was struck by a bullet," he confirmed.

By the time the photos were discovered, Hayes had returned home.

"I was already back home by when I got the phone call and a frantic email from the defense saying, 'Have you ever seen these pictures? What do you think of these?' I was just livid that I was never given this information to begin with."

Before he left the witness stand, Hayes also testified how easily a person armed with a handgun can be disarmed and gave the jury a demonstration. During cross-examination, Nicolini learned that Hickey was not trained by Marty Hayes and that Hayes was giving his expert testimony in this case at no charge. When asked why, Hayes answered, "Because, throughout my career, I have seen people who are being wrongfully prosecuted. I have looked at the evidence, and I decided this is simply wrong. If those people don't have the financial resources to hire experts, then they still need this type of credible witness, so over the years, I've done a few of these without being paid."

Hickey was not a Network member, Hayes explained, and Nicolini asked if the Network's "objective ... [is] to challenge prosecution where self-defense is claimed by the shooter?" Hayes responded, "I would say that the mission of the organization is to help people who are being wrongfully prosecuted."

The Prosecutor's Theory

Material experts who testified on Hickey's behalf included several instructors, ranging from the man who taught an early Arizona concealed handgun licensing class Hickey took, to his mentor, James Yeager, from whom he took many classes and for whom he eventually went on to become an adjunct instructor. Initially, Nicolini grilled Hickey about the concepts and principles Yeager taught him, using notes and handouts from classes, and later, he went over the same material with the instructor himself, discussing avoidance, de-escalation, gunfight tactics and many of Yeager's similes, acronyms and catchy phrases — tools that the instructor used to help students remember important principles.

Alarmingly, out-of-context advice from instructors to "always cheat; always win" and the axiom that one should treat everyone else in a polite manner while simultaneously having a plan to kill them painted an inaccurate picture about Hickey's outlook on life. Nicolini harvested these quotes from the training notes and handouts and made much hay with them, especially during his closing arguments in which he described Hickey in highly inflammatory terms.

The prosecutor told the jury not to consider the case from Hickey's viewpoint, from "what was going on in his paranoid mind," but to apply the reasonable person standard. "This is not a case of self-defense; this is not a case of defending a third person, even if you accept his version of how it went down," urged Nicolini.

"He is lying about how it happened. And you know why he is lying? First of all, he ... has got the same motivation to lie about these facts that any criminal defendant has in this situation, he does not want to be convicted. But I think Larry Hickey has an additional motivation, in this case, he wants to be vindicated; he wants somebody to say, yes, Larry, you exercised your Second Amendment rights to defend yourself and your family like a good American. And you know something else? The same reason why four of his gun instructors have come in here to testify, the people who taught him to use guns and when to use guns and taught him that aggressive mindset, like Jim Yeager, they want to be vindicated, too. But there is no vindication for Mr. Hickey in this case. It didn't happen as he said it happened," the prosecutor alleged.

"Larry brought a gun to a fist fight and used it to shoot two unarmed people, and even if you believed his version of facts, I submit that you must convict him of these charges because the thing is, he was trigger happy. He was a gun-toting, trigger-happy guy, who pulled out his gun in a situation where it absolutely was not required," reads the transcript of parts of Nicolini's closing.

"Reading the transcripts later, I realized this trial was not just about Larry Hickey and his actions," explained Hayes. "This was the Pima County Prosecutor's Office putting the concept of the armed lifestyle on trial because Nicolini attacked the whole concept of taking training, carrying a gun 24/7. He tried to paint the picture that anybody who would do that is really out of whack with society. There was a lot of discussion in his closing about the type of training that Larry took. Nicolini called Larry a liar; he called him a wannabe cop, a wannabe soldier. Frankly, I think it was demeaning to the whole of jurisprudence to see a prosecutor go to those extremes to try to get a conviction when there was nothing in the evidence or record to support his allegations.

"He went overboard."

Messmer reported that he closed out his part of the trial hammering home the fact that "Larry was never the aggressor. I took the jury step by step through what he did to defuse the situation, to deescalate and try to do everything possible to avoid pulling that gun.

"And then I attacked the prosecution's ridiculous attack about too much training," Messmer said. "How is it possible for someone to have too much training? I alluded to similar circumstances that you wouldn't want a doctor to avoid going to training and learning the newest medical procedures, you wouldn't want your lawyer to not keep up on his legal education, and that Larry wasn't just going out there to learn this to be some Rambo. He was actually using this to be an instructor for our troops.

"I think that hit home," Messmer related.

As the last point in both cases, he described the attackers as a three-headed monster. In trial transcripts from the first trial, Messmer is quoted as describing the male assailant's entry into the fight, "Now he [Hickey] is not only dealing with two women, but he is dealing with three people attacking him — this monster, this three-headed, six-fisted, six-footed that can stomp you when you fall down monster — and he adds that the male, a young man in excellent physical condition, is throwing hammer punches to Hickey's head.

"What happens if Larry goes down and they get to his wife?" Messmer asked the jury.

"We know his kid is somewhere around the area; he is coming out, he is looking. We know he was out sometime shortly after that; not only are they possibly going to beat up the wife, but if Larry goes down and he's knocked out, and his gun comes out, then they have a free gun in the hands of these attackers."

Hung Jury

The first trial against Larry Hickey for multiple counts of aggravated assault with a deadly weapon started on September 29 and concluded with closing arguments on October 7, 2009. When the jury returned, nine voted to acquit and three to convict. They were unable to come to a unanimous decision, and the case closed with a hung jury. Had the jury agreed to con-

ALARMINGLY, OUT-OF-CONTEXT ADVICE FROM INSTRUCTORS TO "ALWAYS CHEAT; ALWAYS WIN" AND THE AXIOM THAT ONE SHOULD TREAT EVERYONE ELSE IN A POLITE MANNER WHILE SIMULTANEOUSLY HAVING A PLAN TO KILL THEM PAINTED AN INACCURATE PICTURE ABOUT HICKEY'S OUTLOOK ON LIFE.

vict him, Hickey would have faced a 45-year jail sentence, provided that the convictions on the various charges ran concurrently.

Messmer explained that after the trial, some of the jurors agreed to talk about the case with the defense team. "The feeling we got was that they just would not come off the fact that three individuals did not have a weapon and that it was gun versus no gun. They felt that even though these people probably were the attackers, Larry probably didn't have a right to use his gun at that point in time."

Hayes admitted that he was not surprised when he received two emails from Matthew Messmer, the first telling him that the trial had ended with a hung jury and the second that the State intended to retry Hickey.

Hayes remembered his reaction: "Well, I said, that makes sense because there were really two stories being told. While we had the physical evidence to back up Larry's version of the events, they had more witnesses to tell the other story."

He said that the jurors had to weigh conflicting information between what the physical evidence showed and what the eyewitnesses said.

"The eyewitnesses were also the individuals who Larry shot and they were, frankly, kind of a sympathetic group," Hayes said. "There was a lot of evidence on both sides, and it didn't surprise me there was a hung jury."

When Messmer emailed a second time, he asked if Hayes would consider helping with a second trial. "He asked, 'Are you up for it again?'" Hayes said. "'... Darned right we are. Let's lock and load.'"

Two scant weeks passed between the end of the first trial and the State's announcement that it intended to try Hickey a second time. Though the State dropped several of the charges, if his attorneys did not prevail this time, Hickey estimates that he would have faced a sentence of approximately 30 years. Offered the option of pleading guilty to two felonies, Hickey would have probably served two years in jail, expecting a reduced sentence for good behavior.

"At no time did I ever personally entertain accepting a plea," Hickey exclaimed. "Counsel told me about the risks [of a second trial], but I was pretty adamant with them. The attorney has to do his due diligence, though, so they told me things like the conviction rate for this county attorney's office was 92 percent, and on retrials, it is 95 percent. Then, you don't know what kind of a jury you'll get, and the State now knows your testimony, so they will be more prepared.

"They let me know that I had a tougher fight ahead. It worried me," Hickey admitted. Still, he elected to go back to trial, noting that although the shorter sentence might be easier to contemplate, "It is not justice, so we turned down the plea offer."

New Trial Strategy

Messmer immediately vowed that in the second trial he would not simply present a re-do of the original arguments, and Hayes offered him an innovative solution. "I said, 'Let me run this idea by you.' I told Messmer that Massad Ayoob could testify to everything I testified to in the first trial, plus talk about weapons retention issues and disparity of force issues to a greater degree. We began planning to have Massad serve in the role that I had in the first trial. Then I volunteered to go to Tucson to serve as a defense consultant to help sort out some of the issues as they came up in court."

Ayoob, who had consulted during preparation for the first trial, joined the second defense effort enthusiastically. "I'm not sure there were things that I testified to that Marty could not have handled," Ayoob interjects modestly. "However, the strategy was to have on the defense team someone analogous in their role to the lead investigator who was working at the prosecution table. There you have someone deeply familiar with proper protocols for shooting investigations, crime scene reconstruction, bullet trajectories and angles who can advise the prosecutor on how to best establish his case in front of the jury.

"Marty fulfilled that role for the defense team. It is rare that a defense team has that, and I think it was absolutely critical. The second time around, it allowed a stronger defense to be established."

Ayoob gave testimony about how students are taught to recognize the lethal threat of disparity of force. He told the jury how in Hickey's situation, the male assailant's blind side attack in conjunction with the ongoing attack by the two females tipped the balance creating a deadly situation in which Hickey's decision to shoot was justified.

Civil Suit Settled

Before and during the first trial, Hickey's homeowners' insurance began receiving demand letters from Hickey's assailants wanting to tap into

his insurance to cover their medical bills and collect damages. Expecting
to be acquitted at trial, Hickey directed his insurance company to deny the
demands.

Within 30 days after the end of the first trial, his assailants had filed
a civil lawsuit for monetary damages. Hickey asked his insurer to obtain a
civil attorney for him. Like his insurer, Hickey came to view the settlement
as purely a business decision, recognizing that in a civil case, the plaintiffs
need only convince a majority of the jurors that their argument is more likely
valid than not, unlike the criminal case in which the standards of proof are
considerably higher. Recognizing that a loss in civil court could cost more
than the $100,000 limit of his insurance, Hickey acquiesced, a settlement
was reached, and the $100,000 apportioned primarily to the two who were
shot in the fracas, although all three had attempted to collect. In attempting to get money from Hickey's insurer, the assailants made a number of
depositions, which proved useful later. Messmer called those depositions
ammunition for the defense "because once again, they changed their story."

To claim monetary damages against homeowners insurance, the trio
had to change their stories about where the altercation occurred, from the
middle of the street to its actual location, the Hickey family driveway. "That
is the problem with having to keep your stories straight," Hickey said, speaking carefully and trying not to sound accusatory.

When police interviewed his assailants, not one admitted to striking
Hickey, and they made odd accusations that he didn't say a word to them,
only laughed and started shooting. The original female assailant continued
with that story through the first trial, but in the depositions for the civil case,
she said that Hickey asked them to return to their home, but she chose not
to because she wanted the argument resolved.

In addition, although he had told investigating police officers that he
had not hit Hickey, the male assailant testified in both criminal trials that he
had hit Hickey in the head. Hickey recalled that testimony: "In my mind, that
was like a 'Matlock moment,' an "AH, HA!' like in the TV show *Matlock*. On
TV, that is where the judge says, 'Case dismissed!' Well, that does not happen in real life! But the jurors hear it, and they see this individual squirm on
the stand when they are made to read their own testimony. The jury is not
stupid, thankfully."

The State Tries Again

Messmer resolved that his defense strategy in the second criminal trial would be much more than a do-over of the first. "I think the prosecutor just thought we were going to do a replay and have the same opening and same closing," Messner said. "We really had to go back and learn this stuff even better. On the second trial, it was more important to keep Marty Hayes involved, and his suggestion was absolutely great."

Freed of the ordinary trial restrictions through which witnesses are commonly sequestered, Hayes could be in the courtroom all throughout the trial and, from that broader view, advise on trial strategy. Hayes cited an example of a red herring the prosecutor introduced into the first trial that his advice to the defense helped them avoid in the second. "In the first trial, Nicolini was all concerned about the gun that Larry used. It was a standard Glock 19 loaded with a combination of Silvertip ammunition and some other miscellaneous ammo that was at the bottom of the mag. He was trying to paint the picture of this gun being inherently dangerous, reckless, unsafe, saying, 'It doesn't have a safety on it, does it?' I thought it was kind of weird that he was attacking the gun as much as he was, so I just simply answered the questions as honestly as I could and didn't give him any ammunition to work with."

Hayes continued, "In the second trial, I made it clear to the defense team that you need to establish ahead of time what guns the local police use because they all use .40-caliber Glocks which are generally more powerful than 9mm. So in the second trial, we established through a detective's testimony that their gun was a .40-caliber Glock and guess what? Nicolini knew what we had done, and he never made the gun an issue in the second trial."

Seated in the courtroom directly behind the defense team, Hayes watched, listened and did his best to judge how testimony was being received and what the prosecution had up its sleeve. When something concerned him, he would jot a brief message on a sticky note that he handed to Messmer's paralegal, Jacqueline Britt, who in turn passed it on up to Messmer or Rosenbluth at the defense table with Hickey. "We tried to do it as discreetly as possible so as not to be disruptive," Hayes recalled, noting that neither prosecutor nor judge challenged the activity, and he believes the jury was all but unaware of it.

"When the prosecution was giving their case, I would be looking into how to cross-examine their witnesses and look for discrepancies between their testimony and what I knew about the case," Hayes said. "Understand that 90 to 95 percent of the time, Messmer or Rosenbluth knew that and were already on top of it. I told them, 'I don't know what is in your mind, so I'm going to keep sending these notes,' and they said, 'Just keep sending them.' Occasionally, I would bring up something they hadn't thought about, and we would get that into the cross-examination or the direct examination for some of the defense witnesses."

"I can't believe that we had such luck!" Messmer said. "In addition to Mike [Rosenbluth], we have my legal assistant, Jackie, we have Larry working the trial, but now we also have Marty, who is right behind us and has a different viewpoint and who can tell us what is going on with the firearms. That, too, was very important. We delved into the specifics about the uniqueness of self-defense law even more than in the first trial."

Messmer drew on testimony from Ayoob, as well as bringing out testimony from material witnesses Richard Batory, James Yeager and police sergeant Brian Kowalski, who had been Hickey's instructors. They testified to information upon which Hickey acted when he defended himself and his family. Messmer suggested that in the first trial, they expected Hickey's extensive training to speak for itself. "In the second trial, we needed to ask, 'What was this class about? Why did you take that class? Why was that useful?'" he explained.

Unfortunately, Kowalski fell seriously ill right before he was scheduled to testify, and all parties involved agreed that his testimony from the first trial would suffice. Using transcripts from the earlier trial as scripts, the judge, prosecutor and a "reader" played the roles. Hayes was selected to read Kowalski's words, with several odd moments resulting.

The first came when the prosecutor had asked Kowalski to comment on Hayes' testimony in the first trial, which had preceded Kowalski's. The police sergeant responded in glowing terms, which caused Hayes to chuckle, and the prosecutor to break off from his script and ask, "He is talking about you, isn't he?" After that, the court did its best to move on with the testimony. It was going fine until they reached a point in the policeman's testimony in which he gave demonstrative testimony in addition to his spoken words.

According to Hayes, "In that first trial, Nicolini had asked Kowalski to demonstrate a retention firing position. Apparently, Kowalski got up and showed the jury what that meant. Because this was demonstrative testimony and not verbal testimony, we were kind of stuck. Knowing me from the first trial, the judge said, 'Well, I think Mr. Hayes is qualified to demonstrate that.' So I got up in front of the jury and demonstrated some of this demonstrative evidence even though I'd never been sworn in as a witness," Hayes marveled.

"Frankly, I think that would have been an appealable issue if they had wanted to appeal it, though I don't think it would have gone anywhere because it didn't really affect the outcome of the case, and it did not prejudice either side," Hayes said. "That was a surreal moment. Afterwards, I went back and sat behind the defense and started passing notes again."

Of course, most of the trial was deadly serious. The expert testimony of Massad Ayoob clarified the very real threat of death or crippling injury Hickey faced on November 17, 2008, when he was set upon by the two sisters and the boyfriend. "We had to explain to the jury that there were multiple issues going on," Ayoob began. One issue he clarified was Hickey's fast decision when his strategy changed from fending off the blows to drawing and firing his Glock pistol, explaining how the addition of the young man changed the threat to Hickey.

When the young man jumped into the fight, the circumstances changed "from two females — two fairly good-sized, and one very athletic female — against one medium-sized male," he explained. "Now we had not only the tilting of the balance by the very aggressive, buffed-out young male, but with that, we had the blind side attack of the sucker punch to the head that Larry, with his medical training, realized was very close to rendering him unconscious as he sees flashes of white light."

The danger of passing out introduced an additional justification beyond disparity of force and disparity in numbers, Ayoob explained, describing how disparity of force occurs when an able-bodied person attacks a disabled person. That applies even if the disability occurs during the fight. Applying those definitions to Hickey's situation, Ayoob explained, "Larry knows that in a moment he will pass out. There is absolutely no reason to believe that someone who would join in a three-to-one attack and who would throw a sucker punch from an unseen angle would suddenly turn into the Marquis of Queensberry, as the prosecution said, and let it go at the single punch and say, 'Ah, ha! I have taught you to be a gentleman.' That was one of the prosecution's more ludicrous points," he said chuckling grimly.

"I explained that once he was down, he would be helpless," said Ayoob. "A reasonable and prudent person in his situation, knowing what he knew, could expect to be stomped to death or horribly crippled. There was no reason to believe these people who would commit such an aberrant, violent three-against-one assault, would suddenly turn charitable, merciful, normal and benevolent."

"We had to also explain that Larry knew what they did not: that if they continued to maul him when he was down that they were very like to find a loaded Glock 19 that he was legally carrying, his wife was not only within the line of physical attack but also in the line of fire if they got that gun away from him and he had reason to believe that his little boy was threatened, as well. All those things came together in his mind," Ayoob said.

Ayoob's testimony also showed the jury how Hickey's assailants changed their stories from their initial statements, to testimony in the first trial, to depositions for the civil case, to the testimony the jury had heard in this, the second trial. He pointed out that they had changed their testimony about sequences of events, their locations and what they were doing. "One of the State's witness' testimony about where she was when she was shot was inconsistent with the angle of the gunshot wound and was actually physically impossible. We used a Ring's Blue Gun with a Crimson Trace laser, and that proved to be very effective evidence," Ayoob remembers.

"I think it is another classic example of why certain things need to be articulated at the scene, as I have taught for 30 years," Ayoob said. "The other side is saying you've done all these horrible things and manipulating the story at will. Here, they said, 'It happened in the street,' because they realized, 'Wait a minute, we did attack him on his own property. We can't let that come out,' so they said, 'He came out and met us in the street.'

"Really?" Ayoob wonders. "Why are the blood stains on his property?"

The woman testified that after Hickey shot her in the lower leg, she hopped onto the Hickey driveway. "By some magic, no blood dripped from the massive, hemorrhaging gunshot," Ayoob interjected sarcastically.

"That was one of the things that I explained on the stand: that it would be virtually impossible for that particular wound that was bleeding copiously not to have bled and have left bloodstains on the street," Ayoob recounted. "When they did their civil suit, in deposition, the same witnesses said under oath, 'Did I say it happened on the street? Oh, no, it happened on *his* property,' because the homeowner's liability policy won't cover something that happens on a public street."

"So essentially what you have is these witnesses who blatantly, totally changed their story to whatever served them in whatever setting they were in, criminal or civil. Messmer and his team had to meet it, and I believe they met it successfully," he concluded.

Had things gone disastrously wrong and the jury voted to convict Hickey, both Ayoob and Hayes identified issues they believe would have been grounds for an appeal for a new trial.

Ayoob pointed out, "The judge ignored case law from right there in Arizona, fairly fresh case law in the Harold Fish case, that said that the jury had the right to know anything about the assailant that would cause them to be particularly dangerous even if it was not known to the defendant when they shot them. Now that is a very welcome turnaround from Federal rule of evidence 404B that says prior bad acts by the opponent unless known to you cannot be used in your defense for harming that opponent.

"For whatever reason, the judge chose not to go that way, and the jury never knew that one of those substantial-sized women was athletic and spent a good deal of time working out in a Brazilian jujitsu dojo and had put on her Facebook page prior to the incident that she 'loved to grapple.' But at trial, she's presented as a helpless June Cleaver in a cocktail dress being attacked by the savage, crazed mercenary gun nut, when in fact, she was one of the ones who initiated the attack on Hickey who was attempting throughout to be the peacemaker," Ayoob said.

"The prosecutor won that one," Ayoob accounts. "I think had Hickey been convicted, we would have won on appeal, but it was an uphill fight. That has always been one of the curses of this: attacked by someone with a long, violent history, unless the other side opens the door by blatantly saying you can't believe that someone as nice as the one who was harmed could have attacked this defendant. This prosecutor was wise enough that he did not; he did that by innuendo, but not by statement, so that particular door did not open."

Also kept out of the trial was the videotape of the murder of Constable Lunsford by three considerably smaller suspects during a car search for drugs.

"I think we all thought that was an appealable issue that could have set Larry free if he had been convicted," Hayes said. "There certainly was case law applicable, but the judge felt the video was too graphic and too prejudicial. Well, this was a prejudicial case in which he was being accused with three counts of aggravated assault. And this was in front of him, and I think the jury should have seen it. That was a setback."

Hayes mused further, "Having said that, I think that Messmer's closing argument was the pivotal point in the second trial. I remember a lot of passion and the fact that Messmer really believed that he had a truly innocent individual, which was not the norm for a public defender. He had a lot of passion in his voice when discussing it. In fact, at one point, he had to take a break because he was getting too involved with the argument. He took a break, and then he came back and finished up his closing. To me, that was the biggest part of the case."

Hung Again

On May 25, 2010, when the second trial came to an end, eight members of the jury voted to acquit, two to convict, and two were unable to reach a decision. This jury was quite different than the first. The State had used all of its challenges to disallow any jury picks that admitted to owning guns, had licenses to carry, or had prior police, military or correctional work experience, Hickey remembered.

"Usually, the prosecution wants the law-abiding types, cops, people with a sense of right or wrong. Those were the people I wanted on my jury," Hickey said. "This time, the State assiduously avoided those types of people, and the jury included a mix of retired folks and citizens who Hayes characterizes as being "antsy because they just wanted to get back to their jobs."

According to Messmer, "On the second trial, we had a juror that was a lawyer. In hindsight, we shouldn't have picked him because lawyers overanalyze everything. He's one of the ones who voted against us, and we were absolutely shocked. And he said, 'Hey, I went in there, and I said, 'No, you can't use a weapon even if there are three on one if they don't have a weapon.'"

While Messmer will be the first to say he learned a lot in preparing Larry Hickey's defense, he stresses that attorneys need to know more about self-defense and the law. "I'm glad you are doing this article. I really do think that the lawyers need to be educated about it because it is different when you read on a page what the law is, but when you see this kind of training that Larry had, the kind of perspective that Marty and Ayoob had about this case, it is a totally different thing than what we are used to."

"We certainly would have talked to people around here, but the knowledge that was available to us through Marty and Ayoob was outstanding and made us able to attack the case and gave us ideas that I don't know as lawyers that we would have picked up because we don't always know how to start," Messmer admitted. "It gave us better arguments because we were not thinking as lawyers; we were more taking our law and applying it to actual firearms and that kind of self-defense training. I don't know that we would have gotten that on our own."

After recounting his ordeal from beginning to end, Hickey emphasized that he no longer believes that a trial is about right and wrong, crime and justice. "It seems to be about winning and losing," he mused. For example, he cited how a judge arbitrarily controls what evidence to allow into the trial and what to keep out.

"People need to understand how it works," Hickey said. "You think you are going to be able to present this evidence, and that evidence and everyone will be able to see it clearly. Well, the judge decides what evidence you are going to present."

Because during the fight Hickey's mind had flashed to the video in which three small people kill a large "line-backer sized" police officer, his defense wanted to show the jury the video. The judge would not allow it, though she did allow Hickey to talk about it. "I think the judge was a very fair individual, but that was just a decision she made."

The defense was prevented from presenting material from the Arizona Department of Public Safety's required Concealed Handgun Licensing curriculum that specifically addressed disparity of force when attacked by multiple assailants who are unarmed.

The outcome in a case like Hickey's can also hinge on how the police handle the evidence. Hickey said that at one point during his first trial, he overheard prosecution members talking about the manner in which Hickey had carried his Glock that night. Something he heard made him worried that the prosecution intended to allege that before the shooting, Hickey had his gun tucked in his waistband without a holster, something that would be consistent with running into the house and grabbing a gun. Concerned, he mentioned it to his lawyers, who casually asked the detective who was sitting at the next table if the prosecution had brought Hickey's holster with them. The detective responded, "There was no holster; he didn't have a holster."

Hickey remembered that, by good fortune, the officer who arrested him was due to testify next. Since in court it is not a good idea to ask a question to which you do not know the answer, Hickey's attorney ran through a series of questions starting by asking if the witness took the defendant into custody, whether he gave him a cursory pat down before putting him in the patrol car, and what, if anything the pat down produced.

The officer answered that yes, he took a holster off Hickey and that he put it in evidence. "That holster could never be found, not that we needed it, because the guy admitted to taking it," Hickey recounted. It was later found after the State released Hickey's firearm. When Hickey went to pick up the gun, the clerk asked offhandedly if he wanted "this other stuff." Hickey asked what it was, and the woman gave him some shoes, socks and the missing holster. Further inquiry showed a minor error in the number under which that evidence was logged. Those things just fell through the cracks, Hickey explained.

Hickey characterized the error as, "Not a huge deal, but if it had gone the other way and the prosecutor was able to convince the jury that I was lying and that I was not carrying a firearm in a holster — that I just went in and stuffed a gun in my pants and went out looking for trouble — that makes me wonder."

Throughout a lengthy interview with Hickey, at no time did he express malice or anger toward law enforcement or the criminal justice system. If pushed, he will acknowledge that the system failed him, especially in the early days of his incarceration, but in admitting that, his tone of voice remains even and dispassionate.

"All of the officers that testified were great," he said. "They got up there, and they told the truth about what they observed, their experiences, my demeanor when they responded. I mean, they were great. I don't think there was anything malicious about this prosecution."

Reality

Hickey wants other armed citizens to know, though, that real life bears little resemblance to TV or movie dramas. During classes, roundtable discussions, and on Internet forums, people converse about what might happen. "Very rarely is it about your neighbors attacking you," Hickey said. "It is about a tattooed gang-banger who is robbing the liquor store or the bank. People don't think about your neighbors coming over to kill you or seriously injure you or your family. People think you are going to save the day, and people are going to hoist you up on their shoulders, and it is not always like that. Still, this is the best system we've got. You get your chance in court.

"We learn from others' use of force experiences, and you can learn a lot of court stuff from this one. I want to help people avoid the situation I found myself in and avoid the court fight," he emphasized.

Messmer noted that his defense of Larry Hickey will stand out in his mind as different from other cases in his career. "I thought we did a really good job because we had a great team. Leading up to it, I was absolutely scared for Larry and worried about whether we were going to do the right thing. Once we got to trial, I had no doubts about what we were doing. I knew we were doing it right.

"Sometimes, athletes talk about being in the zone. I felt during these trials that I was in the zone and that the team we had was in the zone. During the closing, I had no doubt that I was able to reach the jury. At least they were listening, and I could tell, doing this as long as I've done it, that I was reaching them."

Messmer feels pride and satisfaction in the outcome of the two trials. "I think, no matter what, no matter how many good cases that I do in the future, because of the uniqueness of this case and all the hard work and the job that we did and especially the resources that were provided to us, this one definitely will go down in memory as one of my better cases, one of my personal accomplishments," he said.

"I would have liked to walk out of there with a jury victory, but we still got the victory, so I'm going to hang it up [as noteworthy] because Larry walked away free, and he was absolutely innocent."

About a month elapsed before the State decided not to take Hickey to trial a third time. "It took two trials, but all my charges were dismissed with prejudice which means they could never come back again," Hickey said. "I can't help but think that the same State that dismissed my charges would not have a problem if I had taken a plea and would be sitting in jail today. To me, that is scary."

As soon as the dismissal was announced, Hickey's attackers had him served with an injunction against harassment, essentially a restraining order that precluded him from owning firearms or coming within a specified distance of them.

"We chose the better part of valor and didn't move back into our home right away," Hickey explained. "We knew that as soon as I showed up, this individual would call the police, and the police would have to make a decision, and that decision would probably be that I would have to go to jail."

He hired a civil attorney, and they requested a hearing. "I knew I had to fight this because it was just ridiculous and had no basis in fact. The woman's statement in the injunction was that back in November 2008, in an argument, Mr. Hickey shot me, and she also made something up about how my wife would park outside of her house and stare at her, so the judge rubber-stamped it," he explained.

On June 14, 2010, following a 2 ½ hour hearing before a city court magistrate, the plaintiff's injunction was quashed. The magistrate took pains to consider all the facts before removing the injunction, retiring to his chambers at one point to consult with Judge Godoy, who had officiated at the two previous trials. Oddly, during the hearing, the plaintiff told the magistrate that she really didn't have any problems with Hickey and that he was welcome to come over to her house to have a soda if he liked so long as he didn't bring a gun along. She stated that she wanted the injunction to prevent Hickey from possessing firearms. The magistrate decided in Hickey's favor. With that decision, Hickey was finally able to return to his home, free of the threat to his freedom and way of life, a black cloud he had lived under since the night of November 17, 2008.

"As an instructor, I teach a lot of foreign weapons classes for a local company that is contracted to teach the military," Hickey said. "My hearing was on Monday, June 14th, and I had orders to be at Camp Pendleton to teach Marines on Monday and Tuesday the 14th and 15th. I didn't get to teach on Monday, but as soon as the judge quashed the order that I couldn't own a firearm, I drove to Oceanside, California, and taught the next day."

Hickey and his family have now returned to live in their home up the driveway from the place the attack occurred. The sisters and their sons still live across the street.

Editor's Note: This article appeared in its original version in the Armed Citizens Legal Defense Network (ACLDN) newsletter. ■

CHAPTER 12:
LESSONS FROM RECENT CONTROVERSIAL CASES

Note: The following first appeared as Mas' Self-Defense and the Law column in Combat Handguns *magazine, July/August 2022 edition, and is reprinted here with the permission of the publisher, Athlon Media.*

When post-shooting pitfalls come under discussion, some naïve souls always cry, "None of that matters! A good shoot is a good shoot!" Whenever I hear that I want to answer, "Yeah, and next Christmas Eve, a chubby guy in a red suit is going to come down your chimney and give you presents, too."

Recent ordeals suffered by people who used deadly force under apparently justifiable circumstances have made national news. Some of their trials were broadcast live and archived for subsequent review by anyone at work when the trials went down. Unfortunately, much of the media portrayed the issues in these cases as if they were parroting the prosecution. An amazing number of people who should know better took the accusations as gospel. Let's look at a couple of examples.

The Totality of the Circumstances: The Rittenhouse Case

When a controversial police shooting in Kenosha, Wisconsin, triggered a riot complete with arson and looting, a 17-year-old named Kyle Rittenhouse, who lived 20 minutes away across the Illinois border, went to help. He was photographed scrubbing graffiti off of vandalized premises and offering first aid to injured people on the streets. Upon his arrival, he found a war zone: police officers at his trial testified that more people on the street were armed than not. Seeing this, Rittenhouse armed himself with a Smith & Wesson M&P 15 .223 rifle that he had given a friend money to purchase for him, with the stated plan that he would take legal possession when he turned 18. Rittenhouse took that rifle from the friend, carrying it loaded with a 30-round magazine.

Later that evening, Rittenhouse was attacked by a man with a serious felony record who had just gotten out of a hospital where he had been treated for suicidal ideation. That man chased Rittenhouse to a point where he could no longer flee and tried to grab his rifle, at which time Rittenhouse shot and killed him. Hostile people in the crowd chased Rittenhouse; three attacked him: one hit him in the head with a skateboard, and Rittenhouse killed him with a single shot. Another threw a flying kick and fled after Kyle shot at him, missing. Yet another pointed a .40-caliber Glock at Rittenhouse's head and received a bullet in the arm that caused him to flee. Rittenhouse ran toward the police with his hands up, trying to surrender, and was ordered by police to get out of the street. He went home, called the police, and turned himself in subsequently. Each element of the shooting was caught on video shown later in court. He was charged with multiple counts of Murder and Attempted Murder and was ultimately found Not Guilty on all charges. The acquittal still outrages many on the political left and those who oppose the right to self-defense.

First, each of his shootings was justified. The man who tried to take his gun with obviously hostile intent reached for a rifle; all the classic elements of self-defense were present. The man who kicked him in the head was attempting deadly force, which warranted a deadly force response. The guy with the skateboard? Clearly an assault with a deadly weapon: self-defense again. Guy with Glock 27 coming toward Rittenhouse's head: obviously justified.

The prosecution tried to claim that it was Rittenhouse's fault for illegally carrying the "deadly assault rifle" in the first place. The judge didn't buy that, and neither did the jury. Evidence showed Rittenhouse had come to Kenosha with benevolent intent, found himself in deadly danger, and had not violated the law by arming himself under such circumstances. The prosecutor tried to show that ball ammunition in the .223 was over-penetrative and could have killed multiple innocent people with each shot; since that didn't happen, that attempt to establish recklessness didn't fly. Had Kyle come to Kenosha on an ordinarily peaceful day, wielded an AR-15 in public, and shot innocent people out of bloodlust, he would indeed have been culpable: but the law demands that *the totality of the circumstances be taken into consideration.* The jury did so, ergo, Not Guilty.

The Initial Aggressor Element: The Arbery Case

You, holding a Remington 870 12-gauge shotgun, confront a burglary suspect who lunges at you, punches you in the face and tries to take your shotgun. You shoot him fatally. Self-defense?

Generally, yes. In this case, *no.* Ahmaud Arbery was a young man, a convicted shoplifter with a history of being aggressive toward police and was also suspected by locals of shoplifting. In a suburban Southeast Georgia neighborhood, he was spotted trespassing at a building under construc-tion. Well-meaning neighbors Gregory McMichael and his adult son Travis, both of whom had some degree of law enforcement experience, went to confront him, followed by another neighbor, William "Roddie" Bryan. The McMichaels in one pickup truck and Bryan, with a video recording going, in another attempted to stop Arbery, who was on foot. At one point, the elder McMichael wielded a .357 Magnum revolver and ordered Arbery to stop, or he would "blow his f***ing head off." As the McMichaels' truck stopped, Arbery lunged at the younger McMichael, striking him and grabbing for the gun, and was shot to death. Arbery was African-American, and his pursuers were Caucasian.

All three men were convicted of murder and given life sentences, both the McMichaels' sentences being without the possibility of parole. How did this happen, and why did the McMichaels receive so much less sympathy and support from the armed citizen community?

None of the pursuers had personally observed Arbery committing a crime. When the elder McMichael pointed a lethal weapon at Arbery and

The Remington 870 and Smith & Wesson 686 were the guns deployed in the Arbery case.

threatened to shoot him, he did not have grounds to detain him as a private citizen. His actions fulfilled all the requirements of a felony charge of Aggravated Assault. That put his pursuers in the position of being the *initial aggressors*, creating reasonable cause for someone in Arbery's position to reasonably believe that he was about to be kidnapped or murdered or both, in turn creating a reasonable belief that he had to counter-attack Travis Arbery in self-defense, and thus voiding Travis Arbery's claim of self-defense.

Lessons

First, Federal Rule of Evidence 404(b) generally precludes you from citing your opponent's previous criminal behavior in your defense if you did not know it when you pulled the trigger since it was not formative to your decision and action. Rittenhouse was acquitted despite his jury not knowing his first attacker was a violent man and a convicted child molester, nor that some of his other attackers had violent histories. The jurors who convicted the McMichaels and Bryan did not know that Arbery was not just a suspected thief but a convicted one.

Second, if we use force or threat of force without reasonable belief that it is necessary, we become The Bad Guy. If the McMichaels and Bryan had held back, kept their distance, called 911 and stayed in contact until police arrived, none of the subsequent events would have happened.

You must always consider the totality of the circumstances. You can never be the initial aggressor. You must act to the standards of the law, the standards by which you will be judged.

Note to readers: *this article is extrapolated from Massad Ayoob's lecture on lessons from controversial cases, put together for the Rangemaster Tactical Conference in Dallas in March 2022.* ■

The prosecution made a big issue of FMJ .223 and the 30-round magazine used in Case 1.

CHAPTER 13:
CONTROVERSIAL CASES: DIVING DEEPER

n the chapter immediately preceding this one, there were space limitations in my *Combat Handguns* article on the Rittenhouse and Arbery cases. We have room to go deeper in the updated *Deadly Force* book.

First, why does the author refer to one case by the defendant's name and the other by the man who was killed? That's because, thanks to the mainstream media, it's how most of the public recognizes those two cases. Long after his acquittal, Kyle Rittenhouse's name was still a household word, while only those who had known the parties or followed the case for professional reasons were likely to recall the names of the men he shot. Conversely, the press made Ahmaud Arbery a martyr, and only "those in the know" generally recognized the names of the three men involved in his death.

Let's look at some things both cases have in common, beyond being televised as they happened and becoming daily front-page news.

If you're involved in a shooting, your life becomes an open book, especially if the incident becomes controversial. Investigators will be talking to everyone they can find who has known you since childhood, looking for testimony that may paint you as bloodthirsty or racist. It is no trick today for police to get a judge to sign a warrant for any electronic device you have access to, smartphone and computers, and go over their contents with the proverbial fine-tooth comb. They will employ high-tech programs developed for investigating white-collar crime and child pornography. Emails, forum commentary, and social media messages you *thought* had been irretrievably deleted will be recovered and very likely introduced as state-of-mind evidence. In Rittenhouse's case, that didn't go much further than showing that the kid was an exuberant teenager who liked girls and played Call of Duty; much more devastating in the other case were recovered materials that indicated racial hatred and included the use of the N-word.

Court defenses are exorbitantly expensive. I have not seen an estimate of the legal expenses of Gregory and Travis McMichael and their neighbor Roddy Bryan in the Arbery matter. Still, we know that security costs during their trial reportedly went over one million dollars. It is estimated that much of the two-million dollars donated to the Rittenhouse defense went for his bail and to pay for his top-flight legal defense team.

Video evidence can be a two-edged sword. These controversial shootings were caught on smartphone video, and those images became landmarks in both trials. In the Rittenhouse case, they helped the defense far more than they hurt it because while the video captured all eight shots fired by the defendant, it also captured the attacks on him by four separate men, which justified him opening fire upon each of them. In the Georgia case, however, while the video showed the decedent punching one of the defendants in the head and then trying to wrestle his shotgun away from him, it also showed the pursuit of the same man by what the prosecution painted as a three-man gang of racists in a two-truck caravan attempting to corner an unarmed young black man. (One pundit likened the defendants to slave catchers.) Ironically, one of the defendants initially leaked that video, thinking it would show clear-cut self-defense.

In each case, men doing questionable things attacked a man armed with a long gun and attempted to disarm him. Two of the four attackers died in the Wisconsin case, and a third was permanently crippled by gunfire. In the Georgia case, the man who made that attempt was shot dead.

Also, in each case, the prosecution held that it could not be self-

defense to shoot an unarmed man. That is a blatant mischaracterization of the law. The principle of disparity of force, explained in detail elsewhere in this book, has been in effect in American law for as long as anyone reading this has been alive. Moreover, a man attempting to disarm another is *a man reaching for a gun!*

Going step by step through the sequence of shots in Kenosha, convicted child molester Joseph Rosenbaum was the first to die. According to the State's own Medical Examiner, who did the autopsy, Rosenbaum's hand was *on* the 17-year-old Rittenhouse's Smith & Wesson AR-15 when Rittenhouse fired the shots that killed him. On that night, Rosenbaum was the first to fall.

Next to come under fire was Maurice Freeland, whose name did not come out until well into the trial. He was the man who took a flying kick at Rittenhouse's head but misjudged the distance, fortunately not making solid contact. Rittenhouse fired two shots at him but missed and ceased fire when Freeland ran away.

Almost immediately, Anthony Huber swung a heavy skateboard at Rittenhouse's head and neck area — a deadly force assault — but did not make enough contact to do as much harm as he apparently intended. Rittenhouse shot him once in the chest, and Huber turned away, staggered a few steps, and collapsed, mortally wounded.

The last to take a bullet was Gaige Grosskreutz, who had lunged at the youth with a .40-caliber Glock 27 pistol in his right hand. When Rittenhouse turned his AR-15 on him, Grosskreutz raised his hands as if in surrender (though still holding his gun), and Rittenhouse held his fire. Grosskreutz admitted in court at trial that only when he swung his pistol down toward Rittenhouse did the young man fire the single shot, which, as Grosskreutz put it, "vaporized" the bicep of his gun arm. The pistol still dangling from the ruined arm, Grosskreutz ran away screaming "Medic!" and Rittenhouse ceased fire.

The defense made it clear — and the jury accepted — that this defendant was in deadly danger every time he fired.

What was different in the Georgia case? As I've explained earlier, the difference was the totality of the circumstances. If Arbery had broken into Travis McMichaels' home and McMichaels had righteously confronted him with his Remington 870, and Arbery had punched him in the head and tried to wrench the shotgun out of his hands, McMichaels would have had every right to fire those three times until the man let go of the weapon and turned away. It was the fact that McMichaels had been chasing Arbery, and his father threatening him with a gun without sufficient cause, which made the three white men the initial aggressors and gave the black man they were pursuing reasonable cause to turn on them and try to take control of Travis McMichaels' weapon.

Every single man Rittenhouse fired upon had been chasing and attacking *him.* By contrast, the three men convicted of murder in Georgia had been the ones chasing Ahmaud Arbery.

In both cases, the defendants took the stand. As discussed in depth elsewhere in this book, self-defense is an affirmative defense. It comes down to: "Why did you shoot him?" And only the person who pulled the trigger can truly answer that.

Why did that strategy win an acquittal in one case and result in convictions in the other? Simply because the defendants came across differently and the fact patterns of their cases differed. Rittenhouse seemed sincere to most observers, and the evidence showed that each time he pulled the trigger, he was the one clearly under attack. The McMichaels, particularly Travis, the one who fired the fatal shots, came across as well as they could have ... but they could not get past the fact that they had not been within the law when they pursued a man they couldn't show had done anything more than harmless trespass and had threatened to shoot Arbery in the head if he did not stop.

In each case, the jury was not allowed to know of prior bad acts by the deceased. Elsewhere in this book, we discuss Rule of Evidence 404(b), which holds that prior bad acts of the person who forced you to harm them generally cannot be introduced on your behalf if they were not known to you at the time you harmed them. Rosenbaum's years in prison for having sex with little boys couldn't come in, nor could the fact that he had just that day been released from a hospital where he had checked himself in as suicidal. (Never forget that suicide is inner-directed homicide, and the suicidal can quickly become homicidal.) Rosenbaum was extremely antagonistic with others in Kenosha throughout the night in question, at one point screaming at an armed man, "Shoot me, n*****!"

Anthony Huber, the man who struck Rittenhouse with the skateboard and tried to grab his gun before being shot in the heart, had a history of domestic violence convictions. He had at various times strangled his brother, held a knife to the brother's belly, kicked his sister, and threatened to burn a house down with his relatives inside. It is a history that casts doubt on some theories that he was benevolently trying to disarm what he thought was an active mass murderer.

Gaige Grosskreutz was forced to admit on the witness stand that he was illegally carrying his loaded, concealed Glock 27; his concealed carry permit expired. However, I've seen no indication of him being charged with doing so.

Ahmaud Arbery was a convicted thief: he had pled guilty to shoplifting and had a criminal record. Local merchants believed him to be "The Jogger," a shoplifter who would enter a store, steal an item and run away without paying for it. Since the conviction and Arbery's very identity were not known to the defendants, this information was not allowed to the jury because it was not formative to the decisions and actions for which they stood charged.

Specific Fine Points: The Rittenhouse Case

Self-defense expert John Murphy is a graduate of the Deadly Force Instructor Course that I've taught for many years with Marty Hayes. After the Rittenhouse trial, Murphy wrote in pistol-forum.com that prosecutor Thomas Binger had tried virtually every dirty trick I had warned about in the instructor class.

Throughout the trial, the prosecution called Rittenhouse's .223 semi-automatic an "assault rifle," even though they knew or should have known that virtually without exception, genuine ordnance experts reserve that term for rifles with fully automatic (i.e., machine gun) capability. Knowing that anti-gun forces have deliberately used this term to falsely demonize the most popular sporting rifle and home defense long gun in America, the prosecution used it to falsely show malicious intent, in this writer's opinion.

One theme of Rittenhouse's accusers was that he had "gone looking for trouble," "crossing state lines" when he went to Kenosha. Rittenhouse was the son of divorced parents who had shared custody of him, and though he mainly lived with his mother in Antioch, Illinois, he often drove the mere twenty miles to Kenosha, Wisconsin, to stay with his dad, who lived in that city. He had also worked as a lifeguard in Kenosha and felt strong ties to the community. Evidence showed that he had gone there with benevo-lent intent. There were images in evidence of him cleaning up graffiti in riot-torn Kenosha, and he had given first aid to one or more injured protesters before the shooting.

To this day, many people still believe Rittenhouse illegally transported the AR-15 rifle across state lines. However, it was proven in court that the gun never left the state of Wisconsin once it was purchased there by the defendant's slightly older friend. Rittenhouse took the rifle from the friend's house after he got to Kenosha and found himself in something close to a war zone; at trial, one of the police officers testified that more of the people on the street that night were armed than were not.

Significantly, the trial judge threw out the charge against Rittenhouse of being illegally armed under the circumstances, ruling that he was within Wisconsin law in that respect.

Prosecutor Binger tried to establish that Rittenhouse acted with malice in his choice of ammunition, at one point suggesting that the 55-grain full metal jacket .223 ammunition he used was designed to "explode" inside the body and was undoubtedly embarrassed when, in front of the jury, Judge Bruce Schroeder corrected him on that falsehood.

Binger then tried the same tactic from the opposite end, implying that Rittenhouse acted with reckless, wanton disregard for human life by using such ball ammunition, on the theory that the bullets were intended to shoot through human beings and likely to kill other, innocent victims beyond their intended target. While that is true of some ball ammunition, the type of .223 ball in the Rittenhouse gun did not do that and does not do that; FBI testing long ago determined that its penetration characteristics are similar to those of standard police service pistol bullets.

When he was cross-examined on this, Rittenhouse seemed a bit lost for an answer. The simplest answer to why he used that particular ammo would have been the truthful one: it was the only .223 ammo readily avail-able to him that night. The ammo issue does not appear to have hurt him in the eyes of the jury any more than did the fact that he, like countless other teenagers, had played Call of Duty.

Prosecutor Binger outraged gun owners everywhere (and probably a good many people in the Kenosha courtroom) when he picked up the evidence AR-15, put it to his shoulder, and swung it around with his finger on the trigger — his muzzle crossing countless people present. He was, of course, pretending to be Kyle Rittenhouse. This is a cheap shyster trick I've seen before, the accusing attorney pretending to be the defendant as he menaces the jury and other onlookers with the defendant's gun that's in evidence. It didn't win the prosecution any friends on the jury and didn't seem to have done so in other cases where the same dirty trick has been played.

A final point in the Rittenhouse trial that hit home with me was when Judge Schroeder ruled that none of the men who were shot would be referred to as "victims." The press dumped on the judge for that, but I applauded him. The unfortunate fact of a self-defense case is that historically, whoever gets shot has always been automatically the "victim," which creates the not-always-true assumption that whoever shot him was a criminal perpetrator. I recall one of my cases where the prosecutor handed me the defendant's gun and said, "Now, I show you the murder weapon." I replied curtly, "It's the death weapon, counselor. The jury will decide if it's a murder weapon." I think that the ruling by Judge Schroeder in the Rittenhouse case should be standard procedure in all such trials.

Specific Fine Points: The Arbery Case

There was a "higher standard of care" element in play in the Arbery case. The easiest way to explain a higher standard of care to a layman is that your accuser will say, "You, of all people, should have known better!"

Travis McMichael, who ended up being the shooter, had performed law enforcement functions while serving in the Coast Guard. His father, Gregory McMichael — who wielded the .357 and shouted a threat to Arbery that he would shoot him if he didn't cease his flight — had worked in law enforcement and had served as a district attorney's investigator. Each should have known that, acting as the "civilians" they now were, they did not have proper cause to threaten anyone with a gun. Their pursuit made them the initial aggressors and tore apart their "mantle of innocence," the legal cloak protecting the person who has done no wrong.

As a direct result of this case, the law changed in the state of Georgia, and "citizen's arrest" was, in effect, eliminated there. Many observers fear that this will have a profoundly negative effect on private citizens who confront genuine criminals in future encounters in Georgia.

We must always consider how our actions and appearance may be seen by others, including even criminal suspects we may face. It apparently did not occur to the white men pursuing Arbery that the young black man they were chasing might see them as an armed, racist three-man lynch mob in a two-truck caravan who had targeted him as a victim for possibly homicidal violence. (We, of course, cannot know if Arbery did perceive them as such, but that was exactly how the prosecution saw it and presented it. It is also how the jury saw it in the initial trial and the second.)

The hate crime issue. It was alleged that Travis McMichael uttered the words "Fuckin' n*****" moments after the shooting. A review of social media posted before the shooting reportedly revealed all manner of racist hate crime language on the defendants' part. Four months after their murder conviction, the defendants were convicted in Federal court of Interference With Rights, a hate crime.

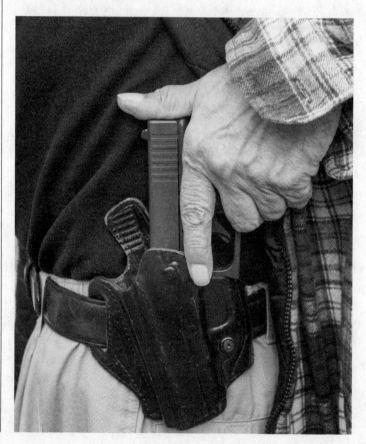

Such words at the scene might have been explained with expert testimony by psychiatrists and psychologists. We humans are verbal creatures. A frightened dog growls or barks; a frightened cat hisses; a frightened human may also utter out-of-character pejoratives. How can the defense explain a long history of racist screeds and epithets, which feed directly into accusations of malice?

In Summary

These two cases were tried so close together they partially overlapped. The trial in Wisconsin ran from November 1 through November 19, 2021, and the one in Georgia from October 15 to November 24 that year. Each took place under a cloud of nationwide disturbance growing out of the death of George Floyd in police custody in Minneapolis, and each unfolded before the eyes of the nation and the world.

What might have been seen as similar issues at first blush turned into profoundly different cases with radically different outcomes. At this writing, appeals are pending for the men convicted in the death of Ahmaud Arbery.

The lessons from both cases, and their trial outcomes, endure. ■

CHAPTER 14:
AFTER THE SHOOTING

I n the old days, we all followed the standard advice from defense lawyers: "Don't say anything to the police." A few years ago, a law professor's 45-minute lecture went viral on the internet with the same message: never talk to the cops. Interestingly, in three-quarters of an hour telling stories of guilty suspects who got hung by their tongue when they tried to outwit trained police interrogators, there's not a single instance of an innocent man getting in trouble for speaking to investigators. There's one case the professor mentions of a mentally ill man whose story was that he confessed to smoke out the actual perpetrator. My take: if you're crazy, maybe you *shouldn't* talk to the police. If you're a guilty criminal, talking to the police means you'll either tell the truth and inculpate yourself or lie to the cops and get caught.

Never forget that when you shoot someone, however necessarily and justifiably, you look an awful lot like a killer, and he looks an awful lot like a victim. The stereotype can take hold quickly if you don't act to let the authorities — from the first responding officer to the designated lead investigator — know what happened. The old saying "You only get one chance to make a first impression" is valid here.

Decades ago, I developed a five-point checklist of things I feel the righteous shooter needs to establish as soon as possible in the aftermath. It's been widely adopted, sometimes with attribution and sometimes without, and is now recommended by entities ranging from the Armed Citizens Legal Defense Network to the US Concealed Carry Association. I'm rather proud of that.

The location of spent casings is not consistent, and in the author's opinion, can't exactly determine the shooter's position. Nonetheless, casings and other evidence should be pointed out at the scene as soon as possible.

Five-Point Checklist

1. Establish the active dynamic. That is, let the authorities know immediately what happened. If you have harmed someone in self-defense, always remember that the active dynamic is not what you did to him; it's what he was trying to do to you or another victim. The active dynamic is his action that forces your lawful response. It's not, "I shot him." It's, "This man tried to kill me." Or, "This man attacked my wife." Whatever it was that led to your use of force.

This makes it clear that the guy on the ground doing a convincing imitation of a victim is, in fact, the criminal perpetrator. It makes it clear that you, the person with the smoking gun who just shot someone, are, in fact, the intended victim.

If one or more of your attackers has left the scene, *explain that now, and give their description.* It will be hard for people to see you as the innocent party if you fail to let the police know that a violent criminal is at large.

> " NEVER FORGET THAT WHEN YOU SHOOT SOMEONE, HOWEVER NECESSARILY AND JUSTIFIABLY, YOU LOOK AN AWFUL LOT LIKE A KILLER, AND HE LOOKS AN AWFUL LOT LIKE A VICTIM.

2. Indicate that you will cooperate with the police by testifying against the man who forced you to draw the gun or signing a complaint against him. There are two roles open in this particular play: victim and perpetrator. As noted, appearances can create mistaken role reversal if things aren't immediately clarified. By making a statement to the police to the effect of "I will sign a complaint against (the person who attacked me)," you reinforce the fact that you are the victim-complainant, the good guy or gal, and the person you're signing the complaint on is the bad guy who forced you to harm him in legitimate defense of self or others. (Note: I would not advise using the phrase "I will press charges." The reason is that legal terminology varies slightly from jurisdiction to jurisdiction. While in many jurisdictions, it is indeed the complainant who presses charges, there are some places where the local terminology is such that the prosecutor "presses charges." If you inadvertently find yourself in one of those places and say, "I will press charges," it sounds to the police as if you have delusions of being the elected chief prosecutor, and you won't be off to a good start. "I will sign the complaint" is neutral and nearly universal.)

The late Jim Cirillo, a friend and mentor of the author, was living proof that after multiple justified homicides, a good person could go on to enjoy life and family.

3. Point out the evidence. The scene will be chaotic. Witnesses will be trampling the scene. So will paramedics and police officers. I've seen cases of the bad guy's gun being picked up by his accomplice or a well-meaning neighbor who didn't want to leave it where a child could find it. I've seen spent casings kicked away from their original resting place or picked up in the treads of emergency personnel's boots or the wheels of an ambulance gurney, thus altering the dimensions of the shooting scene and making it look like something it wasn't. The sooner you point out the evidence to the first responding officers, the more likely it is to be secured. When you've done the right thing, evidence helps you.

4. Point out the witnesses. Witnesses worry about losing time from work to testify in court or being the target for vengeance by criminals. Many "don't want to get involved." Once they leave the scene unidentified, their testimony that would have helped prove your innocence leaves with them. Point out the witnesses to the police at the first opportunity. (Some have asked, "What if the witness is a friend of the attacker and lies about what happened?" The fact is, he was going to do that anyway, so you haven't lost anything. However, your having pointed him out to the police can be seen as an indication that you believed in your innocence, or you wouldn't have steered the police to him, and that can't hurt.)

5. Politely decline further questioning until you have consulted an attorney. Studies show that, in the immediate aftermath of a life-threatening encounter, we may forget some things or get some details wrong. The questions to you will come at random as they occur to the officer, and you will answer them in the same order; in reviewing the cop's notes and his recollection of the discussion later, this can create the false illusion that you were giving a narrative of events in the order in which they occurred, which of course is not the case. But later, when you narrate events in the sequence of their occurrence, it creates a false perception that you have changed your story. Often, frightening things that happened are blocked in short-term memory by a subconscious that doesn't want to recall them; when you say something later that you didn't mention at the scene, it sounds made up. You don't want to answer detailed questions about exact words spoken, distances, or time frames. None of us are human tape recorders. The tunnel vision that afflicts well over half of the people caught up in something like a gunfight creates the literal optical illusion that things and people appear closer and larger than they are. If your memory tells you your attacker was six feet away when you shot him, but he turns out to have been six yards away, you sound like a liar. *Tachypsychia* — the sense of things going into slow motion — is likewise very common. It seemed as if the fight took a whole minute, and you say so, but a security camera shows it was only 10 seconds, and now you look like a liar. The involved victim who had to fight for their survival is the worst possible witness for measuring things in feet or inches or counting how many shots were fired.

Experts recommend 24 to 48 hours between these "critical incidents," as they are now euphemistically called in the emergency services and when the participant is subjected to a detailed debriefing. The Force Science Institute recommends "one full sleep cycle."

That is why my recommendation — practical advice, not legal advice — is to establish the active dynamic, indicate that you'll sign the complaint, point out evidence and witnesses known to you ... and then stop. Be polite. Do not raise your voice. I, for one, would answer subsequent questions with, "Officer, you'll have my full cooperation after I've spoken with counsel."

Second Edition Update

In the years since the first edition of this book came out, the most frequent criticism has revolved around the five-point checklist, just discussed, of things that need to be established immediately at the scene of the incident. I keep hearing, "But all the lawyers tell us *not* to talk to the police!"

When I ask, "Why not?" the near-universal answer is, "Because you'll say something stupid that will make things worse for you!"

I dunno ... maybe I am just lucky enough to get more brilliant students than some of the other instructors.

Here's the deal. Some people, of course, *have* said stupid things in the aftermath — *because they didn't know what needed to be said.*

Look at it this way. We are familiar with humans' "fight or flight" response, quantified well over a century ago by Dr. Walter Cannon at Harvard Medical School. Physicians have argued over the fine points in Cannon's theory, such as the effect of blood sugar, but when the rubber meets the road, Cannon pretty much had it right. If he had anything wrong, it was the name because it's not a two-pronged effect. It's three-pronged: "fight, flight, or *freeze.*" I have observed that if the ones who freeze survive and you can debrief them when you ask, "Why did you just *stand* there?" the answer is almost always, "I didn't know what to do!"

The same is true of the aftermath. People who thought a gunfight would end with the sound of the last shot and when the last piece of spent brass rolled to a stop were indeed clueless about how to handle the aftermath and were prone to making mistakes that compounded their problems. Mistakes such as fleeing the scene ("flight equals guilt") or lying to the police, or mouthing the typical guilty criminal's refrain, "I ain't tellin' you nothin' 'til my mouthpiece gets here!" (That may not be how you say it, but it's damn sure how it will be heard.)

No good deed goes unpunished. After killing a gun-armed robber, Zack Rogers was sued by a person whose life he saved in the incident.

It is often said, "Under stress after a shooting, you won't be able to think straight." Really? You were under extreme life-threatening stress *during* the shooting and could think straight enough to win. What makes people believe their brains will melt into a puddle of mental diarrhea moments later? *You have just defeated an apex predator in a battle to the death,* but now, afterward, you'll degenerate into a mindless blob?

Stop and think. Why could you win the fight and defeat a criminal's lethal attack in the first place? *Because you knew what needed to be done, and you did it. You had enough discipline not to stand over the body, firing more shots into the corpse because you knew when to stop.* How do you handle the aftermath? *Knowing what needs to be said, saying it, and having the mental discipline not to say more than necessary.*

Let's look at some of the arguments I hear from those who insist on the "never talk to the police" mantra.

One argument is, "Look at all the people in the 'Armed Citizens' column in the NRA magazine who shoot people and don't get arrested." My answer is, "Look at them indeed. Do you seriously think that any of those citizens who weren't arrested, or were even announced by the authorities to be justified, achieved that by not telling the police what happened? *Seriously?* It's a fantasy to think that the dialogue will sound like, "Sir, you seem to have shot someone to death. What happened?" "I'm not talking to you without a lawyer!" "Oh, OK, never mind, then." Such an exchange, I submit, will not occur in nature.

Another argument is, "Cops don't have to talk to investigators after they shoot someone, so why should I say anything?" Quite apart from the fact that you're probably *not* a cop, that argument is BS on its face, and anyone who works in law enforcement knows it. The officer involved in a shooting is typically required to give a "public safety statement" at the scene. The police need to know in what direction the bullets went, so they can check and ensure no unseen bystanders have been hit. They need to know where the evidence is. They need to know if other suspects remain at large, jeopardizing the public. Only detailed questioning will likely be held in abeyance until the involved officer can calm down and gather their thoughts. Even then, the cop may be given a *Garrity* warning (or, in California, a *Lybarger* warning) and questioned in detail. In that situation, the officer must answer or risk being fired, but (at least in theory) their statements are made under a degree of duress. They cannot be used against them in a criminal trial proceeding. In short, anyone who tells you, "Cops don't have to say anything after they've shot someone," is telling you that they don't know what they're talking about.

Beretta representative, left, presents Andy Brown with a token of appreciation for his heroism. From some 70 yards, using the Beretta 92 pistol he was issued, Andy slew a mass-murderer who had already killed many with a rifle. His employer did not treat him well in the aftermath.

Yet another argument is, "My not talking to the police can't be held against me." Really? If you *have* read about the many, many shootings in which the police realized from the beginning that it was a legitimate defense of self or others and treated it accordingly, did you notice how many DGUs (defensive gun uses) involve multiple criminals, several of whom fled as soon as one of them was shot? Let's say you were in such a situation and decided you would Never Talk to the Police. At your trial, you can expect the prosecutor or plaintiff's lawyer to tell the jury, "The defendant wants you to believe he was the Good Guy With A Gun. Yet you will learn that after he shot one *alleged* criminal, he didn't bother to tell the police that other alleged dangerous criminals were running loose to jeopardize the public, including all of you jurors. Does that sound like a 'Good Guy With A Gun' to *you,* ladies and gentlemen of the jury?"

I've heard from many attorneys some variation of "I don't care if my client gets arrested. My job is to keep him from getting a long prison sentence!" Well, let's analyze that. The attorney who gives that advice will go home tonight, have dinner with his family, play with his kids and tuck them in to go night-night, and then make love to his spouse and sleep in his bed. He's right: it doesn't impact *him* if *you* get arrested.

If you shot your attacker on a Friday night and are taken into custody, you might not get a bail hearing until at least Monday morning, perhaps later. Jail is not a good environment for decent people. Your whole family will go through the trauma of a loved one being held in jail for a serious crime. You may one day be interviewing for your dream job and have to honestly answer the question, "Have you ever been arrested?" None of that has any direct personal impact on the lawyer who says, "Never talk to the police."

It gets worse. Human nature makes us reluctant to admit that we — or, by extension, our tribe — are wrong. The lead investigator gets his first impressions from you and the first responding officers who had contact with you. If the collective take of all of them is that you were uncooperative (something they associate with guilty people), that will have an effect. The prosecutors work daily with lead investigators and learn to trust those investigators' judgment and perceptions. Remember the mentality ascribed to former U.S. Attorney General Ed Meese, which says, in essence, "If we arrested you, you must be guilty."

"

WHY DO SO MANY FIREARMS INSTRUCTORS PARROT THE "NEVER TALK TO THE POLICE" ADVICE? THOSE INSTRUCTORS USUALLY COME FROM COMPETITIVE SHOOTING OR MILITARY BACKGROUNDS AND DON'T KNOW HOW THE CRIMINAL JUSTICE SYSTEM WORKS IN THE UNITED STATES.

Why do so many firearms instructors parrot the "never talk to the police" advice? Those instructors usually come from competitive shooting or military backgrounds and don't know how the criminal justice system works in the United States. They may not have thought much about how decisions to prosecute or not prosecute are made and find it easier to toss off that convenient one-liner, "Never Talk To The Police."

When you assess conflicting advice, it's essential to understand the experience that informs each advisor. Of the countless defense attorneys I've discussed this with over more than four decades, I've never met one who had defended more innocent clients than guilty ones. During those same four decades plus, as an expert witness, I've turned down far more cases than I've taken and have spoken only for people who the evidence showed me had done the right thing.

It was for those people who had done the right thing that I formulated the five-point checklist in the early 1980s. It has worked well for them since.

Make your own decision. It's your life and your choice. ■

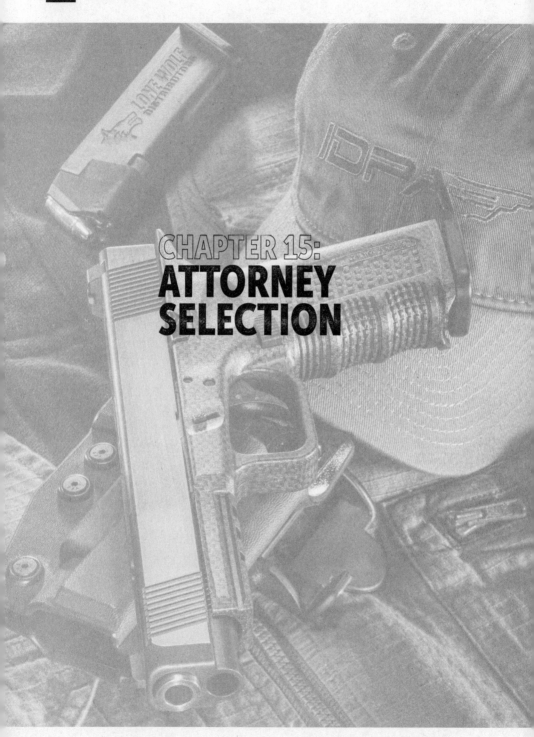

CHAPTER 15:
ATTORNEY SELECTION

Even the most righteous defensive use of a firearm can lead to a false allegation of wrongdoing. It might be an unmeritorious civil lawsuit motivated by greed or revenge or a criminal charge promulgated by a self-styled social justice warrior in a prosecutor's office.

The poet Robert Frost once defined a jury as "twelve people assembled to determine who has the best attorney." There is much truth in this, and people who read this book — people who have accepted the responsibility to protect innocent people — need to take that to heart. Such people are alpha males and females accustomed to being in charge of important matters.

They have to understand that they are not the players when they are on trial anymore.

They are the stakes.

Their attorney is the player. Accordingly, they want the game's best player to represent them at the table.

The "Game"

I don't consider a trial to be a game. Neither should you. But many attorneys do, and it's essential to understand that.

Many people think the best attorney for a shooting case is the most famous criminal lawyer in the region. That's not necessarily true. That "Perry Mason of the community" often got his reputation by pulling rabbits out of hats and winning acquittals for obviously guilty criminals. That sort of legal wizardry employs tactics that are almost 180 degrees opposite of the best skillset for defending legitimate, lawful uses of lethal force.

Never forget that the defense of a genuinely justified use of lethal force is an *affirmative defense!* We are not claiming that we didn't shoot our attacker; instead, we are stipulating that we did indeed shoot him, but we are maintaining that we were correct.

My work over the years has brought me into contact with many criminal defense lawyers. I can usually find time to ask them a few questions unrelated to the particular case at bar. One of those questions is, "Counselor, in all your years in defense bar, how many of your clients were innocent, wrongly accused men or women?"

The answer has always been a relatively tiny percentage who weren't either guilty as charged or at least guilty of some lesser included offense. One with more than thirty years of practice answered, "Oh, it happens. A good one out of a hundred really is totally innocent." Some others have told me they don't think they've ever defended an innocent person.

If that is your professional experience, you will develop a formula of guilt mitigation and establishing some element of reasonable doubt because that's all you, as a defense attorney with a guilty client, have to work with. It becomes your standard, automatic default. Let's examine why that doesn't work for the truly innocent defendant.

A guilty man's lawyer never wants to put him on the witness stand: what can he possibly say that won't be either an admission of guilt or a lie? The lie will open the client to the additional charge of felony perjury. If it appears that his attorney coached him to lie on the witness stand, the lawyer himself has to worry about the criminal charge of subornation of perjury and can hear his license to practice law grow wings and prepare to fly away. So, of course, his default practice becomes, "I never put my clients on the witness stand!"

In contrast, the defendant must take the stand in an affirmative defense. It's not a "whodunnit" anymore: we've already established that it was the defendant who killed the deceased. It's now a "why did he or she do it," *and who besides the defendant can truly answer that question?*

The criminal defense lawyer whose experience is primarily defending the guilty routinely advises, "Never talk to the police!" The reason for that should be obvious: what *can* the guilty man say that won't inculpate him and make his conviction all the more certain? He can lie, but he'll almost certainly be caught in that lie, and lying to the police is another crime in and of itself. "Never talk to the police" probably *is* the best advice the lawyer can give to a potential future guilty client.

But the innocent person who fired in self-defense is poorly served by this advice.

A guilty man's lawyer who gives an innocent client a guilty man's defense will likely end up with a guilty man's verdict.

If the client has established something like "This man attacked me" and pointed out evidence and witnesses from his first contact, he has made it much easier for his attorney to give him a solid affirmative defense. It is defense lawyers who have spent ninety-plus percent of their careers defending at least partially guilty clients who advise "Never talk to the police." A defendant with the mental discipline to go through the "Five Point Checklist" I've described elsewhere in this book will have better paved the way for their attorney to drive them safely through trial to an acquittal.

Desirable Defense Attorney Attributes

All other things being equal, I would much prefer to have a law firm or at least a partnership defending me rather than a sole practitioner. Now, there are some exceptions to this. In the 1980s, I watched Gene Compton, a sole practitioner in Virginia, carry his wrongly accused client Mark Branham on a long, exhausting journey that lasted through three trials before winning the ultimate acquittal.

During that ordeal, focused exclusively on the Branham trial for weeks, Gene paid out of his pocket to keep the office open, knowing that the client couldn't afford his usual fees. This was dedication "above and beyond the call of duty." The attorney, after all, has a duty to their staff to generate enough income to write their paychecks and "keep the lights on." Lawyers with that degree of dedication are not found in every office. A firm with multiple lawyers bringing in multiple fees can handle such things more easily.

During trial, good lawyers don't get much sleep. The other side may be trying to surprise them at every turn, requiring them to burn the midnight oil between trial days. The emotional exhaustion of trial is exacerbated for any ethical attorney who knows they are defending an innocent person, which translates to physical exhaustion and running out of time when you have to do everything yourself without other lawyers taking the slack. Here's an example from the 2021 trial of police officer Derek Chauvin in the death of George Floyd, which was the highest-profile case of its period and triggered riots nationwide.

On April 20, 2021, in my blog (backwoodshome.com/blogs/massadayoob), in an entry titled "Thoughts On the Chauvin Verdict," I wrote: "I don't think the harsh criticism I'm seeing of defense attorney Eric Nelson is warranted. He was David against Goliath, the sole attorney of record that the police union could afford, against no less than three attorneys at the prosecutors' table at any time and more behind the scenes backing them up. At the same time, Nelson's only assistance in court came from a fledgling lawyer who had just passed her bar exam and was acting as an intern. I thought he did an excellent job cross-examining the State's witnesses, and his necessarily long close was more professional than his prosecutorial counterpart's."

Chauvin was, of course, convicted. Many followed that case closely and think there was ample reasonable doubt as to whether Chauvin's kneeling on Floyd for more than nine minutes caused his death — there was evidence that the deceased had enough fentanyl in his system to kill him and maybe enough to kill a couple of people — but I also had a sense of a defense team that was overwhelmed by a much larger prosecution team that also had media-driven public sentiment on its side.

An excellent lawyer, whom I won't name here because it wasn't his fault, lost a murder case in California. A sole practitioner, he learned before trial that his brother had been in a car crash and was not expected to survive. By trial time, he had been without sleep for days, living on black coffee and unfiltered Camel cigarettes. During the trial, I found him groggy, distracted, and "out of it." In mid-trial, he collapsed and was rushed to the hospital by ambulance. There was no one to "pick up the ball" and run with it. His client was convicted and remains in prison.

In a murder trial in Florida, I saw something similar: the trial lawyer was a sole practitioner and a brittle diabetic whose illness was greatly aggravated by the long hours, insomnia and stress of the trial. He had no one to back him up when his disease hit him hard during trial, impairing his focus. The jury found the client guilty of the lesser included charge of manslaughter.

Many military combat survivors will tell you, "No one person can do it alone." That is true to a significant degree in the combat of the courts. That's why I worry about hiring a solo practitioner for the defense.

Don't despair if financial considerations limit you to a public defender. Public defenders get a bad rap because they are notoriously underfunded and overburdened, but don't fall for the stereotype that they'll always give you a sub-par defense. The constant heat of their heavy caseloads has forged some excellent trial lawyers who began as public defenders; the great Roy Black in Miami comes to mind. Elsewhere in this book, Gila Hayes' case study of the Larry Hickey trials demonstrates the splendid work public defenders such as Matt Messmer can do. A good public defender *lives* for the chance to exonerate a truly innocent client.

As noted earlier, you're looking for the best attorney for an affirmative defense, not necessarily criminal defense in general. I, for one, wouldn't want a flamboyant superstar known for courtroom shenanigans; they'll often turn the judge against them, which never helps the client. The sort of lawyer who seems to have majored in Drama and minored in Law tends to aggravate a jury, and the jury tends to see lawyer and client as one, joined at the hip. If the attorney insults or angers them, the only way they can retaliate is to convict his client ... *you.* I want my attorney to be calm, likable and dignified. I want a defense lawyer respected by the prosecutors and the judge alike: the sort of white-maned old lion (or lioness) of the courts that the Bar Association picks to give Ethics lectures at CLE (Continuing Legal Education) training seminars for other lawyers.

The lawyer must know the ins and outs of forensic evidence and proper investigation protocols in shooting cases. How do you find such an attorney near you?

One answer is: use the one the cops use.

It won't be hard to find out what union or fraternal organization (such as FOP, the Fraternal Order of Police, or PBA, Patrolman's Benevolent Association) represents your local police officers or county sheriff's deputies. Reach out to that organization and ask them what criminal defense lawyer they retain for one of their members who is wrongfully indicted after a line of duty or off-duty shooting. That will be an attorney who knows the subtleties of handling a defensive shooting case. If that particular attorney only speaks for police, they will almost certainly be able to refer you to a lawyer who knows what they know and accepts private citizen clients.

Or you can reach out to your post-self-defense support group ... *if you belong to one!*

Post-Self-Defense Support Groups

Over my decades as an expert witness, one thing that has always appalled me has been the enormous cost of legal defense, both criminal and civil, against unmeritorious allegations growing out of genuine self-defense cases. I've seen people go bankrupt. I've seen retirees have to go back to work full time. I've seen people who thought they would die peacefully in a home they owned free and clear to bequeath to their decedents, having to mortgage or reverse mortgage those homes to pay the legal fees. In my most recent murder trial of an armed citizen I helped get fully acquitted, I joined him for a celebratory beer the day after the verdict. He told me that his legal expenses had totaled $300,000 or a little more — and there was still a lawsuit in the wings, filed by the deceased's family.

My colleague Marty Hayes has seen the same thing and did something about it. A highly successful expert witness in the same field as me since 1990 and a former LEO at ranks up to CLEO (Chief Law Enforcement Officer), Marty has also been one of the nation's top firearms and lethal force instructors for decades. He graduated from law school in 2007 and founded the first support group for this sort of situation, the Armed Citizens Legal Defense Network (ACLDN, armedcitizensnetwork.org), the following year.

Hayes explains, "The idea of the Network came from discussing the aftermath of lawful self-defense with my students at the Firearms Academy of Seattle. Most students were very concerned about what to do after a shooting but did not have sufficient money to mount a legal defense. That was the beginning of the Network, and as I was at the time going through law school, I hit upon the idea that instead of becoming a practicing attorney, I would see if my students would pay a little money each year to have the possibility of assistance after an incident. They did, and the effort soon spread nationwide."

The concept quickly caught on and was followed by many imitators, most with different business models. ACLDN is not insurance but instead is member-supported. Members receive several training videos featuring leading experts and attorneys in the field. ACLDN's structure includes an advisory board consisting of Hayes and administrator Vincent Schuck, ace instructors Tom Givens and John Farnam, the same Dennis Tueller mentioned in this book, attorney and firearms expert Emmanuel Kapelsohn, pro-police and pro-gun attorney Marie D'Amico, and master instructor Karl Rehn, and this writer. The board members are available to assist members and their lawyers with trial strategy advice, expert witness appearances and additional support. ACLDN pays lawyers' fees and related costs in criminal defense and civil lawsuits and pays bail if the member has been arrested. Coverage extends to all use of force incidents involving the defense of self or other innocent parties and is not limited to shooting incidents.

As a public service, ACLDN makes its monthly journal available even to non-members at the website listed above. A quick perusal of a few issues will give you an idea of where the organization, and its member lawyers, are coming from. Over the many years, ACLDN has resolved dozens of cases. None have had to go to trial. All have resulted in the most satisfactory outcomes possible. The organization will pay the attorney of the member's choice or select and send in a suitable lawyer if the member doesn't have a particular advocate in mind.

Issues In Selection of Post-Self-Defense Support Groups

While some of these groups offer insurance, many others are pre-paid legal services. The ACLDN is not insurance in any way, shape, or form, but rather a member support group providing a service analogous to a police union or fraternal organization promising to pay for legal defense for a wrongly-accused officer who belongs. Nevertheless, before signing up with any of them, I urge you to do what you would do with real insurance before signing up for a policy: READ THE FINE PRINT FIRST!

Consider the short-lived, ill-fated Carry Guard program once offered by the National Rifle Association. In this writer's opinion, there were many things wrong with it, the cardinal one being their promise to pay every penny of your legal expenses ... *after you were acquitted.*

Now, let that sink in. No attorney will take a criminal defense case on the promise that they will be paid only if — and after — they have won an acquittal. They require a substantial payment up front to draw from regarding legal fees and expenses as they go along. The expenses alone can be high. Volumes of paperwork (reports, depositions, statements, etc.) must be ordered beforehand, and I've seen the providers charge three dollars per page for these mountains of (sometimes triple-spaced) documents. Expert witnesses don't work on later promises of payment either, nor do the court reporters transcribe depositions, etc. The attorney's office staff have to be paid.

Reimbursement requirement is a big red flag. NRA Carry Guard is long gone, but there are organizations today that promise to pay all your legal fees and costs but require you to reimburse them if you lose the case in court. The most innocent man or woman's case can be lost if they have an incompetent lawyer or for several other reasons.

Your support organization is supposed to be your staunch ally in your fight to keep your life as you know it. When it's in the ally's financial interest for you to lose the case, is that entity really your ally?

What I would call a *no-violation* clause could be another deal-breaker for me. This element of the agreement states that if you violate law, rules, or regulation in any way, even though the shooting itself was justifiable, the company does not have to pay for your defense. Let's say you did not realize you were in a hotel that happens to be a "gun-free" zone, and you were carrying your gun in good faith when you had to shoot a rapist in the stairwell, an armed robber breaking into your room or a carjacker in the parking lot.

I have been in numerous establishments posted as "gun-free zones" but posted so poorly that the sign could not be seen until you left the premises, perhaps not even then. I've been in hotels where there weren't any "no guns" signs in the lobbies or doors, but such a policy was stated on the hotel's home page. We travelers rarely look at the fine print on hotel websites. But a "self-defense insurance company" will certainly look there after one of their clients has been involved in a justified shooting on such premises.

Is *"no alcohol on board"* a condition of coverage? If you had a pre-dinner cocktail before a two-hour dinner with friends, I would expect that small amount of alcohol to have metabolized entirely and be a non-issue when you paid for your meal, left the establishment, and had to defend yourself against an armed attacker in the parking lot. However, investigators knowing you left a place of business where alcohol is served, will doubtless check your bill, notice that you had a drink and include that in the report. Under these circumstances, a "no alcohol" policy *might* give the company a legal excuse to dump you and deny coverage.

Will the plan allow you to pick your own lawyer? This element is huge. If the support group insists on sending in an attorney of *their* choice, that might be the lowest-priced novice hungry for his first case. "My Cousin Vinnie" is a most enjoyable movie — I've met law professors who show it at law school — but the title character is the antithesis of what you want working for you when an affirmative defense is needed.

Do your due diligence and find a plan that works for you. Starry-eyed idealists still think, "A good shoot is a good shoot! None of those horror stories will ever happen to *me!*" That's a mindset similar to, "I'll never need a gun for self-defense; none of *those* horror stories will ever happen to *me.*"

But there's another good reason to have post-self-defense support, which many people miss: deterrent effect against political prosecution or unmeritorious lawsuits. Whether in the criminal court arena or the civil, no attorney wants to bring a case he can't win or browbeat the accused into accepting a plea bargain (criminal) or out-of-court settlement (civil). Part of their leverage in achieving that sort of thing, which I consider to be nothing less than legalized extortion when the defendant acted in legitimate self-defense, is the threat to bankrupt them with legal fees if they don't plead or settle. When your attorney can smile at opposing counsel and say, "A third party is paying my client's fees and expenses. Take us to court. We'll beat you there," the deterrent effect is obvious.

I strongly recommend that the armed citizen belongs to a post-self-defense support group for the same reason I recommend every law enforcement officer join their union, fraternal organization or bargaining entity. When wrongly accused in either criminal or civil court, it's good to have a savvy, well-funded organization in your corner, paying for your defense. ∎

CHAPTER 16:
HARDWARE
ISSUES

This book is about the software, not the hardware, of self-defense. Anyone interested in my take on the hardware, I'll refer to my books *Combat Shooting, The Gun Digest Book of Combat Handgunnery, Gun Digest Book of Concealed Carry, 2nd Edition,* and *Massad Ayoob's Greatest Handguns of the World (GunDigestStore.com).* At the same time, since the book you're now reading is about self-defense and defending such actions in court, the fact is that your choice of gun and ammunition fall into the latter arena and need to be discussed here.

If a prosecutor brings you to trial on a charge of reckless driving, do you doubt that he'll make hay with the fact that you were driving a scarlet Corvette Stingray instead of a gray VW bug at the time of the alleged offense? If a plaintiff's lawyer sued you because your dog bit his client, don't you think he'd play up the fact that your pet was a pit bull instead of a miniature poodle? Why would anyone think it would be any different in a case involving a gun?

The attacks on your choice of gun and ammo aren't based on the black letter law; there are no statutes or codes that say you can't carry a gun whose manufacturer named it the Killer Kommando Special or one with a very light trigger pull. Interestingly, the City of San Francisco, California, has an ordinance banning hollowpoint bullets. A State of New Jersey law prohibits the handful of concealed carry permit holders from carrying hollowpoints. However, they can have them at home, and the police are exempt.

The attacks come from trial tactics not taught in law school or available on .gov websites. They'll come from unscrupulous — or sometimes clueless — attorneys who are strongly motivated to paint you as bloodthirsty or negligent to a jury of lay people expressly selected by those lawyers during the *voir dire* process for their lack of knowledge about weapons and self-defense. Some of those attacks are easy for the knowledgeable defense team and defendant to defeat with logical explanations for the choice. And some are hard to win, making them battles best avoided by choosing different equipment beforehand.

Arguments We Can Win

"He chose an especially powerful gun and loaded it with extra-deadly hollow-nosed dum-dum bullets, ladies and gentlemen of the jury. Bullets designed to rend and tear and cause cruel and unusual pain and suffering. And oh, how many bullets he *had,* enough to slaughter a dozen and a half people! What but murderous malice could have motivated him?" That's the kind of argument you can expect. A computer search will get you to the

IF A PLAINTIFF'S LAWYER SUED YOU BECAUSE YOUR DOG BIT HIS CLIENT, DON'T YOU THINK HE'D PLAY UP THE FACT THAT YOUR PET WAS A PIT BULL INSTEAD OF A MINIATURE POODLE? WHY WOULD ANYONE THINK IT WOULD BE ANY DIFFERENT IN A CASE INVOLVING A GUN?

Arizona v. Harold Fish case, in which a retired schoolteacher shot and killed a paranoid schizophrenic who violently attacked him in the desert. Look for the *Dateline* TV episode about the trial. Some of the jurors who convicted him explain how they bought the prosecution's argument that his use of a 10mm pistol and hollowpoint ammunition indicated malice. His conviction was later overturned on appeal over another issue. When Harold Fish died, he still owed half a million dollars in legal fees to the defense attorney who failed to defeat that argument.

Powerful firearms are defensible. I often carry .357s and .45s on my own time. When I had time to hunt, I used a .44 Magnum Smith & Wesson with a 4-inch barrel, which doubled as a defense gun during deer season. I've carried a .45 more than anything else on duty as a police officer. If asked why I carried "such a powerful gun" — and, yes, I've seen that argument

Loaded with 185-grain Remington .45 hollow-points, a Ruger P345 was the death weapon in one of the author's cases. The prosecution made much of the large caliber and the hollowpoints; the defense explained both and won an acquittal.

come up with all those calibers — my answer would be that more powerful calibers have historically stopped gunfights faster. The sooner a gunfight stops, the fewer innocent people get hurt or killed.

The research of Dr. Glenn Meyer, a psychologist and professor from Texas who works with mock juries to determine how various issues impact jurors, has done studies determining that deadlier-seeming "assault guns" make jurors more hostile toward defendants who use them. No surprise: the jury pool is the general public, and the general public has been bombarded with "assault weapon" propaganda for generations by the media and politicians. Does this mean that you should not use an AR-15 for home defense? No, it means that you should be able to articulate that you used that light, easy-to-shoot rifle with its telescoping stock because your petite wife and your grandmother could handle it far more easily and confidently than almost anything else if they needed to shoot to save their lives and the lives of their family. It would be worth your time to explain that it's the most popular sporting rifle in America, advertised in every hunting periodical on the magazine rack.

The author has done multiple "cocked revolver/hair trigger" cases, in some of which the allegation was false. He recommends defensive revolvers be rendered double-action only.

In states with magazine capacity limits, I stay within the limit and carry more magazines. I often carry a 20-shot Springfield XD(m) 9mm with a spare magazine. If asked why I chose to carry that many rounds, I would explain (as I already have in Federal court) that the latest study from the NYPD showed that 3 percent of the time, its officers needed more than 16 rounds, and one study from the LAPD showed 5 percent. Citizens arm themselves for protection from the same criminals the cops face. While 3 and 5 percent don't sound like a lot, ask yourself, "Would I want to be in a situation where there was a 3 or 5 percent chance that I need this thing to save my life and *not* have it?" And, of course, many more situations go beyond 10 or six rounds. The history of fighting armed criminals is that many of them can absorb multiple solid hits before ceasing hostility, sometimes from a state of rage, sometimes because drugs or alcohol have anesthetized them against pain, and sometimes because they're moving fast in the dark and taking effective cover while they shoot at innocent people. We have more bad guys wearing body armor than in the time of John Dillinger, and that can soak

(Top Left) A gun without spare ammo is a temporary gun; spare ammo is strongly suggested. Here's a spare 10-round .45 ACP magazine for a Glock 30 pistol in Glock's inexpensive magazine pouch.

(Top Right) A veteran lawman and firearms specialist developed the Snagmag pocket magazine carrier. The Snagmag is disguised as an ordinary pocket knife.

(Above) Spare ammo is a particularly good idea with a five-shot gun, like this S&W Model 340 M&P. HKS speedloader and Bianchi Speed Strip each hold a full gun-load of five cartridges.

(Top Right) If you can carry one spare magazine, you may not find it hard to carry two. These are .45-caliber Glock 30 mags.

up a lot of ammo before the good guy shooting back realizes it's time to change the point of aim.

Why do we use those hollowpoint bullets, which in my experience, the opposing counsel will make a point of more often than not in an armed citizen shooting? Not *because* the police do — that would open us up to the "wanna-be cop" tar-and-feathering — but *for the same reasons the police do*. Those reasons are:

The "mushroom" shape of the hollowpoint that opposing counsel loves to mention, perhaps hoping to invoke visions of a nuclear cloud over Hiroshima, is also a "parachute" shape intended to slow the bullet down and keep it inside the body of the offender, so it won't pass through and strike an unseen innocent bystander.

> 66
>
> THE GEN5 GLOCK, IN MY OPINION, HAS THE BEST "STREET TRIGGER" THAT ANY MANUFACTURER HAS EVER PUT IN A PISTOL. IT DOESN'T NEED A NY-1 MODULE BECAUSE IT ALREADY GIVES A FIRM, SMOOTH TRIGGER PULL, WHICH MEETS THE COMPANY'S LONG-STANDING 5.5 POUNDS MINIMUM PULL WEIGHT RECOMMENDATION.

Ashley Gibbons reloads exquisitely good ammo, as do many others, but the author recommends factory ammo for defense, citing reasons beyond quality control.

The cookie-cutter shape of the hollowpoint tends to bite into hard surfaces and bury itself there if the bullet misses, instead of ricocheting and going on to endanger innocent bystanders as would the supposedly "humane" bullets the uninformed critics say we should use.

Every department that issues hollowpoints will tell you that since the transition from older ammo, these bullets have been more effective and stopped fights faster. Stopping the criminal immediately from stabbing or shooting, or otherwise mauling the innocent is why there is such a thing as "justifiable homicide" in the first place. The sooner he's stopped, the

fewer innocents he can harm.

Finally, we can make a good argument that since this ammunition stops him faster, the Bad Guy will sustain fewer gunshot wounds and may be more likely to survive the encounter.

If the above arguments had been effectively put before the jury, the verdict in *Arizona v. Fish* might have been different.

Arguments to Avoid

In well over four decades as an expert witness in weapons and shooting cases, I've run across three arguments from the other side which, even though sometimes bogus, are so tough to defeat that it's better not to have to fight them at all. This goes down hard with the naïve folks who believe "a good shoot is a good shoot," which is somewhat akin to the belief that every Christmas, a fat guy in a red suit will come down their chimney and give them presents.

First and foremost is what a layman would call a "hair trigger," a trigger pull lighter than the gun's manufacturer recommends for a defensive firearm. It's common knowledge that good people forced to fight criminals with guns are likely to be nervous and shaky. We've known for well over a century that in the grip of "fight or flight response," blood flow is directed

The expansion characteristics of modern ammo are often attacked in court, but Ayoob has found those attacks easy to defeat. This is a 230-grain projectile from the Federal .45 ACP HST +P load, recovered from flesh and bone after an instant one-shot kill on a hog.

away from the extremities and into major muscle groups and internal viscera to "fuel the furnace" for the strenuous effort that the primal brain believes is about to take place. It's called vasoconstriction. It's one reason frightened Caucasians turn visibly pale and why we all become clumsy under stress. Mixing that with a "hair trigger" is like mixing fire with gasoline.

What, exactly, is a "hair trigger"? It depends on the gun design, just as the question "what is a safe adjustment of brakes" depends on the specific vehicle. The manufacturer's specification for trigger pull weight on that particular firearm, and the "common custom and practice" for adjusting such guns constitute the standards. In the timelessly popular 1911 pistol, the Colt company, which has manufactured more of those guns than any other manufacturer, tells its armorers that 4 pounds is the red-line bottom limit

Use of a powerful handgun such as this .45 auto may be attacked by opposing counsel, but is defensible in court.

The Gun Digest Book of Combat Handgunnery is recommended for more information about the "hardware side" of carrying concealed for self-defense.

of pull weight for a duty gun used for police, military, or civilian defense purposes. The National Rifle Association requires a 4-pound minimum trigger pull on 1911s used in its Distinguished matches and enforces it with referees equipped with trigger-pull weight measurement devices. Do we see a pattern here?

The most popular pistol in the USA today is the Glock. Since its introduction in this country in the early 1980s, this pistol — issued or approved by over 60 percent of America's police at this writing — had a 5.5-pound standard trigger pull. Some departments have gone heavier: Miami and others went with an 8-pound trigger connector. The New York State Police demanded what is now known as the NY-1 trigger, which gives firm resistance from the beginning of the trigger press and brings total pull weight up to around 8 pounds. NYPD demanded more: first called the New York Plus, now known as the NY-2 module, the trigger system in its Glocks approaches *12* pounds, which for this writer, passes the point of diminishing returns. The reason, in all cases, was safety against accidental discharges; with thousands of cops using guns under stress, the firearms instructors in those departments wanted a more significant safety buffer.

In the late 1980s, Glock came out with a target model sporting a 3.5-pound connector; weighed from the bottom tip of the trigger, that was the pull weight, and leverage being what it is, it ran about 4.5 pounds from the center of the pivoting trigger; they later renamed the same part the 4.5-pound connector. However, from the beginning, it was adamant Glock policy that *this trigger pull weight not be used in a duty or defense gun.* Its models with the light trigger, then and now, are listed in catalogs under "sport," not "duty" or "self-defense" pistols. Target models ordered by police departments are, by policy, shipped with 5.5-pound, or heavier trigger pulls.

The Gen5 Glock, in my opinion, has the best "street trigger" that any manufacturer has ever put in a pistol. It doesn't need a NY-1 module because it already gives a firm, smooth trigger pull, which meets the company's long-standing 5.5 pounds minimum pull weight recommendation.

Would installing a lighter trigger in a duty Glock be a problem? Look up the case of *Santibanes v. Tomball, TX* and see for yourself. The short answer is, "Yes."

Before the Glock, revolvers were standard in American law enforcement. Cocked revolvers with light single-action pull proved conducive to unintended discharges. Decades ago, the LAPD set the trend of converting its guns to double-action only. Could, say, a cocked Colt Detective Special with a 4.5-pound pull be seen as "reckless and negligent" for taking a criminal at gunpoint? Look up the Appellate Court decision in *New York v. Frank Magliato,* and find out for yourself that the answer is yes.

Why would 4.5 pounds be considered negligent in a cocked revolver or a Glock but OK for a 1911? Partly because the 1911 has a passive grip safety and an active manual thumb safety the other two guns don't have, and

The author's popular title, *Gun Digest Book of Concealed Carry*, now in its second edition, covers the selection and use of concealed carry methods and related hardware.

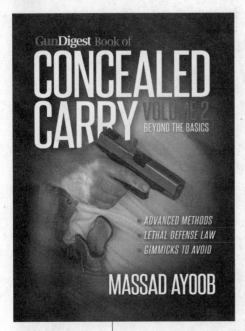

Ayoob's *Gun Digest Book of Concealed Carry, Volume 2,* covers advanced concealed carry methods.

partly because Colt's factory literature, court-discoverable, said so.

My practical advice would be to stay above 4 pounds in a 1911 and 5.5 pounds in a Glock and render a defensive revolver double-action only, which is an easy gunsmithing job.

Why is it an issue at all in an intentional self-defense shooting? Because the so-called hair-trigger gives opposing counsel a hook upon which to hang a false allegation, whether criminal or civil. In the criminal case, it's easier to sell a jury on a theory that the gun went off by accident due to a negligent, excessively light trigger pull, sustaining a manslaughter charge, than to convince them that a good person turned into Mr. Hyde and became a murdering monster. In a civil lawsuit, the motivation is different: the plaintiff's counsel is looking for deep pockets. Few defendants have a million liquid, unprotected dollars that the plaintiff can seize to satisfy the judgment if the jury decides in the civil case that you deliberately,

> " I WOULD AVOID GUNS WITH CONTROVERSIAL NAMES AND DECORATIONS ... WHEN YOU MOST DESPERATELY NEED TO BE RECOGNIZED AS RESPONSIBLE, REASONABLE, AND PRUDENT, DO YOU WANT TO BE GIVING THAT SORT OF FODDER TO A SILVER-TONGUED ATTORNEY WHO IS TRYING TO PAINT YOU AS RECKLESS AND IRRESPONSIBLE WITH FIREARMS?

The Colt .45 has been a classic American home and personal defense weapon in one form or another since 1911. This one, produced circa 1918, is still perfectly functional.

Powerful, high-tech firearms can be controllable. This is a Colt 10mm modified with integral recoil compensator by master pistolsmith Mark Morris.

maliciously killed the deceased. But many people have a million-dollar homeowner liability insurance policy if a burglar was shot, or the same for automobile liability if a carjacker was shot, *and the insurance company has the money!* However, most insurance policies won't pay off on an *intentional tort,* a deliberate act that harmed the plaintiff. But they *will* pay off for a negligent accident. *Voilà!* The theory of "he shot my client by accident when he negligently pointed a hair-trigger gun at him" was born.

The second thing I'd avoid is deactivating or removing a safety device: pinning down the grip safety on a 1911 pistol, for example, or removing the magazine disconnector (which prevents the chambered round from being fired if the magazine is out of the pistol) on a Browning High Power. A jury of laymen with little firearms knowledge is deciding the case: do you want to give opposing counsel the argument, "This person is so reckless with firearms that *he deactivates the safety devices on lethal weapons.*" Seriously?

Finally, I would avoid guns with controversial names and decorations. Like the pit bull in the dog bite case, the theory in trial tactics is that "the pet reflects the personality of the owner." If you prefer a compact 1911 .45,

> "
>
> A FINAL RECOMMENDATION ON AMMUNITION FROM THE COURT DEFENSE SIDE: I URGE YOU NOT TO PUT HANDLOADED AMMUNITION IN YOUR DEFENSIVE FIREARMS — RESERVE THAT FOR PRACTICE, HUNTING, COMPETITION, AND TRAINING. MANY SELF-DEFENSE SHOOTINGS OCCUR AT A "POWDER-BURNING DISTANCE" AND LEAVE GUNSHOT RESIDUE ON THE BODY OR CLOTHING OF THE OPPONENT.

I'd recommend the Colt Defender, not the Auto Ordnance Pit Bull. I've run across two cases, one in which I testified for the defense, where opposing counsel made a massive deal out of the fact that the defendant had a Colt *Cobra*. I've seen people with cartoon "Punisher" skulls on their grips or the back slide plate on their Glock and with gun muzzles engraved "Smile, Wait For Flash" or people who carried Hornady's novelty ammunition, Zombie-Max, instead of the same company's much more defensible Critical Duty, Critical Defense, and XTP ammo. When you most desperately need to be recognized as responsible, reasonable, and prudent, do you want to be giving that sort of fodder to a silver-tongued attorney who is trying to paint you as reckless and irresponsible with firearms?

I doubt anyone reading this would defend their family against home invasion by leaving their front door conspicuously open and placing a loaded shotgun inside the door so that when an intruder entered, he'd be able to grab it and give the homeowner a more challenging gunfight. Some people don't realize that in the "court fight," that's precisely the sort of "firepower" they're handing over to their antagonists when they put "hair triggers" in their defense guns and do any of the other Rambo crap I've discussed above.

A final recommendation on ammunition from the court defense side: I urge you not to put handloaded ammunition in your defensive firearms — reserve that for practice, hunting, competition, and training. Many self-defense shootings occur at a "powder-burning distance" and leave gunshot residue on the body or clothing of the opponent. If the other side falsely argues that he wasn't close enough to hurt you when you fired, gunshot residue (GSR) on his body or clothes may prove otherwise. But to get that evidence in, your defense team will have to do scientific GSR testing within the rules of evidence, which encompass impartial third-party verification. When you load your ammo, and that becomes an issue, you probably won't be able to get it in. The reason is that the other side can argue, literally, "The defendant manufactured the evidence!"

"Your honor, how do we know that the fatal shot wasn't a 'special load' he created to fool the crime lab investigators?" they can say.

I've found this to be the most contentious argument on the firearms Internet. You tell someone the ammo they made themselves may not be the right choice, and they take it personally. I get it. But personal pride has to

The author advises staying above a 4-pound trigger pull in a 1911 and 5.5 pounds in a Glock.
Photo: James House

take second place to family responsibility. If you're falsely accused and can't prove that you're telling the truth, your family will suffer with you through the trial, your possible long imprisonment, and terrible financial loss.

I understand your pride in your handloads. When I won a match with ammo I loaded myself, it made me a little more proud, like feeding my family a meal I cooked from scratch instead of having a pizza delivered. But the forensic verification problem is enormous: *in almost a decade of Internet arguments, no handload fan has ever been able to show me a case where a court accepted a handloader's word or records when it came down to GSR testing to determine the distance to figure out which side was telling the truth.*

I've been a handloader. But I've also been a son

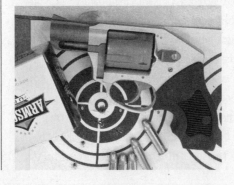

When it comes to revolvers and avoiding the "hair trigger" accusation in court, Ayoob advises you to render your defensive revolver double-action only, which is an easy gunsmithing job.
Photo: Bob Campbell

and son-in-law, a husband and father and grandfather, and those responsibilities take precedence. I load my home defense gun, my carry guns, and
my police duty guns with factory ammunition for verifiability in forensic
testing and also to avoid the argument that "regular bullets weren't deadly
enough to satisfy his blood-lust, so he created his own extra-deadly ammunition." I've seen both occur; research *New Jersey v. Daniel Bias* for the
forensic side and *New Hampshire v. James Kennedy* for the "deadly bullets"
argument.

It's your life, your hardware, your loved ones who'll go through the
ordeal with you ... and it's your choice. ■

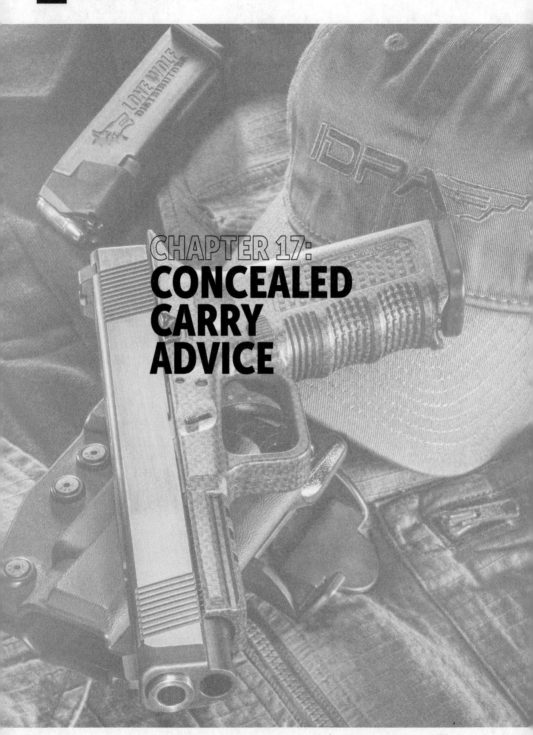

CHAPTER 17:
CONCEALED CARRY ADVICE

T his book would not be complete without some advice on concealed carry. I'd suggest the book I did on that topic, *Gun Digest Book of Concealed Carry, 2nd Edition* (GunDigestStore.com). For now, let's go with something I originally wrote for Harris Publications, which produced one of the magazines I contribute to regularly, *Combat Handguns*. It went viral, which I take as a sign of approval. It's reprinted here with the original publisher's permission.

Ten Commandments for Concealed Carry
By Massad Ayoob

I'm not Moses, let alone God, but the following ten bits of advice are written in stone nonetheless. Not by God but by the vastly powerful mechanisms of logic, law, and reality.

Commandment I: If You Choose to Carry, Always Carry As Much As Is Possible

Hollywood actors get to see the script beforehand, and nothing is fired at them but blanks. You don't have either luxury. Criminals attack people

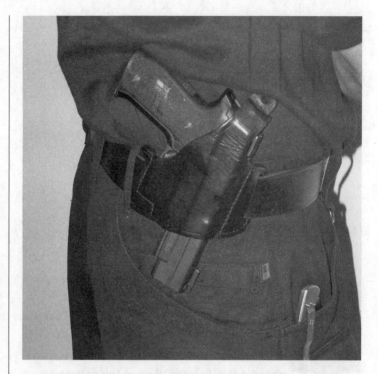

A black pistol in a black holster, with black pants and shirts, is the least noticeable "color combination" when the handgun is open carried. However, while Ayoob supports the right to open carry, he notes that the method is rarely the best tactic.

in times and places where they don't think the victims will be prepared for them. It's what they do. The only way to be prepared to ward off such predators is to always be prepared: i.e., to be routinely armed and constantly ready to respond to deadly threats against you and those who count on you for protection. It's not about convenience. It's literally about life and death.

Commandment II: Don't Carry A Gun If You Aren't Prepared To Use It

The gun is not a magic talisman that wards off evil. It is a special-purpose emergency rescue tool — no

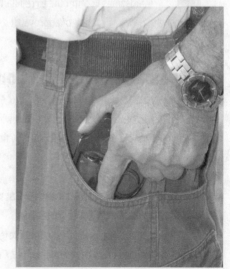

A J-frame revolver in the pocket can be constantly carried with almost any manner of dress.

more, no less. History shows us that — for police and armed citizens alike — the mere drawing of the gun ends the great majority of criminal threats, with the offender either surrendering or running away. However, remember that criminals constitute an armed subculture, living in an underworld awash with stolen, illegal weapons. They don't fear the gun; they fear the resolutely armed man or woman pointing that gun at them. And, being predators, they are expert judges of what is prey and what is a creature more dangerous to them than they are to what they thought a moment ago was their prey.

Thus, the great irony is that the person who is prepared to kill if they must stop a murderous transgression by a human predator is the least likely to have to do so.

Commandment III: Don't Let The Gun Make You Reckless

Lightweight pseudo-psychologists will tell you that "the trigger will pull the finger," and the possession of your gun will make you want to kill

While the author considers .380 caliber marginal at best, tiny pistols like this Ruger LCP, which was made for that round, allow many good people to be armed when they can't carry anything larger.

someone. Rubbish. The gun is no more an evil talisman that turns kindly Dr. Jekyll into evil Mr. Hyde than a good talisman that drives off evil. Those of us who have spent decades immersed in the twin cultures of American law enforcement and the responsibly armed citizenry know that the truth is the opposite: A good person doesn't see the gun as a supercharger for aggression but as a brake that controls natural human emotion. The law itself holds the armed individual to a "higher standard of care," requiring that they do all that is possible to avoid using deadly force until it becomes necessary. Prepare and act accordingly.

(Top) Alertness is paramount to keeping danger at bay. Instead of reading like this, with your head buried in the newspaper like a giraffe at a water hole ...

(Bottom)... Sit erect, bringing the reading matter up to your eye level to improve your peripheral vision and ability to scan the area around you quickly.

> **GUNFIGHTS ARE WON BY THOSE WHO SHOOT FASTEST AND STRAIGHTEST AND ARE USUALLY MEASURED IN SECONDS. LEGAL AFTERMATHS LAST FOR YEARS, AND EMOTIONAL AFTERMATHS, FOR LIFETIMES.**

Commandment IV: Carry Legally

If you live someplace with no provision to carry a gun to protect yourself and your loved ones, don't let pusillanimous politicians turn you into a convicted felon. Move! It's a quality of life issue. The rhetorical theory that sounds like "I interpret the law this way because I believe the law should be this way" — which ignores laws that aren't that way — can sacrifice your freedom, your status as a gun-owning free American, and your ability to provide for your family. If you live where a CCW permit is available, get the damn permit. If you don't, move to someplace that does. Yes, it *is* that simple. And if you are traveling, check sources such as *handgunlaw.us* to ensure that you are legal to carry in the given jurisdiction. Don't let the legal system make you a felon for living up to your responsibilities to protect yourself and those who count on you. If you carry, make sure you carry legally.

More training is always good. Mike Seeklander, left, got rave reviews from this class of already highly accomplished shooters.

(Below) February 2013: The author sets a record while being filmed in a Panteao Press training film, "Massad Ayoob on Concealed Carry."

The record? He successfully concealed more than 50 loaded pistols and revolvers. Do not tell him it's too inconvenient to carry one gun to protect yourself and your loved ones.

Winning an International Defensive Pistol Association match feels good. Here, the author accepts the Stock Service Revolver Champion award from Bill Barron, match director for the South Mountain regional IDPA championship in Phoenix, Arizona. IDPA matches help you hone your defensive shooting skills.

Massad Ayoob shoots his Springfield Armory XDm 5.25 in an IDPA ESP Division, note the cover garment. *Photo: Yamil Sued*

Guns are killing
our kids!
Vote Y...

COMMON
SENS...

HOW
CHIL...

...IFE-SAVER
AN ASSAULT
WEAPONS

LIFE-S...
BACKGR...
CHEC...

Your rights to self-defense are constantly under attack. The author has attended many anti-gun rallies and legislative public hearings where he has spoken in defense of gun rights. Get involved! Photo: EyeJoy/iStock.com

" WHEN YOU CARRY A GUN, YOU CARRY THE POWER OF LIFE AND DEATH. IT IS A POWER THAT BELONGS ONLY IN THE HANDS OF RESPONSIBLE PEOPLE WHO CARE ABOUT CONSEQUENCES AND ARE RESPECTFUL OF LIFE...

Commandment V: Know What You're Doing

Gunfights are won by those who shoot fastest and straightest and are usually measured in seconds. Legal aftermaths last for years, and emotional aftermaths, for lifetimes. Get educated in depth in the management of all three stages of the encounter beforehand.

Commandment VI: Concealed Means Concealed

If your local license requires concealed carry, keep the gun truly concealed. The revealing of a concealed handgun is seen in many quarters as a threat, which can result in charges of criminal threatening, brandishing, and more. A malevolent person who wants to falsely accuse you of threatening them with a gun will have their wrongful accusation bolstered if the police find you with a gun where they said it was. Yes, that happens. Some jurisdictions allow "open carry." I support the right to open carry in the proper time and place but have found over the decades that there are relatively few ideal times or places where the practice won't unnecessarily and predictably frighten someone the carrier had no reason to scare.

Commandment VII: Maximize Your Firearms Familiarity

If you ever need that gun, it will happen so quickly and terribly that you'll have to be swift and sure. If you don't, you'll still be handling a deadly weapon in the presence of people you love. Making gun manipulation second nature — safety and draw-fire-hit — is thus doubly important.

Commandment VIII: Understand The Fine Points

Don't just read the headlines or editorials; read the fine print. Study the laws of your jurisdiction. What's legal in one place won't be legal in another. Cities may have prohibitions that states don't. Remember the principle, "ignorance of the law is no excuse."

Commandment IX: Carry an Adequate Firearm

A Vespa motor scooter is a motor vehicle, but it's a poor excuse for a family car. A .22 or .25 is a firearm, but it's a poor excuse for defense. Carry a gun loaded with ammunition with a track record of quickly stopping lethal assaults. Hint: if your chosen caliber is not used by police or military, it's probably not powerful enough for its intended purpose.

Commandment X: Use Common Sense

Common sense — encompassing ethics, logic, and law alike — must be your constant guide and companion when you carry a gun — not idealism, not rhetoric. When you carry a gun, you carry the power of life and death. It is a power that belongs only in the hands of responsible people who care about consequences and are respectful of life and limb and human safety, that of others and their own.

Editor's Note: This article appeared in its original version in Combat Handguns *magazine.* ■

Classic combat revolvers are far from obsolete. These StressFire Instructor candidates at Lethal Force Institute learn to shoot and teach the wheelgun. The author says training such as this can be admissible in court following a shooting, allowing you to articulate how you understood the nature of a threat at the time you defended yourself. *Photo: Massad Ayoob*

"

THE GUN IS NOT A MAGIC TALISMAN THAT WARDS OFF EVIL. IT IS A SPECIAL-PURPOSE EMERGENCY RESCUE TOOL — NO MORE, NO LESS.

CHAPTER 18:
LATEST TRENDS

y primary occupation is teaching judicious use of deadly force. My second is writing about self-defense and weapons. Third on the list is my work as an expert witness in weapons, homicide and assault cases. I could be wearing any of those hats when someone asks, "You've been doing this for decades; what new trends are you seeing?"

The answer is ... not many. Lethal force law is one of the most mature and stable bodies of law in American jurisprudence. As you'll see elsewhere in this book, controversies such as Stand Your Ground laws haven't really changed things as much as the pundits say.

But that's not to say that there's nothing new.

Between the first edition of this book in 2014 and this second, the most significant change has come from something discussed in depth in that early edition, the Zimmerman case. It ushered in a new and deceitful strategy of accusation.

Not until the dead teenager's smartphone was finally unlocked did investigators learn how deeply young Trayvon Martin had become involved

Ayoob, right, observes as lighting experts determine ambient light at a crime scene. This could be a critical element for the jury to weigh.

in "thug life." There were indications of illegal drug sales and use, trafficking in illegal guns, burglary and streetfighting. It's reasonable to believe that, like many teenagers, Trayvon Martin had gone to great lengths to keep his parents from learning of his transgressions. His mother was a professional with a master's degree, and his father had put the gang-banging of his younger years behind him and become a productive citizen. It appears that genuine tough love caused his mom to send him hundreds of miles north to live with his dad. When the divorced parents learned that their unarmed 17-year-old son had been shot and killed, they understandably sought legal counsel. They ended up with Benjamin Crump, who hired high-powered PR man Ryan Julison to create the trope of a child (remember the pre-pubescent photo of Trayvon, who towered over Zimmerman?) hunted down and killed by a racist monster.

Elsewhere, this book explains the evidence that led to Zimmerman's acquittal. But the Crump/Julison strategy of smearing the target and making the shooting a national issue had proven successful and would be repeated again and again. In 2014 in Ferguson, Missouri, it was Crump and Julison's "hands up, don't shoot" myth that caused the city to burn in the wake of Officer Darren Wilson fatally shooting the "gentle giant" Michael Brown. Incontrovertible evidence showed that the supposedly white racist policeman — who, on his last call, had resuscitated a black child who had stopped breathing — was punched in the head through the open window of his patrol SUV by Brown, who then tried to disarm the officer and shoot him with his own gun. The first wound was on Brown's arm, at near contact according to the gunshot residue surrounding the entry, and Brown's DNA was on the officer's SIG P229R pistol. Since he had just tried to disarm a cop and shoot him with his own gun, when Brown fled, Wilson naturally pursued, and when the larger man turned and lunged at him, he shot him until he fell.

You can review the transcript of the grand jury hearing, which, in a departure from the usual procedure, was made public. The "hands up, don't shoot" narrative fell apart under cross-examination, which is why the officer was not charged. However, his law enforcement career was destroyed, as was that of his uninvolved wife, who was also a Ferguson officer. Had they remained, they would have been targeted by individuals like the one who went to prison for shooting at George Zimmerman and missing his head by inches because he wanted to avenge "a murdered black child."

And so it has continued since, in case after high-profile case. Many of these have resulted in protests, riots, and even death.

Consider the shooting of Jacob Blake in Kenosha, Wisconsin. The trope was "unarmed black man shot seven times in the back in front of children by (presumably racist) white police officer." From the beginning, a smartphone recording of the incident showed a knife in Mr. Blake's left hand as he attempted to enter an automobile he did not own or have permission to use, as police officers screamed at him to drop the knife. There was a child in the car, and police were aware that there were warrants out on Blake for sexual assault and domestic violence. When an officer struggling with Blake at the driver's door of the vehicle perceived Blake turned toward him with the blade, he shot him.

It became another "racist police brutality" *cause célèbre*. Kenosha burned. During the rioting there, resulting from this shooting, the Kyle Rittenhouse case discussed elsewhere in this book took place.

It seemed that the Kenosha Police Department did not tell the officer's side. That did not emerge until weeks later when the Wisconsin Attorney General's office told the public what had really happened.

The lesson? Law schools and police academies have always taught, "We must not discuss our cases in the press; it will all come out in court." Crump and Julison had changed the paradigm, blatantly weaving false narratives to the press that were not answered with the truth until too late. When the accused does not deny the accusation, their silence is seen by the public as an admission of guilt. *Qui tacet consentire videtur, ubi loqui debuit ac potuit* (He who is silent, when he ought to have spoken and was able to, is taken to agree).

Some police entities have recognized this and fought back successfully. The Los Angeles Police Department and the Las Vegas Metropolitan Police Department developed the policy that with any potentially controversial shooting, they would call a press conference as soon as possible, play dispatch recordings, show bodycam and dashcam footage of the incident, and explain what happened, assuring the public that the investigation continues. Despite many shootings in both communities, neither has had rioting except for spillover from the death of George Floyd in Minneapolis, a

> "
> APPLICATIONS FOR CONCEALED CARRY PERMITS SKYROCKETED, TOO, AND MANY AMERICANS FOUND THEM UNOBTAINABLE BECAUSE THE LICENSING UNITS OF THE ISSUING AGENCIES SHUT DOWN, SOMETIMES BECAUSE THEY WERE DECLARED "NON-ESSENTIAL" DURING THE PANDEMIC OR THERE SIMPLY WEREN'T ENOUGH COPS TO PROCESS THEM.

conflagration that sent its embers throughout the nation. Other law enforcement agencies have followed this wise policy. Getting the truth out keeps lies from germinating in the fertile fields of public opinion.

The Roaring (Twenty) Twenties

An inflammatory confluence of circumstances significantly affected armed citizens, law enforcement, the criminal justice system and American society beginning in 2020. In Minneapolis, a black man displaying signs of Fentanyl overdose —confirmed at autopsy— died while a white police officer knelt on his shoulder for nearly ten minutes. The result was nationwide violence known as the George Floyd riots.

Other disturbances were taking place. Fueled by Black Lives Matter rhetoric and the Antifa movement, the city of Portland, Oregon, allowed rioters to take over a police station and, for an extended period, an area of the city encompassing six square blocks. I have been unable to find an estimate of the number of residents who were trapped in that area without police protection. Still, I suspect if a like number of Americans had been on an ocean liner seized by Somalian pirates, the U.S. Government would have sent the Navy and SEAL Team Six to rescue them. Instead, placating the rioters became the order of the day.

Concurrent with that was the COVID epidemic and the resulting shutdown of businesses nationwide. Authoritative news sources estimated that police services would be severely cut due to officers who contracted the virus and the necessary isolation of other cops with whom they had come into contact. Americans had a growing sense of being on their own and understandably perceived their long-accustomed level of safety and security collapsing around them. A drought of ammunition accompanied shortages of toilet paper and sanitizer, and firearm sales skyrocketed. It was estimated that some ten million Americans had bought guns for self-protection for the first time.

Applications for concealed carry permits skyrocketed, too, and many Americans found them unobtainable because the licensing units of the issuing agencies shut down, sometimes because they were declared "non-essential" during the pandemic or there simply weren't enough cops to process them. The difficulty in obtaining permits may have been one factor driving the trend toward so-called "Constitutional Carry," that is, the legalization of concealed carry without a permit for any adult with a clean criminal record. By the end of the first quarter of 2022, half the country — 25 of the 50 states — had legalized permitless carry.

Concurrently, it became known as fact and not a conspiracy theory that billionaires with "progressive" agendas were spending millions to elect prosecutors who promised to seek *decarceration* — releasing criminals from jails and prisons — and to elect politicians with "defund the police" agendas.

All these simultaneous trends contributed to people having a sense of being on their own and needing self-protection more than ever.

The Changing Face of the "Mob"

The "rules of engagement" for armed citizens changed most visibly in riot situations. "What do we do when Antifas drag us out of our cars during a riot? Can we shoot to defend ourselves?" became the hot question for self-defense instructors nationwide.

Here is this writer's answer.

The following appeared in the August 2020 edition of the *ACLDN Journal,* "DEFENSE AGAINST MOBS: An Interview With Massad Ayoob" By Gila Hayes.

[Editor's note: Reprint edited for stylistic consistency.]

eJournal: Thank you, Mas, for agreeing to talk to us about surviving mob violence. It is a timely topic on which our readers have many questions. May we start by defining our terminology? What are the different meanings of the terms "rioters," "a mob," or "political protesters?"

Ayoob: The terms, unfortunately, mean different things to different people, Gila. If you look at the dictionary, a mob is a crowd of people, usually a relatively large crowd, especially one that is disorderly and intent on causing trouble or violence. Now, just within that definition, you will see the term stretched here and there. Let's say a rock star is being mobbed by his adoring fans and autograph seekers. It's a mob of screaming fans, they appear to be disorderly, but there is no collective intent to harm. So, I am not sure that "mob," as we use the word today, would apply to that correctly.

Rioters are people causing tumultuous damage often accompanied by arson and looting, which is large-scale theft.

Finally, we have the protesters. In the ideal situation, protesters have gotten a license from the police department to march, the streets will be closed off for them, and they calmly do their march, maybe chanting slogans, and that would be the extent of it.

Going back into the 18th century, it has been understood that as the law applies, a mob, essentially, is an organism all moving in the same direction with the same unlawful purpose, with a homicidal intent and usually, to some degree, a specific target. It has been said that just as every member of the mob shares the criminal and civil responsibility for damage caused by the mob, they also share the responsibility for the fear they have created in the victim who opens fire. Therefore, if you aimed at Rioter A, but you hit Rioter B, too bad, a target is a target, and they started the fight, and they lost.

The mob violence once was essentially geared to what, since the 19th century, has been called a lynch mob. What we are seeing here today is a different pattern of encounter.

Let's go back in history to January 14, 1881. Everybody who has seen cowboy movies and read history has a picture in their mind of Wyatt Earp standing in front of the jail with a sawed-off shotgun holding off a mob that wants to lynch a prisoner. That actually happened in 1881. There were primarily four lawmen: Wyatt Earp, his brother Virgil, County Sheriff Johnny Behan and Ben Sippy, who was the town Marshal.

The man they were protecting was named Michael O'Rourke, who, I believe, at the time, they were actually holding in a local saloon. He had shot and killed a very popular mining engineer in Tombstone, AZ, which was a mining town, and the other miners were absolutely furious, so they worked up a lynch mob.

The lawmen stood off the mob, I believe that no one was shot, although there may or may not have been warning shots. They made it clear, "We know you are going to murder this man, but we have a duty to bring him to justice and let the courts do their job. If you try to get past us and take him, we will kill you." The mob realized, "They're not kidding!" and turned around and left.

Continuing into the 20th century, probably one of the most famous of the Texas Rangers is Frank Hamer. It is an interesting irony because Hamer killed a great many people in gunfights in the course of his career, and a great many were Hispanic because so much of his work was along the Mexican border. There are people who call him a racist simply because he shot someone of a different color. It is a proven, documented fact that many times Frank Hamer stood alone against lynch mobs and protected black men that the white mobs, infiltrated with KKK, wanted to take out and hang. I don't recall that he ever had to shoot any of those, but had he done so, his actions would have been justifiable.

Probably the classic case of an armed citizen defending against a mob goes back to 1925 and the then-famous case of Dr. Ossian Sweet. He was an African American physician in the city of Detroit, which was very, very segregated at the time. He moved into a nice, upscale home in what previously was an all-white neighborhood and a whole lot of the white folks — remember this time was a peak of KKK influence — decided that they wanted him out of there.

On a day when he had ten members of his family and friends inside his home, they surrounded his house, screaming all sorts of epithets, and finally started throwing rocks through the windows. Shots were fired from inside

"

PROBABLY THE CLASSIC CASE OF AN ARMED CITIZEN DEFENDING AGAINST A MOB GOES BACK TO 1925 AND THE THEN-FAMOUS CASE OF DR. OSSIAN SWEET. HE WAS AN AFRICAN AMERICAN PHYSICIAN IN THE CITY OF DETROIT, WHICH WAS VERY, VERY SEGREGATED AT THE TIME. HE MOVED INTO A NICE, UPSCALE HOME IN WHAT PREVIOUSLY WAS AN ALL-WHITE NEIGHBORHOOD AND A WHOLE LOT OF THE WHITE FOLKS — REMEMBER THIS TIME WAS A PEAK OF KKK INFLUENCE — DECIDED THAT THEY WANTED HIM OUT OF THERE.

the house, killing one member of the white mob and wounding another. Everyone who was in the Sweet household at the time was arrested and charged with murder. In the first trial, they were all tried together, and the jury hung. So, there was a second trial, and they apparently decided if we can't get them all together, we will get them one at a time.

The first trial was that of Ossian Sweet's younger brother, Henry, and the NAACP hired Clarence Darrow to defend him. Darrow gave an absolutely brilliant argument on the sanctity of the home, the right to protect the home and the principle of the Castle Doctrine. The all-white jury acquitted, and at that point, I think the prosecutor saw the handwriting on the wall and dropped the rest of the cases.

Now, what you had in every one of those cases is the rule that a member of the mob shares the responsibility and, therefore, all share in the general jeopardy from the fear created in people who defend themselves against the mob. All the members of the mob were there for a single, dedicated purpose of harming and killing certain people. That is the kind of lynch mob for which the rule was geared.

If you fast-forward to the latter 20th century, the classic example is the so-called Rooftop Koreans. In 1992, the Rodney King riots in Los Angeles left 50-some dead: the death toll would later rise to 63 as some of the more severely injured people died. It caused over $1 billion in property damage. Thousands of people were injured, some of whom would never be made whole.

It was the acquittal of the four officers who arrested King that triggered the riots, but something else was also going on. In a neighborhood known as Koreatown, a female Korean shop owner named Soon Ja Du had shot and killed a 15-year-old black girl named Latasha Harlins. She accused Miss Harlins of shoplifting, and the young girl threw a drink in her face and was shot in the back of the head by the store owner. The African American community was, understandably, infuriated when the store owner was convicted of voluntary manslaughter but sentenced to probation with fines and community service. As a result, the Koreatown area was pretty hard-hit during the riots.

The Koreans armed themselves. They claimed there was absolutely no police presence. The police had withdrawn and were not responding to 9-1-1 calls. The Koreans staged on the rooftops where they had a decent field of fire, and they made it clear, "The city is burning. You are not going to burn this community. We will shoot you."

eJournal: Were there many actual shootings?

Ayoob: Well, there history diverges. I cannot find any documented cases; there were, certainly, warning shots. Of course, none of us here recommend warning shots. To answer your question, I cannot find any documented cases where it was confirmed that they had shot anyone.

eJournal: Well, with no police response, there would be no post-shooting investigations. Who is to say who caused the death of whom?

Ayoob: There are stories and rumors that a bunch of the dead were killed by armed citizens, including the so-called Rooftop Koreans. People were on their own! They were on their own in a dystopian situation through no fault of their own. As of 2017, a follow-up investigation in the Los Angeles Times reported that no one knows who killed 23 of the slain.

That set a paradigm, and we have seen after Hurricane Andrew in Florida and after Hurricane Katrina: when there was looting, and there were

armed people present protecting the stores, those stores were not looted; those stores were not burned.

We saw it in 2014 with the riots in Ferguson, Missouri. Very seldom did they actually have to shoot those people. The understanding was, well, yes, someone might call standing in front of your store with an AR-15 "going armed to the terror of the public," but there was no alternative. The police had been called back on the orders of the city fathers. Left on their own, the people in Ferguson did what they had to do. Off the top of my head, I cannot think of any cases where the prosecutor was stupid enough to prosecute the people who used guns to protect.

eJournal: Six years later, has the landscape of the criminal justice system changed?

Ayoob: In the recent rash of riots, at least one store owner in the Midwest has been arrested for shooting and killing a man whose body was outside the pawnshop when the police got there. Whether he was shot outside the building or inside the store and then staggered outside to die, I do not know, and I have not seen any public determination at this time. The pawnshop owner claimed self-defense, and they arrested him on the charge of murder, last I knew.

What we are seeing that is different in the current 2020 situation is most aptly described by a friend of mine who is a very street-wise police supervisor in a major, high-crime city. He said the difference this time is that the mob is not working with one mind, one purpose and one target. What we have is the Antifa types and the opportunistic looters basically seeding themselves in among those I would call the legitimate protesters — the people who are there in good conscience and good faith, to cause no physical harm to anyone and to voice what they believe is a very important concern.

My friend said the crowd today is not a mob; the crowd today is an ocean in which the predators swim, hide and are essentially affecting camouflage. They emerge out of the ocean to set fires to buildings, to violently assault people, and then to melt back into the protection of the crowd. They are using the crowd in the same way that Saddam Hussein used human shields: taking women and children and settling them in camps surrounding all the military bases during the Iraq war when he was afraid the Americans would obliterate his military bases.

That changes things entirely in the 2020 riot situations. If you look at some of the discussions among the more militant people on certain forums and social media, you'll find things like, "I will load my .308 with military ball, so I can shoot through bad guys and get three of them with one shot." One guy said he was going to load hardcast hunting bullets in a .44 Magnum so he could get three rioters with one.

You just want to slap those idiots in the head because you do not know who is behind the guy who is attacking you. Maybe — and we have seen this happen — it is a legitimate protester trying to grab and pull him off of you and saying, "This is not what we are about!" Do you want to kill that person with an over-penetrative bullet?

Everyone cites the Reginald Denny beating. Without question, if Reginald Denny had a gun, he would have had a right to kill all four of those evil bastards that stomped him. One literally crushed his skull with a cinder block. His skull was in fragments; he had profound brain damage. He had

to rehabilitate for years to learn to walk and talk again and is still, to this day somewhat impaired from that horrible beating. None of the four actually served more than four years in prison.

eJournal: What if he misses and shoots someone standing nearby videotaping or just trying to get out of the area?

Ayoob: Well, here comes the problem. Reginald Denny has been the first to publicly thank the people who rescued him — all of whom were good, black people from that community who were horrified to see what was happening. So, now, you have been hit in the head and stunned. The guys attacking you happen to be black, and now you are surrounded by black folks. What if you shoot one of your rescuers?

In Seattle, recently, you saw video of the courageous African American security guard who disarmed an AR-15 from the rioters who had taken it from a trashed, abandoned police car.

eJournal: If you were there, would you think he was an immediate threat to you?

Ayoob: You don't know who's who! You are going to have to be really careful. Do not be thinking that this is the amorphous mob that the lynch mob laws were talking about.

What you have got here are sharks that swam out of the ocean, and there might be a little wave of good-faith protesters coming out of that ocean trying to pull the sharks off of you. You don't know for sure. Target selection and target determination are going to be absolutely critical.

I see people that are saying, "Oh boy! I am going to start carrying my Krinkov 7.62x39 with my [gestures] wink, nudge wrist brace, and that will be my car gun." Well, son, you fire that inside the car with the windows up without any hearing protection, I guarantee you will suffer some degree of permanent hearing damage. If you are using military ball ammo, you're going to kill at least two people and maybe three if you have a crowd behind.

eJournal: What are likely criminal charges for harming the people behind your intended target?

Ayoob: We all know that the single most common physiological altered perception that we are aware of is auditory exclusion — we don't hear what other people are yelling because we are so focused on the threat. That is going to be increased profoundly by deafness — maybe temporary but probably permanent — from firing a high-powered weapon inside a closed vehicle, shooting from the inside of the car out. You cannot hear that the person behind them is screaming, "What are you doing? Get away from that car! You are making us all look bad!" You wound up killing that person, too. You previously posted on the Internet, "Boy, oh boy! Now I can get two or three with one shot." If you did not care who was behind them, and particularly if somebody's iPhone shows the person behind them, the term for that in law is depraved indifference for human life.

eJournal: We are talking about murder.

Ayoob: We are, or at least manslaughter. A whole lot of people have not thought past playing Call of Duty or the next season of Walking Dead. Your other problem is getting caught in traffic because people are blocking the highways, if you do have to abandon the vehicle, what are you going to do with the AR-15, what are you going to do with the Krinkov? People seeing you will think, "Oh my, there is a crazy man with a machine gun!" The cops might shoot you; an armed Antifa might say, "Here's my chance!" and shoot you; maybe three football players who are present as protesters might jump you for the gun.

A WHOLE LOT OF PEOPLE HAVE NOT THOUGHT PAST PLAYING CALL OF DUTY OR THE NEXT SEASON OF WALKING DEAD. YOUR OTHER PROBLEM IS GETTING CAUGHT IN TRAFFIC BECAUSE PEOPLE ARE BLOCKING THE HIGHWAYS, IF YOU DO HAVE TO ABANDON THE VEHICLE, WHAT ARE YOU GOING TO DO WITH THE AR-15, WHAT ARE YOU GOING TO DO WITH THE KRINKOV? PEOPLE SEEING YOU WILL THINK, "OH MY, THERE IS A CRAZY MAN WITH A MACHINE GUN!" THE COPS MIGHT SHOOT YOU...

I would suggest staying with handguns. Just because vehicles might be involved, don't look at it like a state trooper or FBI agent who is highly likely to have to fire deep penetrating bullets into an automobile. I would be looking at a crowd scenario from just the opposite angle, and if I thought I had to go into a place like that during such a time, my 9mm load would not be 147 grain subsonic, or the 124-grain +P bonded Gold Dot that I'm carrying today. I would probably be going with a 115-grain +P+ going at 1,300 feet per second. With the 115, we're looking at a wound track that is only about 10 inches long but very wide which is consistent with quicker debilitation. When you are in a crowd situation, you do not have a safe backstop, only the body of the offender. You have got to bear that in mind.

eJournal: The experience of shooting in a moving, jostling crowd is so far beyond the training and preparation of most as to create a real disconnect between actual marksmanship ability and the realistic defensive shooting within the setting we are discussing today. I have to ask, if you decided to draw and introduce a gun into arm's reach of a hostile, milling throng, what would you do? Draw to a retention position? A protected gun position? Low ready?

Ayoob: Well, I would not draw to Position Sul because it traps both of my hands at the centerline. Drawing to retention would be better. If I don't immediately intend to shoot, hand on the holstered gun with the other hand free to block and parry, I think, would be better yet.

eJournal: So, you don't necessarily want that gun out until you have identified a threat you think you will have to shoot?

Ayoob: Well, remember that other people do not know who we are. Let's say there are two or three well-intentioned protesters who came to march because they believed everything BLM said, and they want to do good. They're well-intentioned, good human beings, but each of them is the size of a pro-football linebacker. They hear from behind them the scream, "He has got a gun!" They see you struggling with people who a few minutes ago were walking with them, who now are obviously in fear of you. You are going to have them on top of you because they will come to the conclusion that you are the fascist that Antifa warned them about, or you are like the crazy, white racist who drove into a crowd of people in Charlottesville, Virginia, killing one and sending 19 more to the hospital. There is a whole lot of potential there for mistaken identity.

eJournal: What is your opinion about resorting to alternate weapons — perhaps pepper spray, batons where they're legal, knives? In other words, in very crowded situations with large numbers of people, is the gun our best defense?

Ayoob: Certainly pepper spray. A baton big enough to fight with is hard to conceal. In some states, Florida, for example, it is not a license to carry a handgun; it is a license to carry a weapon. There, you are allowed to carry concealed nunchaku, you are allowed to conceal a telescoping baton of the ASP type. Ask yourself, though, how much good is that going to do? Are you any good with that? Are you trained in it? How many people do you think you can fend off with it at once if three of them are jumping you and trying to get it away from you? A knife is not going to work too terribly well against a whole lot of folks, either. You might get two or three, but someone is going to come up on the sidewalk behind you with a brick and hit you in the head. With a gun, one of two things will happen. Either they will all flee at the sight of the gun or the sound of the shot, or they will try to be heroes and converge on you.

eJournal: How has shooting violent protesters worked out in the courts?

Ayoob: Here in Washington, you saw the Hokoana trial. Mr. Hokoana was at a protest, and some of the Antifa appeared to him to be roughing up people who he perceived as innocent. He wound up pepper-spraying some of them, and at that point, the big, buff Antifa guy came at him. His wife perceived that man to be armed with a knife with which he was about to stab Hokoana. She drew her pistol and fired one shot, hitting the guy in the abdomen. He doubled over, and she and her husband ran away.

I think his initial use of the pepper spray probably would have been justifiable, and I'll tell you, being a little more familiar with that case than most, there is reason to believe she is telling the truth. If she is telling the truth, if she had shot that guy, stood her ground and stepped on the knife that he dropped before anybody could remove it from the scene, she would have had a much better argument for self-defense than she did.

It was a five-week trial that cost a great deal of money and ended in a hung jury after the majority of the jury had wanted to convict. Mr. Hokoana had posted on social media that he was ready to "crack heads" and said, "I am going to go full melee," at a politically-charged event where I know there is going to be a demonstration, where I know Antifa are going to be and there is a real good chance that there is going to be violence, "I am going to go full melee."

Someone asked him on social media if he was going to carry a gun, and he said, "No, but my wife's going to carry hers." They went to a university setting that they knew is a gun-free zone, intentionally breaking the law going there with a gun. I think she would have had a strong doctrine of competing harms argument, except if you know there is going to be violence and you have an option, why did you go?

eJournal: It appears that by posting your intent to crack skulls and going, you agree to fight.

Ayoob: The Statute of Winchester about mutual combat from the middle of the last millennium had the *homicide se defendo* principle. Part of that was, "Look, we are fed up with the flower of our young men from the dukes and the counts down to the poorest of the peasantry killing each other over arguments about bullshit pride. If two of you go out to fight, one of you will not get a pat on the back and the other a hole in the ground. The horizontal one will go to the hospital or the grave, and the vertical one goes to jail."

eJournal: Yes, you are both responsible.

Ayoob: When you agreed to fight, your mutual combat voids the mantle of innocence. It shreds the mantle of innocence.

eJournal: Was Ms. Hokoana, deciding to go despite knowing about the plans to fight, innocent?

Ayoob: Well, her argument could have been, "My husband wanted to go, so I figured I had better go to protect him." I think if she had made that argument, that would have been understood under the doctrine of competing harms, the doctrine of necessity, the doctrine of two evils. It did not come across that way to the jury. The jurors said afterward, we simply did not find her testimony credible. That was made worse because the couple fled after the shooting, so you had the "flight equals guilt" thing going.

IF THEY HAD PICKED UP THE KNIFE THEY SAID THE ANTIFA GUY DROPPED, SOMEONE WHO JUST HEARD THE SHOT MIGHT SEE THAT JUST IN TIME TO CONCLUDE THAT THEY WERE PLANTING A "DROP KNIFE" ON AN UNARMED MAN. THEY'D BE RUNNING WITH A KNIFE IN HAND, AND THEY'D BE OBSCURING FINGERPRINTS AND DNA EVIDENCE. WOULD THEY HAVE TIME TO PULL OUT THEIR SMARTPHONE AND TAKE A PICTURE OF THE DROPPED KNIFE? PROBABLY NOT. YOU WOULD HAVE TO ASSESS THE CROWD.

Tremendous social pressure had been applied. Right now, the Antifa and BLM and such are favored by politicians and most of the media. If it looks like you went there to fight these poor, downtrodden people, you'll be cast as the bad guy.

You cannot expect to get too much sympathy, and you cannot expect to get too many of your friends and like-minded people on the jury.

eJournal: I would like to ask about fleeing from ongoing danger after a shooting. I could understand feeling so alone and threatened by large numbers of violent protesters converging on the person who shot their comrade that running away to a safer location could look like a pretty good option. If you shoot to defend against attack by a member of a mob and decide to retreat to a safe place, how do you defuse the "flight equals guilt" perception you identified as part of the reason the woman in your real-life example was unable to convince a jury of her innocence?

Ayoob: Gila, I don't know of a really good answer for that. If they had picked up the knife they said the Antifa guy dropped, someone who just heard the shot might see that just in time to conclude that they were planting a "drop knife" on an unarmed man. They'd be running with a knife in hand, and they'd be obscuring fingerprints and DNA evidence. Would they have time to pull out their smartphone and take a picture of the dropped knife? Probably not. You would have to assess the crowd. If they're backing off, stand your ground and straddle the attacker's dropped weapon.

Are there other people there who are on your side? In another case where a young man shot a protester-turned-rioter who was chasing him and trying to smash him in the head with a skateboard, a group of conservative sympathizers surrounded the shooter and protected him from the downed man's compatriots until the police could get there to take control of the scene.[17] Will that be possible in something like this that one of your readers could get caught up in? We just don't know.

eJournal: What is the likely outcome for some poor, unfortunate person, maybe a businessman who is just walking home from work, not realizing what is building up around him, who just gets caught up in a riot and becomes a target for the violent members of the mob? Can he shoot to avoid having his head bashed in?

Ayoob: If it came upon you that quickly, you still have your innocence maintained. You are the victim, caught up in the maelstrom by fate. What

I would suggest, though, if you are walking to work, you would kind of notice, "Uh oh, something is kind of happening up ahead." Now would be a really good time to go into some place that is safe, make some phone calls to get help and to find out what is happening, and stay there where it is safe.

If you are driving, there is an app called Waze which, so long as it knows where you are going, warns and alerts you to traffic jams and other problems ahead. If the streets are blocked by protesters, rioters, or just by construction workers, you are hopefully going to know in time to avoid it.

eJournal: What if bad luck strikes, your smartphone is dead, so your app doesn't help, or you can't exit the freeway in time? Is it enough just to have a gun in the car? Just last week, I corresponded with a man who drives over a bridge going to his office and, because he is going to work, has his gun in his briefcase. How he carries was not the focus of his question, but it made me wonder how well he would be able to take care of himself in a riot. What say you? Gun on body? Gun in bag?

Ayoob: Gun on body! If it is in the bag, it is going to be much slower to get out. If you have to step out of the vehicle, you can't reach the gun when you need it, and if you are separated from the vehicle, which is probably now unlocked with an open door, someone else is going to get it.

eJournal: The idea of getting out of the car at all is kind of chilling, but I'm not sure the popular suggestion to drive through a mass of protesters is going to work out well, either.

Ayoob: If you are in a car, I have a couple of suggestions. In every case we have seen of someone driving out of it, we are seeing, again and again, people being charged for doing so, even though the people were blocking them illegally, and they had very articulable reason to believe they might be dragged out of that car and beaten if they didn't. There is one thing none of them did, and I hope all of our members and readers get this: if you have got to drive out of a mob, turn on your damned flashers and lay on your damned horn! These are universal signals of emergency traffic coming through, and let that be seen on all of those dozens of iPhone videos: you were in emergency mode, trying to get out of the way, telling people, "Get out of the way, I am afraid."

eJournal: What speed? Just chugging through at five miles an hour or moving more quickly?

Ayoob: You have got to remember that different vehicles have different safety devices. Some airbags will only trigger with an impact of 14 miles an hour; some will trigger lighter. This brings us to the interesting case in Michigan of the lady in a parking lot dispute that was started by the other people. She got out of the car finally and pulled a gun, so everybody was saying, "Well, gee, why couldn't she just back out and drive away?"

One, the primary assailant was at the back of the car, pounding on it. Two, I spoke with John Correia, who told me he had spoken with those folks [search "Interview with Jillian and Eric Wuestenberg, Detroit Firearms Display (John's Briefs)" on Youtube, or visit the Active Self Protection channel] and she said they had what she called the nanny program on in the car. If the car senses a human being behind it, it will stop, and you cannot override it. Apparently, that is what happened in that situation.

eJournal: Does a violent protester breaking a car's side window or windshield pose such a threat to the car's occupants as to justify use of deadly force to stop him or her?

Ayoob: In my opinion, you are justified, although that might not be the opinion of the prosecutor. My opinion is based on the reason that they are trying to invade the passenger compartment. Why are they breaking the window? Why do you crack the walnut? You crack it to get what's inside and consume it. It is not reasonable and prudent to believe anything else.

Many states have passed laws that said the Castle Doctrine that protects you inside your home extends to inside your vehicle. The car is treated like a domicile. Even in states where that is not the black letter law, the situation is clear.

Antifa are now carrying the emergency rescue glass breakers, and that brings me to the other safety equipment I am now keeping in my car: a pair of safety glasses for every passenger, and I keep a pair of active hearing protectors in my vehicle. I know that cops shooting through their windshields in desperate situations do suffer some degree of permanent hearing loss. This, of course, would go to the power of 10 for the people with the short-barreled .223 AR pistols and such.

66

IF THE RIOTERS ARE THROWING PROJECTILES — ROCKS AND SUCH — INTO THE CAR, THE SPALL FROM THE BROKEN GLASS IS GOING TO COME INTO THE CAR. IN A WORST-CASE SCENARIO, INJURY FROM THE GLASS COULD CAUSE PERMANENT BLINDNESS. USUALLY, I DON'T WEAR GLASSES, BUT YOU'LL NOTICE I HAVE BEEN WEARING GLASSES ANY TIME I AM IN A CAR. EVEN BEFORE I BECAME A COP, I HAD SEEN CAR CRASHES WHERE THE WINDSHIELD DISINTEGRATED.

We have both participated in tactical vehicle penetration tests. You know when you shoot a windshield, some of the glass spall will come toward the direction of the shot, meaning that if you are shooting from the inside shooting out, you are still going to get some of the glass back in your face. That happens so quickly there is not time for the eyelids to blink and block it, and anyway, eyelids will not block much.

If the rioters are throwing projectiles — rocks and such — into the car, the spall from the broken glass is going to come into the car. In a worst-case scenario, injury from the glass could cause permanent blindness. Usually, I don't wear glasses, but you'll notice I have been wearing glasses any time I am in a car. Even before I became a cop, I had seen car crashes where the windshield disintegrated. The theory is that if the windshield disintegrates into tiny pellets, you're less likely to be decapitated by a large shard of glass. But those pellets come flying through the passenger compartment. The eye protection is for the threat from the outside or danger from the inside going out.

eJournal: If we have established that breaking windows to reach people in a car's passenger compartment poses a true, immediate danger to life...

Ayoob: In my opinion, it does, but that might not be the opinion of the prosecutor, who is an elected official. These things are tending to happen in the "Blue" cities that elect the "Blue" officials. If we have a district attorney who wants to keep getting his campaign donations for reelection from George Soros like the prosecutor in Saint Louis does, or from Michael Bloomberg, he is not going to see it as they are cracking the walnut to get at the meat inside and devour it, he is going to see it as, "Oh, you killed them for vandalizing your car."

eJournal: If we are blocked in and unable to drive away and rioters are breaking into cars adjacent to ours, at what point do we perceive that threat as extending to the occupants of our car?

Ayoob: Well, when it turns toward you, it is coming to get you. If I see two guys who look a lot alike and one is breaking into the other guy's car, I am not getting involved. I don't know who is who! Most of us would jump to the conclusion that it is a rioter or a carjacker but know this: one thing we may be seeing in these riots is gangbangers using all the tumult and absence of law enforcement to kill other gangbangers. If they are coming toward me and I am seeing them doing that to others, all the bets are off, and I will do what I have to do.

eJournal: So, it becomes a question of "when?" Will you wait until they have begun striking the car?

Ayoob: If they are hitting the car, that may render escape impossible depending on the kinds of weapons they are using. If that is happening, I will engage. I was involved in one case in Florida, not a riot, that involved a group of hostile people who were attacking a young man in his car. One of them allegedly was hitting the vehicle with a baseball bat. The other, with a bare fist, punched through the safety glass of the side window and hit the driver in the head. The driver took his .38, shot him in the chest and killed him. He finally got his car in reverse and got out of there.

He was charged with manslaughter for killing an unarmed man. Our defense team won an acquittal for him on the manslaughter charge, but that case did not have the political overtones. There was no cross-racial element, and there was no political gain.

eJournal: A question about windows: windows up, windows down, windows open a tiny amount?

Ayoob: I would suggest windows very slightly down. Some people tell me that rolling the window down just an inch will actually give it a greater tensile strength and resistance, but it also lets you better hear what is going on outside. One problem with the windows being rolled up, particularly if you have the radio going, the air conditioning going, or in the winter, the heater going, is that you end up in an almost silent bubble.

eJournal: Mas, this is such a big subject! I am worried that I have failed to ask you about important topics. What should be our biggest takeaway? What would help us be best prepared in this time of increased danger?

Ayoob: Follow the news and follow what is happening. Know what the trends are. Gila, my final advice, and I think the best advice I can find, comes from the poet and humorist Ogden Nash, "When called by a panther, don't 'anther.'"

eJournal: Stay away, run away, don't engage! All good strategies, and seriously, you have outlined a lot of areas of risk that we may not have previously identified, offered options for defense that we might not have considered, and emphasized not answering that panther by not voluntarily going to where protests are underway. Thank you for all of your time and knowledge! ∎

APPENDIX

Psychological Aftermath
Of A Citizen's Use Of Lethal Force
By Anthony Semone, PhD

Because of the work of Artwohl, Christensen, Lewinski, Ayoob and many others, much is now known about the psychological effects experienced by a person in association with self-defensive use of deadly force. At the onset of the confrontation, for example, it is common for the person to experience tunnel vision, auditory exclusion, alterations in perceived time, and the loss of fine motor control, among others. In the time frame following the encounter, it is unsurprising to observe symptoms associated with the altered state of consciousness produced by the encounter with death, including memory impairment, dissociative symptoms, and disruption to basic biological functions such as eating, sleeping, and sexual behavior. At points further along the temporal dimension from the shooting, flashbacks, social withdrawal and isolation, avoidance, and hypervigilance may well occur. (This listing of symptoms is not exhaustive.) While these data are largely gathered from subjects in the law enforcement community, they have been extrapolated here to the private citizen who has employed deadly force.

    The rate of a person's recovery from the symptoms of complex stressful events will vary as a function of their pre-existing resilience with respect to the stressing stimulus complex and the efficacy of post-stimulus exposure to corrective interventions. Resilience is understood as "the capacity to recover quickly from difficulties; toughness," and it can be brought about in any given individual by graded exposure to the stressing stimulus complex. That exposure can be via mental imagery, mindfulness techniques, and/or scenario based training. Interventions employed for post-exposure recovery typically involve initially Critical Incident Stress Debriefing. Extended debriefing and graded exposure to stimulus complexes that continue to provoke negative experiences can be employed to ameliorate persistent symptomatology. Social support, however, is the major source for developing both resilience and symptom reduction secondary to the intimate understanding of the complex psychological response to a deadly force event.

> ## "
> THE RATE OF A PERSON'S RECOVERY FROM THE SYMPTOMS OF COMPLEX STRESSFUL EVENTS WILL VARY AS A FUNCTION OF THEIR PRE-EXISTING RESILIENCE WITH RESPECT TO THE STRESSING STIMULUS COMPLEX AND THE EFFICACY OF POST-STIMULUS EXPOSURE TO CORRECTIVE INTERVENTIONS.

Private Citizen — Law Enforcement

Generally speaking, private citizens do not share with law enforcement officers those factors central to developing resilience. For the most part, private citizens are not members of an insular group whose esprit de corps permeates its daily existence. Private citizens do not typically undergo the extensive psychologically-based selection process that looks for resilience, nor do they benefit from resilience-producing experiences of academy training. In fact, it is reasonable to hypothesize that a significant percentage of private citizens undergo minimal training, if any at all. Also, law enforcement officers, as part of their governmental appointment as "keepers of the peace," have available to them the additional protections afforded by a network of professionals including psychologists, clergy, medical assistance programs, defense attorneys, and more. Indeed, any given use of deadly force by an officer has the potential of availing him of qualified immunity and summary judgment against potential legal consequences.

However, private citizens who use lethal means to counter an imminent attack that reasonably threatens him or her with grave bodily harm or death may well do so at their own peril. That seems on the face of it inarguably true. Absent training, absent a cohesive supportive community, absent embedded professionals who are proximately available to him or her, the private citizen is left mostly alone to deal with the aftermath of that use of deadly force, and with a greater likelihood of the occurrence of complex psychological consequences. More critical, however, in this author's view, is this: private citizens do NOT have formal, visible governmental authority and sanction to engage in protecting and serving the public, even with deadly force. So there is an embedded social, cultural, and political prejudice against private citizen use of lethal means of self-defense. Private citizens who secure the means and take the responsibility for their own safety and that of their loved ones are seen as vigilantes or lone wolves. They are seen as inveighing against the collective and they frighten others because of their individualist ideology.

Hence, it is precisely in the presence of this deeply embedded societal bias that the use of lethal force will undergo scathing scrutiny from that citizen's social, cultural, and political systems. And that scrutiny may well bring with it the full weight of governmental and media effort, especially when the use of force involves the death of a racial minority. As recent history has amply documented, neither private citizen (nor law enforcement officer for that matter) will escape that consequence (though arguably the LE will be more protected). This author would propose that, in the vulnerable citizen, the durability of the "poetic justice" inherent in the Mark of Cain will be the most enduring of symptom complexes with which the citizen will have to contend.

Hypothetical Use-of-Force Scenario

You have just been required to use deadly force to ensure your continued life. In doing so, you met all requisite legal conditions, just as your father and your prolific reading of self-defense literature taught you. Upon recognizing that the attacker was down and out, you replaced your weapon in your truck while dialing 911 to report a self-defense shooting. You have your hands in the air as the first arriving officer orders you to turn around and get on the ground. As you are doing that you have a knee in your back, propelling you forcefully to the pavement. You then become aware of another sharp pain in your neck as what seems to be another knee immobilizes you. You experience a very rapid heart rate, irregular in character and you

> THE STRESS WILL CONTINUE WITH THE INTERACTION AMONG YOU, LAW ENFORCEMENT, AND THE PROSECUTORIAL SIDE OF THE LEGAL SYSTEM: FROM INITIAL ARREST AND INCARCERATION, TO PROBABLE CAUSE HEARING(S); PRELIMINARY HEARING(S); RESPONSE TO CONTINUED JAILING; SECURING BOND (WHERE POSSIBLE GIVEN THE CHARGE); CONTINUING THREATS AGAINST YOUR FAMILY ...

fear a heart attack. You are transported by EMS to your local hospital where you are diagnosed with an anxiety attack and released to the custody of law enforcement officers. (You will subsequently be diagnosed with cervical vertebral fractures and under go surgical repair. You will also undergo medical treatment for rotator cuff injury.) "Ah, excuse me Officer Friendly, I'm not the bad guy here."

The stress will continue with the interaction among you, law enforcement, and the prosecutorial side of the legal system: from initial arrest and incarceration, to probable cause hearing(s); preliminary hearing (s); response to continued jailing; securing bond (where possible given the charge); continuing threats against your family because you defended yourself successfully against a member of the community; threats against you while in jail; securing your own defense counsel; securing the funds (you may well go bankrupt) necessary to support a defense team, to include at least one investigator, one crime scene reconstructionist, one use-of-force expert, one prior firearms trainer as a fact witness (assuming you had any training), and of course one defense attorney where defending you will not be his or her first rodeo as an attorney who specializes in self-defense cases.

Now, let us assume that you get through the many pretrial motions, unfavorable rulings given by an anti-gun judge, and that you luck out and you meet your burden of production and are allowed to enter the defense of self-defense. However, your use of force expert is sharply curtailed in what he is allowed to introduce as expert testimony, the judge having ruled in a Frye hearing that such testimony requires the use of licensed psychologists or psychiatrists. Since your expert is not one of those professionals, he is precluded from testifying about those issues for just that reason, notwithstanding his credentials as an expert in the use of deadly force. Of course said judge was able to drag out some broadly construable case law as justification for his decision. In any case, that's what you're left with, but I digress.

And if it seems the gods are against you, consider further that you live in a jurisdiction that has gone progressively statist for the last three elections, electing politicians opposed to private citizen carry of lethal weapons. Those elected officials also represent the exact constituency reflected in the social, cultural, and political group of the individual whose life you admit to having taken. And it is precisely at jury selection that multiple additional stressors come into play deriving from the fact that the jury is not made up of your peers, but rather those of the decedent. And it is just here that the societal impact of your defensive use of deadly force will begin to have its say on the outcome of your legal case. Media outlets in the community will pounce immediately upon the shooting as the grist for their anti-gun mill and echo the dismay of the paper's similarly-biased readership.

Now, consider this: when, for example, you first contacted your wife following your being detained by LE and taken to jail, with the one phone call you were allowed by the jailer, your wife, amidst sobs, reported to you that your 11-year-old daughter came home from school also in tears as she reported one of her classmates having announced for all to hear that, "Your Daddy is a BAAADDDDD MAAANNN. He killed a poor, innocent boy who my Mommy told me had just turned his life around. I don't ever want to play again with you."

You and your family begin to feel shunned and distanced by your neighbors. Your children are ignored by their peers and no longer have their usual play-friends to "hang with." As a consequence of this social system response to your defensive shooting, your family becomes increasingly disenfranchised from its social system. Your and your family's responses to the reaction of the milieu in which you live will amplify further the shame and humiliation. Why?

The media will report this: You have just taken the life of a poor, disenfranchised boy that, according to all reports was unarmed – "after all, it was just a 'toy gun.'" The newscaster will report in somber tones on the nightly news report, that the teenage boy was from an impoverished neighborhood; that he never had the "privilege" you have enjoyed your entire life; and, besides that, quoting a family member: "how was he gonna get the money to pay for the new clothes for the coming school year? Stealing from you, while not the correct thing to do, didn't deserve the death penalty."

This encounter will not, however, have been your first experience with "The Mark of Cain." And it will not be your last. The psychologist (whom your defense attorney retained pro bono), in his continuing debriefing process with you, advised you, as the old song goes: "(It's) only just begun." Indeed so, it has only just begun, because in these times the defender must now anticipate the second judicial attack, the civil suit.

It Does Not Get Any More Real Than This

What follows is taken in part from public records and in part from this author's direct interview with the person (hereinafter "D") who used deadly force in a confrontation with a neighbor in his community. After five hours of deliberation, the jury by unanimous decision found him Not Guilty of all charges. He had been charged with 1st degree Murder, 3rd degree Murder and Manslaughter. Be mindful that the shooting took place in 2012, but it was not until 2013 that the case even came to trial. Since the jurisdiction in which it took place did not provide for bail since the primary charge was 1st degree murder, D remained in prison for virtually one year before the trial even began. Because he was deemed by the classifying officer to be a vulnerable prisoner, for his protection he was placed in solitary confinement for that entire time.

In late Spring of 2012, in a small suburban community, a confrontation took place between D and his next-door neighbor. It was not the first such encounter between the two, the latter reportedly angry over property-line boundary violations committed by D's dogs that were defecating on his property. There were as well arguments apparently having to do with a di-lapidated, termite-infested shed in D's backyard. Over time, there apparently had been escalations in the acrimony between the two neighbors, including an occasion on which D believed that his neighbor had poisoned his dogs. D also saw him as responsible for tipping over log piles as well as killing a rabbit that was being fed by D's girlfriend. (At the end of the trial, the DA admitted that the decedent may well have been a bully, but that didn't mean he deserved to be killed.)

D's primary response to those incidents was to call his local township police and file a report. On interview, he reports to this author that he did in fact do that but that the police response either never took place or was ineffectual. He added that one officer advised him to send a registered letter to the attacker telling him to stay off his property. It is important to recognize that the attacker, a former Marine, was a person who was well liked by a number of people in that neighborhood. As well, the attacker had a sign posted in is yard that read: "Intruders will be shot. Survivors will be shot again."

In any case on the day of the shooting, a confrontation took place between the two men as D was leaving his property in his truck. As he was backing out from his driveway, he saw his neighbor approaching at a brisk pace and reportedly hollering, "I'm going to go over and get those dogs." D testified, "I thought he was going to kill my dogs (and) hurt B (his girlfriend). (So) I stopped my truck and got out. I put it in park, took off my seat belt and got out. He was right there; he said I'm going to fix you. I grabbed the pistol off the seat. The way he said "I'm going to fix you." It was like a growl. He was raging, he was seething. .... I thought he was going to kill me. (I) could see (him) pulling something out of his pocket.... (I) thought it was a gun. I fired.... I stopped shooting when he was no longer a threat. (I) then called 911 to get help for (him)."

Managing the Aftermath

The interview between D and this author (a portion of which is reproduced below) took place four years after the shooting incident and three

> " MY INTERNAL EXPERIENCE (IS) A COMBINATION OF SADNESS AND A BIT OF ANGER. I'M SAD THAT THIS IS WHAT I'M KNOWN FOR NOW. THAT'S THE BIG ASPECT OF IT. EVERYTHING I'VE ACCOMPLISHED UP TO NOW, ALL THE ACCOLADES, THEY MEAN NOTHING NOW ... FOR MY OBITUARY I'M GOING TO HAVE TO COME UP WITH THE CURE FOR CANCER (TO ERASE THE STIGMA OF THE SHOOTING).

years from the verdict. In D's own words (save for omitting names and locations and for enhancing grammatical structure), here are some of his comments about the long-term psychological effects of the deadly force encounter. Note specifically those comments he gives about the critical need he felt for being able to tell his whole story; for being able to feel understood, and understood by peers, by people who were connected to the self-defense community. As well, note his disdain for the legal system, despite the verdict. His report of his psychological experiences post-shooting are as compelling a narration of the effects of the Mark of Cain as this author has ever read or heard:

Most impactful (experience) from verdict to this date psychologically I would have to say (is) the public's reaction and how people look and act towards me now.

It's something (the shooting) that is brought up once a week from other people.

It's always having to deal with the elephant in the room. Meeting new people... do they know? Do they not know? Sometimes people will ask about it; sometimes people will have gallows humor or make a joke about it.

Two weeks ago I was out with two people talking and one guy said he was having trouble with his neighbor. The other guy said: Well don't ask (him) about that. He meant it as a joke but I didn't take it that way. He was referring to me.

You have to let it roll off your back. Some people don't realize how life altering this situation was. They see me walking around and looking okay and assume I'm okay, but I'm not. You have to learn to deal with it or you won't be able to associate with anybody. It's the new normal. (Emphasis added)

My internal experience (is) a combination of sadness and a bit of anger. I'm sad that this is what I'm known for now. That's the big aspect of it. Everything I've accomplished up to now, all the accolades, they mean nothing now.

For my obituary I'm going to have to come up with the cure for cancer (to erase the stigma of the shooting).

And a little bit of anger that people aren't more sensitive to the situ-

ation. A person died; (that's) not to be joked about; the seriousness of the entire situation; there were no winners; making a joke is not very sensitive; I don't see people making those comments to a woman who had been sexually assaulted.

(I felt) trepidation at your (referring to this author) contact but I hope that it can help me turn a bad situation into a positive. I could very easily have said after the acquittal I'm not going to speak about this again. This would not have been a benefit to anybody. But I still have my demons, but it helps to get it out. (I) still have some trepidation to bring it out because it brings up upsetting thoughts and feelings. But that's what the new normal is.

(It) irks me when I see phony PTSD; if you really had it you wouldn't be talking about it the way you are.

Lawyers are the winner. System is the winner. They (prosecution) lost (but) they still made their money.

Both the decedent and I were the smallest part of the whole thing. (The) prosecution (is) making a big deal about being out for justice. Baloney! There are two people's lives and he and I were just two small parts to further individual agendas (and) careers. (This trial) was supposed to be about truth and justice. (It's) Not.

Prosecution didn't really have anything to convict me on. They had four shell casings. I admitted this. What's the purpose? This wasn't like OJ. One week to get it done. The judge said to jurors, expect a week, jurors getting antsy so we went long in the evenings. We shortened our defense case; but it was over.

Disappointed in the pace (of the trial). (I) always thought that high paid people in these positions should act accordingly. I didn't have my day in court. Winning is the goal. We're here not to hear you story. We're here to get you home. Defense attorney didn't want to carry it on.

I had my mother call Massad; see what he thinks about the case. Massad's comment was "What's he even being charged for." I said finally somebody understands.

When I was in (the) class: I'm now in the company of other people who understand!! Ordinary folk do not understand. There are people who do know what I'm talking about. Part of the reason I did (the presentation at the class) is just that; when I was reading and learning nobody ever talked about the aftermath; it's now coming to the fore. More prevalent. More questionable prosecutions.

I had hoped for the opportunity to sit down and talk to the Prosecution but that doesn't happen anymore. It's not like (TV).

So the more opportunity to give voice to what happened to a knowledgeable audience, the better. Still (it) sticks in my craw that I couldn't say my piece. What was reported in the newspaper was a lie. Couldn't explain. I did not get my whole story out.

(We used a) forensic psychologist to see what I was all about psychologically. (She was) a help to (my attorney) to understand. (Prosecution) was trying to paint me as a gun nut. (Psychological) testing made an impression on jury. That was a big help.

Trial covers the range of emotions from anger to sad to funny. Prosecutor looked ridiculous hammering on her (defense psychologist) credentials (but) she put him in his place.

Irks me even today the cursory investigation. They got blinders on immediately. Forensics team (was) told you are going to a murder scene. Rush to judgment as to murder. This is now four years since the shooting. You called on the day. Good karma.

(The prosecutor) was up for reelection – charge what you want. (There was all the) media attention for him (to help) in his reelection. Maybe only his 3rd or 4th case he tried himself. He thought (he had) a slam-dunk. Tried to block my self-defense defense. But I knew I had to be the first one to 911.

I'M THAT GUY. (Emphasis added) Just something you have to deal with. I meet a girl. When do you bring that up what I did? Do you wait till they are emotionally invested? I never read about that anywhere.

How do I explain the four-year gap? Another residual is that I need to get my record expunged. Especially because (on employment applications) it's now (have you) ever (been) "charged with a crime." Now I have to go get a lawyer to get my permit back.

Still follows me to this day. In January of this year, (I was) in a bar and a guy killed another guy, (who was) six feet behind me. Actor shoved an *older guy and broke his neck. Blood all over. Put me back in another place. I showed arriving officer my driver's license and the officer talked with me about 15 seconds. I asked the officer for any info about the guy and got ignored.*

I'm not anti-cop. (although my) local department is under DOJ scrutiny. (I have had) three surgeries from excessive arresting force; ruptured two disks in (my) neck; rotator cuff injury and surgery.

(The shooting) will produce major changes in your life!

Caveat Emptor

Even a cursory review of the Defendant's statements provides eloquent testimony to the pervasive and enduring psychological effects secondary to his justifiable use of deadly force. These statements he made are occurring four years post shooting event. As he talks, it has all the vocal quality of what clinically is known as "talking in real time," that is, as if in the time and space of the occurrence of the event.

When this author asked him how he got through it all, his immediate response was family and (real) friends. He was clear in pointing out that his use of deadly force separated his friends from his acquaintances, and within the latter group, even those whom he had known for many years had abandoned him. He lost all his financial resources and has to depend upon family to survive again. The injuries he sustained secondary to his arrest left him unable to work, forcing him into continued dependence upon his family as he awaits a favorable decision on his disability payment status. He is now in the process of moving to another state where he will be closer to his family of origin and where he believes he will be able to be regarded as a person in his own right, and not as "That Guy."

As noted earlier, private citizens encounter the complex stress associated with their use of deadly force as the "lone survivor." There are no fellow officers who arrive, lights on, sirens loud to provide a secure perimeter. There is no officer to whom he is especially close to provide a secondary weapon to replace the weapon he used in the engagement. Transport to secure environment does not happen. There is no police chaplain to notify the family of the shooting and to provide them with reassurance as to their loved one's safety. There is no immediate response from a police psychologist/police surgeon to conduct a defusing with the relevant officers and who will provide formal incident debriefing for the officer following the IACP OIS protocol.

The bottom line, however, is that private citizens who chose to go armed in the service of the protection of our life and the lives of those we hold close to our heart, well, we do that at our own psychological peril. ■

This article appeared in the book, Straight Talk On Armed Defense: What The Experts Want You To Know *edited by Massad Ayoob and available at* GunDigestStore.com.

ABOUT
DR. ANTHONY SEMONE

Dr. Anthony Semone has amassed considerable education, experience, and training within a broad range of psychological disciplines. In doing so, he has afforded himself the ability to work within the fields of Forensic Psychology, Clinical Neuropsychology, Clinical Psychology, and Police Psychology.

Dr. Semone holds certifications from the NRA as an instructor in Home Firearms Safety, Personal Protection and Pistol, as well as in Law Enforcement/Security Firearms; from the Smith &Wesson Academy as a Reduced Light Training Instructor, Advanced Instructor in Police Use of Force and Risk Management, and as a Master Use of Force and Control Instructor; from the Lethal Force Institute as a Stressfire Instructor in Combat Pistol and Shotgun; and from the PA State Police as Lethal Weapons Instructor. He is also certified by the Lethal Force Institute as a Police Instructor in the Ayoob/ Lindell Method of Weapon Retention and in the Kubotan/Persuader. He has taken advanced firearms training from such internationally recognized instructors as Ray Chapman, Marty Hayes, Chuck Taylor, Clive Shepherd, Bob Taubert, Bert DuVernay, Tom Aveni and Clint Smith.

Dr Semone has been qualified in both state and federal courts and has provided in those contexts expert testimony on Use of Force, Body Alarm Reactions and their Impact on Eyewitness Identification, Post-Shooting Trauma and PTSD. He has assisted the Massachusetts State Police and the Baltimore County (MD) Police Firearms Training Units in designing instructional programs so as to incorporate known psychological principles to enhance the efficacy of those programs. He is presently involved in gathering data on the relationship between heart rate variability and decision-making ability in officer use of force.

1   Martinez, Ramiro, *They Call Me Ranger Ray*, New Braunfels, TX: Rio Bravo Publishing, 2006, Page 84.

2   Lee, Cynthia, *Murder and the Reasonable Man*, Pgs. 129–130.

3   Law Dictionary: http://thelawdictionary.org/imminent-danger/#ixz2tp77H34L

4   Branca, Andrew, *The Law of Self Defense*, 2013, page 14.

5   Jordan, Bill, *No Second Place Winner*, pgs. 15-16, published by Police Bookshelf, PO Box 122, Concord, NH 03302, copyright 1965 by Bill Jordan

6   Tennessee V. Garner, 471 U.S. 1 (1985),471 U.S. 1, Appeal From The United States Court Of Appeals For The Sixth Circuit, No. 83-1035.

7   Illinois v. Wardlow (98-1036) 528 U.S. 119 (2000) 183 Ill. 2d 306, 701 N. E. 2d 484.

8   http://statelymcdanielmanor.wordpress.com/2013/07/09/george-zimmerman-hollow-points-and-reality/.

9   http://articles.washingtonpost.com/2012-04-12/lifestyle/35450681_1_trayvon-martin-story-george-zimmerman-unarmed-teenager.

10 National Review, http://nationalreview.com/article/353633/angela-coreys-checkered-past-ian-tuttle/page/0/1.

11 http://www.thedailybeast.com/articles/2013/07/19/angela-corey-s-overzealous-prose-cution-of-marissa-alexander.html

12 http://jonathanturley.org/2013/07/18/zimmerman-prosecutors-angela-corey-under-fire-for-public-comments-and-allegedly-threatening-action-against-harvard-law-professor/

13 http://www.blogtalkradio.com/traceyandfriends/2013/07/31/hump-day-with-tracey-jeff-and-sticks.mp3

14 http://www.backwoodshome.com/articles2/ayoob143.html

15 https://armedcitizensnetwork.org/

16 http://www.policeone.com/policeonetv/videos/1736783-reality-training-lunsford-incident/).

17 Albuquerque, NM, June 2020.

The Complete Guide to
GUNS PAST
AND PRESENT

You'll find all the guns you love, and many you never even knew about, in this handsome second edition of *The Illustrated History of Firearms*. This special project from Gun Digest and the experts at the NRA Firearms Museums is the most comprehensive visual gun reference ever published. The story of the gun starts in the 14th Century and continues with today's technological marvels. You'll learn about all of them and their worldwide influence in 320 pages with more than 1,700 full-color photos, bound in a hardcover format with a crisp dust jacket. Whether you want to learn more about firearms history or need a gift for your favorite gun enthusiast, this is the book you need!

Product No. R8090
$39.99

Order online at
GunDigestStore.com
Or call
920.471.4522

FREE SHIPPING
On Orders over $59!

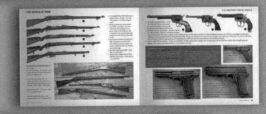

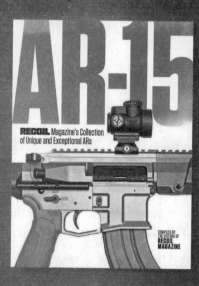
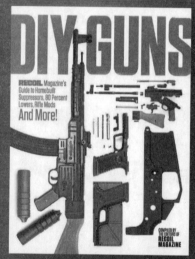